Beckett, Joyce and the Art of the Negative

EUROPEAN JOYCE STUDIES

16

General Editor: Fritz Senn
Associate Editor: Christine van Boheemen

BECKETT, JOYCE AND THE ART OF THE NEGATIVE

Edited by
Colleen Jaurretche

Amsterdam - New York, NY 2005

The paper on which this book is printed meets the requirements of "ISO 9706:1994, Information and documentation - Paper for documents - Requirements for permanence".

ISBN: 90-420-1617-5
©Editions Rodopi B.V., Amsterdam – New York, NY 2005
Printed in The Netherlands

CONTENTS

Acknowledgments

Bibliographical Note

Introduction
    Colleen Jaurretche   11

Joyce's Aesthetic of the Double Negative and His
Encounters with Homer's *Odyssey*   15
    Keri Elizabeth Ames

"Nichtsnichtsundnichts": Beckett's and Joyce's
Transtextual Undoings   49
    Dirk Van Hulle

The Unnamable: Denegative Dialogue   63
    Russell Kilbourn

Mingled Flesh   91
    Ulrika Maude

Beckett's Purgatories   109
    John L. Murphy

The Uncanny in Beckett   125
    Lois Oppenheim

Death Sentences: Silence, Colonial Memory and the
Voice of the Dead in *Dubliners*   141
    Nels Pearson

Something for Nothing: Beckett's *Dream of Fair
to Middling Women*   171
    John Pilling

Joyce's Negative Esthetics   181
    Jean-Michel Rabaté

The Joyce of Impossibilities   197
    Fritz Senn

"Wanting in Inanity": Negativity, Language and "God"
in Beckett   213
    Asja Szafraniec

From Ideology of Loss to Aesthetics of Absence:
The Endgame in Beckett's *The Lost Ones*   235
    Yuan Yuan

ACKNOWLEDGMENTS

I wish to thank Christine van Boheemen-Saaf for her invitation to work on this issue of the *European Joyce Studies* Annual, for her editorial advice, and for her suggestion to include Samuel Beckett in its scope.

My thanks to Nora Elias of the UCLA Department of English for her efforts in preparation of the manuscript; she has worked in heroic ways to make this project a reality. As always, my thanks go to Jack Kolb for his ever-listening ear; to my Joycean colleagues for their support; and to Geoff and Ryan for their patience and love.

BIBLIOGRAPHICAL NOTE

The following conventions will be used to refer to the following standard editions of Joyce's works. Because this series has no precedent for reference of Beckett's works, individual authors will cite their preferred editions.

CW James Joyce, *The Critical Writings of James Joyce,* ed. Ellsworth Mason and Richard Ellmann. New York: Viking Press, 1959.

D James Joyce, *Dubliners: Text, Criticism, and Notes,* ed. Robert Scholes and A. Walton Litz. New York: Viking Press, 1969.

FW plus page and line number. James Joyce, *Finnegans Wake.* New York: Penguin, 1967.

JJA plus volume and page number. James Joyce, *The James Joyce Archive,* ed. Michael Groden, Hans Walter Gabler, David Hayman, A. Walton Litz, and Danis Rose. 63 vols. New York and London: Garland, 1977-1979.

JJI Richard Ellmann, *James Joyce.* New York: Oxford University Press, 1959.

JJII Richard Ellmann, *James Joyce.* Revised edition. New York: Oxford University Press, 1982.

Letters I, II, & III   James Joyce, *Letters of James Joyce.* Vol. I, ed. Stuart Gilbert. New York: Viking Press, 1957; reissued with corrections 1966. Vols. II & III, ed. Richard Ellmann. New York: Viking Press, 1966.

P James Joyce, *A Portrait of the Artist as a Young Man.* New York: Penguin, 1993.

S James Joyce, *Selected Letters of James Joyce*, ed. Richard Ellmann. New York: Viking Press, 1975; London: Faber, 1975.

U plus episode and line number. James Joyce, *Ulysses,* ed. Hans Walter Gabler et al. New York and London: Garland Publishing, 1984, 1986.

INTRODUCTION

COLLEEN JAURRETCHE

> I can connect nothing with nothing.
> —T.S. Eliot, *The Waste Land*

> ...sharing a joke with nothingness.
> —Virginia Woolf, *To the Lighthouse*

> Perhaps it is nothing that is our true state, and our dream of life is inexistent.
> —Marcel Proust, *In Search of Lost Time*

Negation is the dark metaphysical heart of modern literature. Yeats composes poetry from "any rich, dark nothing";[1] at the center of *A Passage to India* the Marabar Caves resound with emptiness; and Lily Briscoe is confounded by the blank space on her canvas. Samuel Beckett and James Joyce write with deep awareness of ancient, medieval and modern philosophical and theological traditions that express negation and its correlative states—absence, void, emptiness and nothingness—as central to language and representation. The essays in this volume emphasize its importance to the central meditation of literary modernism: the nature of mind and its expression in words. The collection does not strive to present a system for reading Beckett and Joyce, nor does it seek to draw comparisons between the authors. Rather, the essays in this volume point out absence as the chief condition (and therefore parallel) of Beckett's and Joyce's literary worlds, and suggest the inherence of negation to modernist thought.

Given the abundance of essays on Beckett included in this volume, it is tempting to speculate on the relative affinity of Beckett and Joyce to its theme; however, neither author is more nor less obfuscatory, and neither has a greater or lesser relationship to negation. Each confirms the activity of perception as the defining feature of mind and philosophical core of language.

---

[1] W. B. Yeats, "The Gyres," in *W. B. Yeats: Selected Poems and Four Play*, ed. M. L. Rosenthal (New York: Scribner, 1996), 178.

In keeping with their respective delight in recondite knowledge, Beckett and Joyce drew their vocabulary for absence from its arcane history. That history begins with negative theology, the strain of mystical discourse through which the West articulates the ineffability of God. Sometimes termed apophatic and sometimes termed *via negativa*, the tradition originated with Plotinus and flourished in the sixth-century theology of Dionysius the Areopagite. It conceptualizes God as unknowable and yet, paradoxically, only known through language. This philosophy is at the foundation of the idea that reality derives from language; language, in turn, exists in relation to senses and mind. Apophatic thought finds it apotheosis in St. John of the Cross' *Dark Night of the Soul* which Joyce tells us is at the center of the night of *Finnegans Wake*. From the dark corner of Euclid's *Gnomon* cited at the beginning of *Dubliners* to the phenomenological questions raised by the "Real Absence" (536.05) of *Finnegans Wake*, Joyce's artistic roots lie in Western culture's earliest concepts of presence and absence. So do those of Beckett. Wolfgang Iser says that Beckett's work demonstrates unknowability as the only meaning and purpose for art, and Shira Wolosky identifies "inexpressibility" as a major topos in Western literature.[2] If we proceed, like the voice of *The Unnamable*, by "...aporia pure and simple...Or by affirmations and negations invalidated as uttered..." (291), we are forced to conclude, like Moran in *Malone Dies*, that "Nothing is more real than nothing" (192), an assertion as bold and bare as the empty tomb.[3] Thus *Waiting for Godot* begins "nothing to be done" and offers silence both as a form of enunciation and "divine aphasia": to echo Beckett's own words on Joyce's *Work in Progress*, art is the "*absolute absence of the Absolute.*"[4]

The voice of *The Unnamable* tells us about the condition of "feeling nothing, knowing nothing...wanting nothing" (348) in ways that nonetheless convince us that sensations become words become worlds. Just how this occurs is the subject of essays in this collection, although Joyce and Beckett's critical writings on the visual arts resonate for their own writings. In his words on paintings by the van Veldes, Beckett says, "the work, considered as pure creation, whose function stops with its genesis, is

---

[2] Wolfgang Iser, "The Pattern of Negativity in Beckett's Prose," *Georgia Review* 29, no. 9 (Fall 1975): 706-719; Shira Wolosky, *Language Mysticism: The Negative Way of Language in Eliot, Beckett and Celan* (Stanford, Calif.: Stanford University Press, 1995).

[3] Samuel Beckett, *Three Novels: Molloy, Malone Dies, The Unnamable* (New York: Grove Press, 1958).

[4] Samuel Beckett, *Our Exagmination Round His Factification for Incamination of Work in Progress* (Paris: Shakespeare and Company, 1929), 22.

consecrated to the void."[5] His words parallel Joyce's relation of art to absence, of word to picture. Joyce's 1912 critical essay upon William Blake states that the connection between visual and verbal art lies in "the pure clean line that evokes and creates the figure on the background of the uncreated void."[6] These quotations point out the relation between perception and language that is explored by many of the essays in this collection. Many years later, in correspondence to his son Giorgio, Joyce echoes his own words on the void, "My eyes are tired. For over half a century, they have gazed into nullity where they have found a lovely nothing."[7]

Our eyes now continue that gaze. Keri Elizabeth Ames's reconstruction of Joyce's Homeric sources reminds us that the search for literary sources, like all quests, has at its center that which is not there. Dirk Van Hulle writes about how Beckett and Joyce weave worlds of language that reveal nothingness behind phenomena: Joyce through superfluity, Beckett through restraint. Russell Kilbourn writes about strategies of "denegation" in *The Unnamable*. Ulrika Maude analyzes surface and embodiment in *The Lost Ones*. John Murphy looks at the historical relation between purgatory and ideas of non-being as he analyzes the worlds of the dead in *The Lost Ones*, *Play,* and *How It Is*. Lois Oppenheim argues that Beckett's theory of representation depends upon an understanding of absence in relation to the uncanny. Nels Pearson equates ineffability to colonial oppression or usurpation of language in *Dubliners*. John Pilling examines the ways in which *Dream of Fair to Middling Women* employs "negational strategies" that call into question the definition of the novelistic form. Jean-Michel Rabaté brings together Joyce, Lacan, and silence to offer a theory of negation and negative theology as aesthetic discourse. Asja Szafraniec examines how negative theology directly addresses its own rhetoricity in Beckett's work. Fritz Senn reminds us that in the most basic sense we cannot read, translate, dramatize, and interpret Joyce's work, and yet we must. And Yuan Yuan comments upon the relation between negation, loss, and literary theory as he looks at Beckett's disintegration and reconstitution of the subject.

---

[5] Translated by John Pilling in his *Samuel Beckett* (London: Routledge & Kegan Paul, 1976), 20.
[6] *CW,* 221.
[7] *Letters III,* 358. The original Italian reads: "Ho gli occhi stanchi. Da piu di mezzo secolo scrutano nel nulla dove hanno trovato un bellissimo niente."

As the essays support each other, there is no recommended sequence of reading; they are arranged alphabetically by author. Their collective theme is the generative subject of this book: an appraisal of negation as the core of perception, and its intrinsic relation to the workings of language.

Claremont McKenna College

JOYCE'S AESTHETIC OF THE DOUBLE NEGATIVE AND HIS ENCOUNTERS WITH HOMER'S *ODYSSEY* *

KERI ELIZABETH AMES

"Ah, Dedalus! The Greeks! I must teach you. You must read them in the original" (*U* 1.79-80), declares Buck Mulligan to Stephen. The proclamation that one "must read them [the Greeks] in the original" can hardly be taken lightly, given that it occurs in a book which Joyce has chosen to title *Ulysses*. As Fritz Senn observes, "the question of experiencing great literature merely through the medium of restrictive translations is written into the book."[1] He notes further that "Mulligan's amicable gesture (or taunt) seems balanced by a reciprocal comment in the library chapter.... To match Mulligan's boast of reading in the original, Stephen echoes the phrase and connects it with the late Latin of a theologian."[2] The passage to which he refers reads: "—Saint Thomas, Stephen smiling said, whose gorbellied works I enjoy reading in the original, writing on incest" (*U*, 9.778). A most urgent and obvious question is thus incited by Joyce's book but never answered: did Joyce himself take Buck Mulligan's advice? Did he read the Greeks in the original? Or, like Stephen, did he appreciate Latin texts in the original instead?

One might think by this point in Joyce studies that the answer to whether Joyce read "in the original" is already well established and exhausted, and in a volume focusing on negative aesthetics with my chosen title, one likely expects the answer to be Molly Bloom's. But the correct answer is yes and no,

---

* For Fritz Senn in all of his authenticity, with gratitude for our continuing textual debates and his incisive criticism on earlier versions of this essay, and for Wendy Doniger, who waved her magic wand and asked me the questions that incited this inquiry. I wish to thank the Zürich James Joyce Foundation for supporting this research in 2003. I also thank Luca Crispi for his superb suggestions on further sources and the members of the 2003 Zürich Joyce August Workshop for their comments on my work in progress.
  [1] Fritz Senn, "'In the Original': Buck Mulligan and Stephen Dedalus," *Arion* 2 (1992): 216.
  [2] Ibid.

closer to Molly's ambiguous first word in *Ulysses*: "Mn" (*U*, 4.57), which Leopold first interprets to mean "No, She didn't want anything" (*U*, 4.58). Molly's "Mn" actually means no and yes, for it indicates that she does not want Leopold to buy her anything for breakfast but only wants tea with cream and bread (*U*, 4.318, 366). So Joyce too could have answered "Mn" concerning his own reading "in the original." For Joyce did indeed read Latin works "in the original" during the course of his education at Belvedere and University College Dublin, while he cannot be said to have done so proficiently in the area of Greek classical texts at any point in his life. Yet the matter of how well Joyce knew the *Odyssey*, and the translations upon which he relied while writing *Ulysses*, still remains a point of contention and ignorance.

The urgency of resolving this issue was announced to me when I received a review of an article that I submitted to the *Proceedings of the Modern Language Association* in which the reviewer informed me that I should not be using my own translations of Homer's *Odyssey* to support my comparative efforts with Joyce's *Ulysses*. This anonymous reviewer insisted that "the Butcher and Lang translation of the *Odyssey* should be included since this was the only translation that Joyce ever read."[3] Despite the helpful criticism of this reviewer regarding the rest of my work, I knew that this claim was dead wrong. Nevertheless, it unmasks a very significant misconception about the nature and extent of Joyce's acquaintance with Homer's *Odyssey*. Most of my readers will immediately recall that Joyce of course read Charles Lamb's *Adventures of Ulysses*. But that knowledge alone is hardly sufficient ground upon which to defend an intertextual project comparing Homer's Greek poem with Joyce's novel. My determination to justify using my own translations in my comparative work led me to try to ascertain exactly what translations of Homer Joyce read and when he read them. I also sought to learn whether Joyce's own acquaintance with the *Odyssey* would bear out the value of Homer's Greek poem for readers of his work. Surprisingly, establishing Joyce's encounters with Homer proved much more difficult and perplexing than I initially imagined, despite the variety of work already done on classical themes in Joyce.[4] Allow me to trace the available evidence

---

[3] Personal correspondence from the *Proceedings of the Modern Language Association*, in an anonymous review of "Narrative Reticence in Homer's *Odyssey* and Joyce's *Ulysses*" (2 April 2002).

[4] W. B. Stanford, Hugh Kenner and Fritz Senn of course remain pioneers in this realm. Other contributors to scholarship on this topic include Brian Arkins, Lillian Doherty, Sidney Feshbach, John Gordon, Margaret Mills Harper, Declan Kiberd, Morton Levitt, R. L. Lind, Margot Norris, David Norris, John Rickard, R. J. Schork, Michael Seidel, Constance Tagopoulos, Bjorn Tysdahl, and David Wykes.

regarding Joyce's encounters with the *Odyssey* in any form, an endeavour which will first require me to elucidate Joyce's level of competence in Latin as well as in Greek, and I will then draw a few conclusions about how Joyce himself read Homer and what translations of Homer Joyce scholars should rely upon and quote in their comparative efforts.

First of all, Joyce did own and read Homer in the original Greek, but his expertise was so minimal that he cannot justly be said to have known Homer in the original. Any typical young classical scholar in the second year of studying Greek would already possess more facility with Homer than Joyce ever managed to achieve.[5] R. J. Schork establishes Joyce's expertise in Latin

---

[5] Wolfhard Steppe was so skeptical of Joyce's competence in ancient Greek that he discredited the accuracy of a letter in which Joyce writes "I am writing a series of epicleti—ten—for a paper" (*Letters I*, 55) and disputes the accuracy of "the explanatory footnote claiming that *epicleti* were 'derived from *epiclesis* (invocation')" (*Letters I,* 55); see Wolfhard Steppe, "The Merry Greeks (with a Farewell to *epicleti*)," *James Joyce Quarterly* 32 (1995): 598. Steppe found it "difficult to believe that, back in 1904, Joyce would have been capable of coming up with the epicleti notion." (ibid., 603). He contends that Joyce's word is actually "epiclets—little epics, so to speak, a series of short narrative pieces (the classicist's answer to the novelettes Gerty MacDowell would prefer—*U* 13.110)" (ibid.). At Steppe's request, John O'Hanlon examined the original document in the University College Dublin library and reported, "The word is 'epiclets' with a short JJ 's' which Gilbert and Curran evidently mistook for an 'i.' For a second opinion, I noted that the U. C. D. librarian also read 'epiclets,' for that is the form of the word in the brief extract from the letter included on their index card in the catalogue" (ibid., 604). Steppe concludes that this "Unknown Librarian of University College, Dublin...was possibly the first person ever to see and understand what Joyce put down...and was not taken in by what Gilbert had printed" (ibid., 604). Steppe comments that the word *epiclesis* itself finally does occur in Joyce's notes, but not until around 1933 (ibid., 612; see *JJA,* 37:110). Another similar error, due to the challenge of deciphering Joyce's handwriting in final consonants which Joyce hardly ever inscribed very meticulously, is found in the single word sentence "Poser" (*U,* 16.1386), which appears in his notes as well. Philip Herring at first writes "poses" (Philip Herring, ed., *Joyce's Ulysses Notesheets in the British Museum* [Charlottesville: University Press of Virginia, 1972], 385), but that word is later corrected to "Poser" (Philip Herring, ed., *Joyce's Notes and Early Drafts for Ulysses: Selections from the Buffalo Collection* [Charlottesville: University Press of Virginia, 1977], 267). The single word sentence is quite clear in the original notes following the same question found in the final version in expanded form: "Can real love exist between married folk? Poser." (*JJA,* 12:67, bottom). Hence Joyce's final letters are consistently difficult to decipher, and here the 's' and the 'r' are very closely similar in Joyce's unusual scrawl, just as the 's' and the 'i' are in the epiclets instance.

and his lack thereof in Greek quite thoroughly and convincingly.[6] Schork comments that Joyce's scores on his Latin exams at Belvedere were "extraordinarily high,"[7] eliminating any suspicion that Joyce was a mediocre classical linguist. Yet if Joyce's Latin was so superb because of his formal education, at what point did he begin to learn Greek? Denis Rose and John O'Hanlon contend that after Joyce had "what was described by his physician as a 'nervous breakdown' (*Letters I*, 97), and he took upon himself a 'rest cure' (*Letters II*, 387). As if seeking direction, he embarked upon a course of research beginning, logically enough with the Greek language....Although the Greek is modern Greek, it is clear that one of Joyce's purposes was to facilitate a systematic study of the *Odyssey*."[8] This course of events lends a new autobiographical resonance to the words in *Finnegans Wake*, "unconsciously explaining, for inkstands, with a meticulosity bordering on the insane, the various meanings of all the different foreign parts of speech he misused" (*FW*, 173.33-36). In his meticulous if somewhat insanely obsessive approach to learning Greek, Joyce was undeniably not seeking a through, philological knowledge of the language but instead likely enjoyed acquiring enough linguistic insight to fuel and foster his purposefully erroneous "misuse" of various permutations of foreign words . His ancient Greek studies progressed far enough to enable him to scrawl the first line of Homer's *Odyssey* in Greek from memory on a tablecloth, albeit without the proper accents and with two glaring spelling errors, an extra lambda in "malla" and a final alpha instead of the correct epsilon in "ennepa."[9] Mulligan asserts that

---

[6] R. J. Schork, *Latin and Roman Culture in Joyce* (Gainesville: University Press of Florida, 1997), and *Greek and Hellenic Culture in Joyce* (Gainesville: University Press of Florida, 1998).

[7] Schork (1997), 275.

[8] Danis Rose and John O'Hanlon, eds., *James Joyce: The Lost Notebook* (Edinburgh: Split Pea Press, 1989), xiii. Joyce's documents from this period of study have been preserved and can be found at the State University of New York at Buffalo (MSS VIII.A.1, 2, 4, 6); see Rodney Wilson Owen, *James Joyce and the Beginnings of Ulysses* (Ann Arbor, Mich.: UMI Research Press, 1983), for discussion of their contents. Further on Joyce's forays into modern Greek, see Schork (1998), 240-259.

[9] Ellmann reproduces the drawing on Plate X in *JJI* and Plate XXXVII in *JJII*. Ellmann offers two dates, "the beginning of 1926" (*JJI*, 585; *JJII*, 573) and "about 1923" (*JJII*, Plate XXXVII). Wolfhard Steppe inclines toward the 1926 dating and further observes "a pedant, however, will insist on eleven adjustments in order to get Joyce's line straight. Its imperfections tell us that Joyce never cared to attend to the very *elements* of Greek: the values of its single letters" (Steppe [1995], 601). Steppe offers a rather exhaustive analysis of Joyce's engagement with Greek and the errors and failings which nonetheless persisted. As Steppe writes, Joyce's "notebooks attest to the zeal with which the writer of *Ulysses* applied himself to the study of (modern

one "must" read in the original, while Stephen argues for the pleasures of doing so. Joyce himself would seem to have followed and ignored both pieces of advice in varying degrees. Still, his fascination and fixation with both Greek and Latin words throughout his life should not be denied.

Most scholars concede that Joyce's fascination with Greek did not result in any remarkable competence in the language, either in modern or classical Greek.[10] Schork addresses the question of Joyce's knowledge of ancient Greek brilliantly, noting that early on Joyce admitted unequivocally his own inability to read Greek: "In a Collegiate essay, 'The Study of Languages,' (1898-1899), Joyce wrote, 'the writer humbly acknowledges his ignorance of Greek' (*CW*, 295)."[11] Schork further suggests that Joyce himself made "an accurate evaluation of his own proficiency"[12] to Harriet Shaw Weaver in a letter of June 24, 1921, writing, "I forgot to tell you another

---

rather than classical) Greek" (Steppe [1995], 600), and Steppe offers numerous interesting examples of Joyce's Greek knowledge and its errors emerge in his notes, as well as how those notes are reflected in *Ulysses* (see Steppe [1995], 599-603). He notes that the word *epiclesis* appearing in Joyce's notebook around 1933 is "preceded by several more entries that have a (pseudo-) Hellenic ring, mixing Greek and Latin characters rather freely (and disposing completely of the Greek 'e's dear to Henry Flower of old)" (Steppe [1995], 617); see Steppe's examples and note his warning that "much of this demi-semi-Greek notation was misrepresented by France Raphael (*JJA*, 41:55)" (Steppe [1995], 617, and *JJA*, 41:55). This conglomeration of Latin and Greek words reveals how Joyce's preoccupation with classical languages was joined by his disregard for engaging in accurate and reliable philological work. For more on such classical linguistic word play, see Schork (1997), 1-39, 217-243, and (1998), 260-274.

[10] See Schork (1997, 1998); Brian Arkins, "Joyce and Greek," *Notes and Queries* (1996): 444, and *Greek and Roman Themes in Joyce* (New York: Edwin Mellen, 1999); and Steppe (1995). Schork discounts Arkins' claim that "Joyce knew a certain amount of classical Greek" (Arkins [1996], 444), on the basis of his "inaccurate and inadequate evidence" (Schork [1998], 297). Yet Joyce did know a "certain amount" of Greek, enough to write words and use lexicons and coin neologisms, but that amount certainly did not constitute solid proficiency, thus inciting Schork's criticism of the claim. I cannot read modern Greek and so cannot judge the quality of Manto Aravantinou's argument in that language that Joyce's modern Greek was adequate if not fluent, but a review of her work by M. Byron Raizis condemns Aravantinou's lack of scholarly rigor, noting that "several of the words on her page 129 are not found in the texts or in any known lexicon or concordance" (review by M. Byron Raizis of "TA HELLENIKÁ TOU TZAÍEMS TZÓYS [THE GREEK OF JAMES JOYCE], by Manto Aravantinou [Athens: Hermes, 1977]," *James Joyce Quarterly* 16 [1976]: 523). We can safely presume that Joyce's modern Greek skills surpassed his classical Greek ones, but that in neither case is he completely proficient.

[11] Schork (1997), 256.
[12] Schork (1998), 245.

thing. I don't even know Greek though I am spoken of an erudite....I spoke or used to speak modern Greek not too badly (I speak four or five languages fluently enough) and have spent a great deal of time with Greeks of all kinds from noblemen down to onionsellers, chiefly the latter. I am superstitious about them. They bring me luck." (*Letters I*, 167; *SL,* 284; emphasis added).

Joyce announces his fluency in "four or five" languages, presumably including English, German, French, and Italian. He admits to knowing no classical Greek while having lost most of the modern Greek he used to speak "not too badly." Yet Joyce's own announcement here seems a bit overly self-denigrating according to Schork's assessment of his Greek skills. Schork offers fascinating examples of neo-Hellenic words in *Finnegans Wake*, evidence which reveals Joyce's tremendously vast multilingual vocabulary and which makes Schork's statement "I deduce that Joyce's oral and graphic reproduction of Greek, ancient or Modern, was fluid"[13] quite compelling. Even so, the serious flaws in Joyce's Greek knowledge never seem to have perturbed him enough to inspire him to redeem them.

For Joyce's facility in Greek should not be confused with rigorous philological knowledge. Joyce himself read the original Homer in Greek much like a detective decoding a cryptogram word by word, not at all like a trained classical scholar. Schork explains that Joyce made various rather feeble if still zealous attempts to decode Homer's Greek, albeit in a rather rough and unscholarly manner. Schork discusses the few lines of the Greek *Odyssey* that appear copied in Joyce's notebooks (*Od.* 2.420-421, 9.366-67),[14] but he first explains why Joyce could not be properly said ever to have read Homer in Greek:

> There is evidence that he briefly tried to work with the Homeric text. His Trieste library included a school edition of Book 1 of the epic, complete with copious notes of every sort and a line-by-line translation into grotesquely literal Italian. On several pages of the book, Joyce wrote occasional notes, almost all of them involving a mechanical transfer of a vocabulary word from the commentary into the text...His mastery of grammar, syntax, and the apparatus of a scholarly commentary for a Latin text would have aided him in addressing the Greek text of Homer. This mechanical process, however, does not mean that Joyce could 'read' even a single verse of the original

---

[13] Schork (1998), 256.

[14] Also see Owen (1983), 96-104, especially his "Collation of Selected Greek Manuscripts" (99). As Owen admits, "Joyce's motives for recording these lines remains obscure" (ibid., 102). For my own suggestion of how these Homeric lines relate to Leopold's own anonymity as "L. Boom" (*U*, 16.1260, 1262, 1265, 1274, 1275, 18.1264), see Keri Elizabeth Ames, "The Convergence of Homer's *Odyssey* and Joyce's *Ulysses*" (Ph.D. dissertation, University of Chicago, 2003), 320-321.

Odyssey. Rather, with the appropriate lexical assistance and syntactical clues, he would have been able to decipher the meaning of individual words and to explain how they functioned in the context. All the evidence from the school text of the *Odyssey* indicates that Joyce was following the process I have just described. Such effort, which can sometimes yield sophisticated results for a single word or phrase, falls short of a claim to be able to 'read' the original—and Joyce would be the first to admit that such was the case.[15]

Schork provides support for this contention with his reference to a copy of Book I of Homer's *Odyssey* in Joyce's Trieste library "with many notes and an interlinear 'translation' into Italian; several pages of this work are annotated (mainly vocabulary) in Joyce's handwriting."[16] Yet Schork neglects to provide a definitive list of the Homeric translations which Joyce consulted.

While Joyce seems to have exerted himself to decipher Homer's Greek in this rather crude manner, it is surprising that Joyce never seems to have sought out a Latin translation of the *Odyssey*. The *Odyssey* in a Latin translation never appears anywhere in Joyce's reading or libraries, although his Latin reading did include Cicero, Ovid, Sallust, Caesar, Horace, Livy and Lucretius.[17] Quite oddly, he never sought to become acquainted with Homer in the one classical language at which he was adept.[18] Joyce could have read Andronicus' *L'Odyssia* easily and thoroughly in what Schork calls his "first second language,"[19] for it would have been available in almost any public library. Perhaps lack of interest was the cause; Richard Ellmann assumes that Homer held little interest for Joyce during his early adulthood, and the course of his studies certainly seems to support that contention. Ellmann writes, "At this time [1902] Joyce had no interest in Homer. He told Padraic Colum that the Greek epics were before Europe, and outside of the tradition of European culture. The *Divine Comedy* was Europe's epic, he said. He distrusted Plato, as Herbert Gorman says, and described Hellenism in an early notebook as

---

[15] Schork (1998), 85 (emphasis added); see further, 86-90.

[16] Schork (1997), 256. Schork refers his readers to Michael Gillespie, *James Joyce's Trieste Library: A Catalogue of Materials at the Harry Ransom Research Center* (Austin: University of Texas Press, 1986), 120, item #219.

[17] See Schork (1997), 245-247.

[18] No Latin translations of the *Odyssey*, nor any Latin commentaries, are ever mentioned in Joyce's school curriculum or personal libraries, described by Thomas E. Connolly, *The Personal Library of James Joyce*, University of Buffalo Studies 22 (1955); Richard Ellmann, *The Consciousness of Joyce* (New York: Oxford University Press, 1977); and Michael Patrick Gillespie, *Inverted Volumes Improperly Arranged: James Joyce and His Trieste Library* (Ann Arbor, Mich.: UMI Research Press, 1983), and Gillespie (1986).

[19] Schork (1997), 2 and 29.

'European appendicitis'" (*JJII*, 103). Yet Danis Rose and John O'Hanlon aver, "There can be little doubt but that Joyce first read Victor Bérard's *Les Phéniciens et l'Odyssée* (1902) in the Zentralbibliothek Zürich. On the front cover verso of MS VI.D.7, the unit 'P&' represents the title, and 'ZG 116/117' are the call numbers in the library for the two volumes of the work."[20] Such definitive evidence for Joyce's early study of Bérard contradicts Ellmann's claim that Joyce had no early interest in Homer whatsoever, while demonstrating how Joyce could later condemn and dismiss exactly what he had devoted his time and energy to studying during his writing.[21] Moreover, Rose and O'Hanlon propose that Joyce's study of Bérard was incited by his reading of Walter Leaf's *Troy: A Study in Homeric Geography*, another book which never appears in any of Joyce's libraries.[22] They assert that Joyce meticulously copied notes "(avidly, more than he needed or could have used) from Walter Leaf's reconstruction of daily life in ancient Troy."[23] Rose and O'Hanlon detail another instance where "Joyce once again overstretched the simple truth" by neglecting to mention his reading of Bérard and exaggerating how much of *Ulysses* had already been written in a 1938 letter to Louis Gillet.[24] Joyce's own equivocations only complicate the issue of the depth, breadth, and chronology of his own reading, but we must acknowledge that his insatiable curiosity led him to reading about the Greeks quite early, no matter what else he suggested.

We thus have good ground to doubt Joyce's protests regarding his interest in the Greeks. In this vein, Joyce's own declared regret to Vladimir Nabokov regarding collaborating with Stuart Gilbert for the sake of exposing and explaining his use of the Homeric intertext should not be construed as evidence of his own disillusionment with the intertextuality he has nurtured, but rather as a reflection of his complete disgust and dissatisfaction with how his novel's relationship with Homer's *Odyssey* had been received and interpreted by the public. Richard Ellmann describes the circumstances of Joyce's admission of remorse:

---

[20] Rose and O'Hanlon (1989), xxx.

[21] On Joyce's study and use of Bérard, see Rose and O'Hanlon (1989), xxx-xxxii; Michael Seidel, *Epic Geography: James Joyce's Ulysses* (Princeton, N.J.: Princeton University Press, 1976); and Michael Groden, *Ulysses in Progress* (Princeton, N.J.: Princeton University Press, 1977), 76-91.

[22] Connolly (1955), Ellmann (1977), and Gillespie (1983, 1986).

[23] Rose and O'Hanlon (1989), xxviii, see xxviii-xxxiv on Leaf. Copying far more than he could ever have used perhaps reflects more of the "meticulosity bordering on the insane" (*FW*, 173.34).

[24] *Letters I*, 401, and Rose and O'Hanlon (1989), xxix.

Joyce's attitude toward [Gilbert's book] gradually altered. Vladimir Nabokov recalled a conversation with him at dinner in the Léons' flat in about 1937. Joyce said something disparaging about the use of mythology in modern literature. Nabokov replied in amazement, "But you employed Homer!" "A whim," was Joyce's comment. "But you collaborated with Gilbert," Nabokov persisted. "A terrible mistake," said Joyce, "an advertisement for the book. I regret it very much." (*JJII*, 616)[25]

This single comment to Nabokov should not by any means negate the significance of the Homeric intertext to *Ulysses*, especially given the fact that Joyce's statement to Padraic Colum denigrating the Greeks cannot be accepted at face value, either.

Yet no matter what classical research Joyce engaged in, he still seems to have neglected to read any Latin translation of the *Odyssey* in which he would have enjoyed thorough competence. It might even qualify as an aversion on his part to exploring the Latin translation, because it is very difficult to believe that he would not have known of its existence after his fine training in Latin.[26] After all, as R. L. Lind explains, "Roman literature begins with Homer, for the first Latin book of any consequence was the translation of the *Odyssey* into saturnian meter by Livius Andronicus."[27] Fritz Senn, however, thinks the Latin translation could easily have been overlooked by Joyce and that we cannot assume Joyce consciously and purposefully ignored it.[28] At any rate, while there is no evidence that Joyce read it or commented upon it anywhere, it cannot be definitively ascertained that Joyce made an overt and undeniable choice to avoid reading it. At least we can be confident that Joyce was never examined on the Andronicus translation while in school. For at the same time that Schork establishes that Joyce's Greek was so elementary, Schork affirms Joyce's remarkable expertise in Latin, detailing

---

[25] On Joyce's relationship with Nabokov, see Michael H. Begnal, "Joyce, Nabokov, and the Hungarian National Soccer Team," *James Joyce Quarterly* 31 (1993-1994): 519-525.

[26] Joyce's translation of Horace's *Ode* III.13 (cited in Kevin Sullivan, *Joyce Among the Jesuits* [New York: Columbia University Press, 1957], 75-77, and Herbert Gorman, *James Joyce* [New York and Toronto: Farrar and Rinehart, 1929], 45-46) shows his care for syntax and his sensitivity to style, betraying the linguistic gifts yet to blossom fully. See Sullivan's discussion of the method of Jesuit pedagogy by which such passages were taught, involving oral reading, translation, metrical identification, parsing of grammatical perplexities, and comments on the historical and cultural context relevant to the passage at hand (Sullivan [1957], 76-77).

[27] L. R. Lind, "The Uses of Homer," *Classical and Modern Literature* 10 (1989): 10.

[28] Personal conversation, Zürich James Joyce Foundation, 27 April 2003.

the history and compass of Joyce's Latin study in an appendix entitled "Joyce's Latin Curriculum."[29] He writes:

> Joyce read widely in the translations of Greek literature and in works on them and general Greek culture. In the Wake Notebook VI.B.20.33 there is an entry on 'Wolf's Theory of Homer.' At the time, that theory would be familiar only to specialists interested in the possibility that the Homeric epics were the oral productions of an unlettered poet... In general, however, a fair assessment of Joyce's competence with the *ipsissima verba* of ancient Greek can be illustrated by a glance at his rendition of the Greek alphabet on the back cover of a Wake notebook (VI.B.21); it is incomplete and slightly out of order, the hesitant script of an enthusiastic tyro.[30]

Thus Joyce did dabble around quite extensively with Greek but never applied himself to its mastery with the vigour that he invested in his Latin. Joyce's expertise in Latin was thus joined with a life-long dalliance into modern and ancient Greek that cannot properly be characterized as competence. Given his extensive knowledge of Latin, along with his study of French, Italian, and German, Joyce certainly knew the intricacies of inflected languages and recognized the problems with translations. As a matter of fact, he was so concerned about the flaws inherent in translations that he set out to learn Dano-Norwegian in order to be able to read Ibsen in the original. His letter to Ibsen in that language apologizes so fluently for his language skills that it leaves little doubt that Joyce was a linguist of exceptional talents.[31]

---

[29] See Schork (1997), 245-247. For a listing of the texts included in Joyce's studies in English at Belvedere, see Kevin Sullivan's appendix (1957), 237-240. For copies of the actual examination reports of scores, see Bruce Bradley, *James Joyce's Schooldays* (Dublin: Gill and Macmillan, 1982), 110-111, 116-117, 130-131, 140-141. Also see Kevin Sullivan's appendix (1957), 236-237. Joyce's course of study can be determined quite specifically in all of his subjects, including Latin, English, French, Italian, Logic, Natural Philosophy, and Mathematics, in large part because the examination papers still exist. Eileen MacCarvill collected all of Joyce's examinations, which were issued by the Intermediate Education Board for Ireland and the Royal University of Ireland, for a project that was never completed (photocopies of disbound proofs, Zürich James Joyce Foundation, 1992).

[30] Schork (1997), 29-30.

[31] Joyce fully acknowledged the value of reading any text in its original language. Ellmann describes the breadth of Joyce's reading thusly, and then observes that Joyce was inspired to learn Ibsen's language in order to read his plays in their original language: "He set himself to master languages and literatures, and read so widely that it is hard to say definitely of any important creative work published in the late nineteenth century that Joyce had not read it....To read Ibsen in the original, Joyce began to study Dano-Norwegian" (*JJII*, 75-76). Joyce then wrote to Ibsen in his own

Nevertheless, he made no serious effort whatsoever to learn enough Greek to read Homer with the same degree of expertise with which he had read Dante, Vergil, Ibsen, Hauptmann, and others in their original languages.[32]

Indubitably, then, Joyce chose to struggle on his own with Homer's Greek text, but given his linguistic limitations in Greek, he was mostly compelled to rely upon translations. Joyce himself claimed that his interest in Homer, and in Odysseus in particular, emerged early, due to his encounter with Charles Lamb's *The Adventures of Ulysses* at the age of twelve.[33] Joyce once offered a rather puzzling comment to Herbert Gorman, suggesting why

language. At least in its English translation, Joyce's letter is so eloquent that his apology to Ibsen for his lack of linguistic competence seems like false modesty: "My own knowledge of your language is not, as you see, great, but I trust you will be able to decipher my meaning" (*JJII*, 86). Joyce's German was adequate to translate Hauptmann (*JJII*, 87), but Yeats was not overly impressed with his efforts, writing to Joyce that he had given his Hauptmann translations of *Before Dawn* and *Michael Kramer* to "a friend who is a German scholar to read some time ago, and she saw, what indeed you know yourself, that you are not a very good German scholar'" (*JJII*, 178). Joyce also made some effort to learn Irish, as Frank Budgen recalls: "he soon abandoned Irish in favor of Norwegian, which he studied to such purpose that later he was able to translate James Stephens' poem 'The Wind on Stephen's Green,' into Norwegian (as well as into Latin, Italian, German, and French)" (Frank Budgen, *James Joyce and the Making of Ulysses* [Bloomington: Indiana University Press, 1960], 32).

[32] On Joyce's Italian and French studies, see *JJII*, 59-60. William Henry, who taught Latin and Greek at Belvedere, taught Stanislaus in Greek, as Stanislaus testifies in *My Brother's Keeper* (New York: Viking, 1958), 73, while Henry taught Joyce in Latin after Joyce chose to study Italian instead of Greek (*JJI*, 47); see further Bradley (1982), 113-114. Early on, then, Joyce decided not to learn Greek but to concentrate on Italian instead.

[33] On the edition of Lamb Joyce most likely read and why it matters, see Alastair McCleery, "The Gathered Lambs," *James Joyce Quarterly* 31 (1994): 557-563, and "The One Lost Lamb," *James Joyce Quarterly* 27 (1990): 635-639. Hugh Kenner discusses Lamb and his influence on Joyce in *Ulysses* (Baltimore: Johns Hopkins University Press, 1987), 23-24, as does David Wykes, who proposes that "As Joyce discovered when he came to know Homer, Lamb represents a liberalizing of the Greek epic's structure; Joyce himself liberalizes it even more" (David Wykes, "The *Odyssey* in *Ulysses*," *Texas Studies in Language and Literature* 10 [1968]: 304); see 302-305 on Joyce's use of Lamb. Stanislaus Joyce confirms his brother's early fascination with Lamb: "…his first interest as a boy in the figure Ulysses was aroused when his class was reading Lamb's *Adventures of Ulysses*. The boys were asked which of the heroes they admired most. My brother chose Ulysses in reaction against the general admiration for the heftier, muscle-bound dealers of Homeric blows." (Stanislaus Joyce [1958], 43).

Ulysses was his favorite hero and referring to his first encounter with the hero through Lamb:

> I was twelve years old when I studied the Trojan War but the story of Ulysses alone remained in my recollection. It was the mysticism that pleased me....[34]

Joyce's fascination with Lamb is thus incontrovertibly significant. But if the recollections of Joyce's schoolmate William G. Fallon are correct, Pope's translation made a significant impression upon the young Joyce as well. Joyce wrote on Pope's translation of the *Odyssey* while at Belvedere for his English teacher George Dempsey. Fallon recalls,

> Joyce always maintained that he owed Mr. Dempsey a debt for the way he had been taught English...The subjects he prescribed usually provided scope for any of us with imagination. Joyce availed of his liberality. On one occasion we had Lamb's *Shakespearean Tales,* and elementary text-book. Joyce instead handed in a composition on the essays of Elia. I remember, too, that after we had made some progress in Pope's *Essay on Man* in class, our task was to comment on the lines:
>
> 'Honour and shame from no condition rise;
> Act well your part, there all the honour lies.'

---

[34] W. B. Stanford, "The Mysticism That Pleased Him," *Envoy* 5 (1951), 62. Stanford consequently wonders, "What did Joyce mean by 'mysticism' in this context, and from what source did he, knowing no Greek, first derive it?" (ibid., 62). Joyce commented further along these same lines to Georges Borach: "only the *Odyssey* stuck in my memory. I want to be candid: at twelve I liked the mysticism in Ulysses" (Michael Seidel, *James Joyce: A Short Introduction* [Oxford: Blackwell, 2002], 100). I refer you to Stanford's article for his answer, although the question remains an open one. McCleery examines the debate insightfully (1990), 635-636, 638-639, and Bjorn Tysdahl explores the impact of Lamb upon Joyce, arguing that "Lamb's *Ulysses* could teach Joyce something about the options available to a writer who wanted to use Homer freely....The portrait of a peace-loving and inventive Bloom...can be appreciated more fully against an awareness of what Lamb does to Homer's long and loving account of a country at peace with itself and its neighbors" (Bjorn Tysdahl, "On First Looking into Homer: Lamb's *Ulysses* and Joyce's," in *Classic Joyce*: *Papers from the XVI James Joyce Symposium, Joyce Studies in Italy* 6, ed. Franca Ruggieri [Rome: Bulzione Editore, 1999], 287, 288). On the influence of the medieval mystical tradition upon Joyce, see Colleen Jaurretche, *"The Sensual Philosophy": Joyce and the Aesthetics of Mysticism* (Madison: University of Wisconsin Press, 1997).

'And Joyce,' Mr. Dempsey added, 'you may write whatever you like.' Yes; Joyce selected to write on Pope's translation of the *Odyssey*. Absit omen! He was no more than sixteen years old at the time. Connolly suggested that he must have picked it up at one of the second-hand bookstalls. This was his first introduction perhaps to the famous tale of which he was later to give his own twentieth century rendition.[35]

In dispute of this possibility stands Kevin Sullivan proposal that Joyce's very first encounter with the story of Troy occurred at Clongowes while reading *Peter Parley's Tales About Ancient and Modern Greece*, in addition to *Peter Parley's Tales About Ancient Rome*. Sullivan explains, "It may have been on Parley's imaginative excursion into ancient Greece that James Joyce first heard of the man called Ulysses. It was certainly in Parley…that he first encountered the gods, goddesses, and heroes of a vanished golden age."[36]

But what other translations might Joyce have used as inspiration for *Ulysses*? W. B. Stanford reports that

> Professor Stanislaus Joyce has kindly informed me that his brother had studied the following writers on Ulysses: Virgil, Ovid, Dante, Shakespeare, Racine, Fénelon, Tennyson, Phillips, d'Annunzio and Hauptmann, as well as Samuel Butler's *The Authoress of the Odyssey* and Victor Bérard's *Les Phéniciens et l'Odyssée*, and the translations by Butler and Cowper.[37]

Hugh Kenner refers to this claim of Stanford's and further comments that

> Stannie recalled Jim using only two translations, Cowper's and Butler's (the latter published in 1900, hence the most up-to-date version available when *Ulysses* was being thought out). Stanislaus Joyce's freedom to inspect his brother's working books must be located before the 1914 war broke out,

---

[35] Ulick O'Connor, ed., *The Joyce We Knew* (Cork: Mercier Press, 1967), 42.
[36] Sullivan (1957), 44-45.
[37] W. B. Stanford, *The Ulysses Theme* (Dallas: Spring Publications, 1968), 76. Furthermore, Kevin Sullivan's discussion of Lamb's declared debt to Chapman in his own redaction would seem to imply that Joyce must have had at least some passing acquaintance with Chapman. Sullivan also offers insight into how Chapman's translation would have impacted Lamb's version enough to give it the sense of mysticism Joyce appreciated; see Sullivan (1957), 94-97. I wonder how much attention Joyce would have devoted to Cowper, though, because his classmate Eugene Sheehy remembers that Joyce "considered that the poet Cowper was only fit to write the rhymes which are found in the interiors of Christmas crackers. When requested, therefore, to write an appreciation of *The Task*, he finished off two pages of scathing disparagement of its author with an adaptation of Hamlet's farewell to the dead Polonius: 'Peace tedious old fool!" (O'Connor [1967], 19-20).

since shortly after that Stannie was interned and Jim subsequently left for Zurich. So it seems probable that his testimony chiefly pertains to the nascent stages of Joyce's book. Frank Budgen's recollection of Joyce using Butcher and Lang comes from later years, when Joyce was studying Victorian-Homeric diction in order to parody it in 'Cyclops'....[38]

The prevailing assumption, which my anonymous *PMLA* reviewer also made, that the Butcher and Lang translation was Joyce's only source for *The Odyssey*, surely derives from Frank Budgen's recollection: "As a work of reference for his *Ulysses* he used the Butcher-Lang translation of the *Odyssey*."[39] Budgen does not, however, state that it was the only translation Joyce used, and it is difficult to determine at what date Budgen remembers this occurring, although it seems likely that it was in Paris.[40] Regardless of the dating of Budgen's memory of Joyce's use of Butcher and Lang, the assertion that Butcher and Lang was the only translation Joyce used is definitively revealed to be a misconception. For my own part, I cannot imagine Joyce admiring Butler's book while utterly ignoring his fine translation, and Stanislaus assures us that was not the case. It would make no sense for Joyce to have esteemed *The Authoress of the Odyssey* so highly, as is universally agreed, while neglecting Butler's translation entirely.

Surprisingly enough, Ellmann's biography, which retains its status as something of a Bible for Joyce scholars despite recent insistence upon the need for new approaches to Joyce biography, never establishes when and where Joyce read *The Odyssey* and whose translations he read.[41] Ellmann only

---

[38] Hugh Kenner, *Joyce's Voices* (London: Faber and Faber, 1978), 110-111; see further his *The Pound Era* (Berkeley: University of California Press, 1971), 44-50.

[39] Budgen (1960), 323.

[40] Read Budgen (1960), 318-324, and make your own attempt to fix the date of his recollections. The construction of his narrative obscures the exact timing of his memories, but his mention of finding Joyce different in Paris than he had been in Zürich appears on 318; later on 323 he discusses Joyce in Zürich again. That the Butcher–Lang translation influenced Joyce substantially is not to be disputed; for instance, Herring offers a long list of citations of words and phrases in "Penelope" which he believes to be derived therein and which would far seem to surpass any possible coincidences; see Herring (1972), 497.

[41] Morris Beja, Ira B. Nadel, and William S. Brockman concur on the value of Ellmann's work while also proclaiming the need for new biographical work on Joyce. Brockman contends, "Ellmann's scholarship has dominated Joyce studies for decades for good reason" (William S. Brockman, "Learning to be James Joyce's Contemporary: Richard Ellmann's Discovery and Transformation of Joyce's Letters and Manuscripts," in *Joyce and the Joyceans*, ed. Morton Levitt [Syracuse, N.Y.: Syracuse University Press, 2002], 68); and Beja insists, "No Joyce scholar or critic can fail to be in Ellmann's debt" (Morris Beja, "Citizen Joyce or My Quest for Rosebud,"

establishes Joyce's early encounter with Lamb and his choice of Ulysses as the topic for his school essay "My Favourite Hero."[42] The same ease with which Ellmann documented the enormous breadth of Joyce's other reading is thoroughly absent in respect to Joyce's acquaintance with Homer. Most recently, Brian Arkins has clarified matters in the most sensible and most convincing way, by listing the books of Homer which Joyce owned:

> Joyce owned both the *Iliad* and the *Odyssey* in the original Greek. He also owned translations into English of the *Iliad* by Edward Earl of Derby, and by A. Long, W. Leaf and E. Myers, as well as a study of the *Iliad* by W. L. Collins. For the *Odyssey* Joyce possessed a bilingual version in Greek and Italian of Book 1; an Italian edition of Book 14; translations of the whole work by W. Cowper and by T. E. Shaw; and a German commentary on the words and phrases of the *Odyssey* by O. Henke.[43]

in Levitt [2002], 15). Beja discusses how "Ellmann's work looms over any attempt to write a biography of Joyce" (ibid., 16), including his own biography on Joyce (Morris Beja, *James Joyce: A Literary Life* [London: Macmillan, 1992]). Ira B. Nadel concurs with him on the need for a new approach to Joyce's life with the complaint that "Joyce biography has for too long erased Joyce's contradictions....A new life of Joyce should not reinforce Joyce the revered artist but reveal Joyce the individual, with his foibles, masks, misunderstandings, resentments, and obsessions" (Ira B. Nadel, "Joyce and Blackmail," in Levitt [2002], 31). Ellmann's failure to establish the translations of Homer which Joyce read is not redeemed by Schork, substantiating the need for more biographical work. The autobiographical nature of Joyce's fiction only makes this task all the more urgent. Ellmann thinks that Joyce found some substantiation for the autobiographical basis for his fiction in Samuel Butler, who "insisted, as Bérard denied, that the *Odyssey* was just like other fictional works in being covertly autobiographical....Joyce concurred, so far as his own book was concerned." (Ellmann [1977], 28; see his full exposition on the influences of Butler, Victor Bérard and Francis Bacon, 26-31). Beja's comment, "Of course with Joyce, even more than with most writers, there is a complex and intricate connection between the life and the art" (Levitt [2002], 15) explains why any decent biography on Joyce almost inevitably expands our understanding of his work. Brenda Maddox's *Nora: The Real Life of Molly Bloom* (Boston: Houghton Mifflin Company, 1988) is a testimony to the power and talent of the biographer who is also literary critic, exposing the connections between life and text

[42] *JJII*, 46, and Gorman (1929), 45.

[43] Arkins (1999), 22. Arkins also comments on the striking similarity between Thoreau's translation of the *Iliad* and the end of "The Dead," revealing another translation of Homer which Joyce very likely encountered even though no one had been able to identify exactly where and when that encounter occurred. See Arkins (1999), 21, and *JJII*, 251.

Arkins refers readers to Ellmann's list of Joyce's 1920 library.[44] Notably, Arkins never mentions Butcher and Lang.[45] Moreover, two Greek texts with Italian commentary, one of Book 1 of the *Odyssey*, and the other of Book 14, seem to have been owned by Joyce as well.[46]

This assortment of possible early encounters with the myth of Ulysses, along with such a variety of translations of Homer, has contributed to the persistent uncertainty surrounding Joyce's various encounters with Homer. But as a whole they finally serve to assure us that Joyce supplemented his untrained forays into Homer's Greek by reading numerous translations of Homer at different times in his life, including those of Lamb, Cowper, Shaw (Lawrence), Pope, and Butler, in addition to that of Butcher and Lang. It would make sense for Joyce to have cherished Lamb in adolescence, to have studied it along with Pope and Cowper for his Intermediate Examination in 1894,[47] and then to have turned to Butler and Shaw (Lawrence) during the earlier stages of writing *Ulysses* in Trieste and Zürich, and then finally to have read the Butcher and Lang translation in order to incorporate its style and tone further into his novel in Paris. It is worth emphasizing that Stanislaus does not mention Butcher and Lang at all,[48] perhaps lending credence to the notion that Joyce read their translation in Paris at a rather late stage in the writing of *Ulysses*. It is surely fair to claim that Joyce was less than systematic in his Homeric studies and approached them with none of the intellectual rigor with

---

[44] See Ellmann (1977), 98-134. In his list of books consulted while writing *Ulysses*, Michael Patrick Gillespie includes the Earl of Derby's translation of the *Iliad*, and Cowper's translation of the *Odyssey* (Gillespie [1983], 99). Gillespie's catalogue of the Trieste library also lists the Earl of Derby's *Iliad* (Gillespie [1986], 119, #217), and Cowper's *Odyssey* (Gillespie [1986], 120, #218). Connolly includes the *Iliad* by Lang, Leaf, and Myers (Connolly [1955], 19, #144), and T. E. Shaw's *Odyssey* (Connolly [1955], 19, #145). T. E. Shaw is also known as T. E. Lawrence.

[45] Butcher and Lang's translation does not appear in any of Joyce's libraries as listed by Connolly (1955), Gillespie (1983, 1986), or Ellmann (1977), nor is it mentioned in Gillespie's lists of books Joyce owned in Zürich, nor in his list of books Joyce consulted while writing *Ulysses* (Gillespie 1983). Thus Budgen's recollection alone, rather than Joyce's ownership of the translation itself, has led to the prevailing assumptions regarding its influence upon Joyce.

[46] Homer, *Il Libro XIV dell'Odissea* appears on Gillespie's list of books Joyce owned in Zürich (Gillespie [1983], 95), as well as in Gillespie's catalogue of his Trieste library (Gillespie [1986], 120). Homer's *L'Odissea, Libro 1* is included in Gillespie's list of books Joyce consulted while writing *Ulysses* (Gillespie [1983], 198), a copy which had an interlinear Italian translation (Gillespie [1986], 120).

[47] Arkins lists the questions on Lamb in that exam (Arkins [1999], 14-15), as does Bradley (1982), 109.

[48] Stanford (1968), 276.

which he had been trained in Latin. He definitely seems to have exposed himself to an amalgam of Homeric translations in English, a commentary in German, and even Italian translations of Books 1 and 14, but he apparently never invested himself in any Latin translation or commentary. The pervasive doubt about precisely which translations he used at what points in time at the very least indicates that he never devoted himself to one certain version at the expense of all the others.

Herein lies his aesthetic of the double negative: Joyce seems to have decisively rejected reading nothing which related to the realm of the myth of Odysseus. We can be certain that Joyce did not limit himself to reading in the original, any more than he limited himself to any one specific translation. In general, Joyce's avid reading and research seems guided by an extraordinary inclusivism, in which he pored over the most elite and scholarly work at the same time as he steeped himself in the colloquial language and popular press and music of the time. The only sort of Homeric document likely excluded from his reading is a Latin translation of Homer; otherwise, Joyce read much more broadly and widely than most recognize, perhaps best exemplified by Rose and O'Hanlon's work on the lost notebook (VI.D.7) in which Joyce took notes on newspaper articles, modern Greek, contemporary slang, Aristotle's *Rhetoric*, William Wycherley's *The Plain Dealer*, and the work of Victor Bérard, Walter Leaf and W. H. Roscher.[49] Joyce's inquisitiveness seems to have directed him toward a true diversity of source material in which he deemed very little to be irrelevant or beneath his notice.

Consequently, preserving the version of the *Odyssey* to which Joyce was responding in critical work, which was the well-intentioned advice of my anonymous *PMLA* reviewer, is an impossible goal. There is no decisive and definitive translation of Homer's *Odyssey* that must be quoted in intertextual studies of Homer and Joyce, unless any particular study is an attempt to examine the influences of Joyce's own knowledge of a single translation of the *Odyssey* upon *Ulysses*. To convey the implications of the many translations by which Joyce would have been influenced, one would have to quote from each translation listed above. For textual analysis of a single brief passage, comparing the many versions Joyce read might indeed be fruitful, but in a book length study, quoting every Homeric translation that Joyce read for every piece of evidence would prove cumbersome and confusing for the reader, not to mention daunting and arduous for the scholar and horrifying for

---

[49] See Rose and O'Hanlon (1989). Brian Arkins claims, "After Homer, the most important Classical author for Joyce was Aristotle" (Arkins [1999], 23). For a thorough summary of all of the classical texts Joyce owned, see Arkins (1999), 22-25.

the publisher, who would be faced with extremely lengthy manuscripts filled with quotations from Joyce's variety of Homeric sources.

But intertextual studies do not require the fulfillment of such a demand, because they do not depend solely upon the influences upon the artist, nor upon his or her intentions. Brian Arkins notes that Julia Kristeva, who, after all, invented the notion of intertextuality,[50] claims that "any text is the absorption and transformation of another."[51] While writing *Ulysses*, Joyce absorbed and transformed many variations upon Homer's *Odyssey*, proven by his dependence on a broad array of translations.[52] In some sense, he then emulated what might have been the method of oral bards in ancient Greece, if one accepts Albert Lord's premise that

> a song has no 'author' but a multiplicity of authors, each singing being a creation....the song has a specific though flexible content....All singers use traditional material in a traditional way, but no two singers use exactly the same material in exactly the same way.[53]

Homer's poem can be considered his own version of his inherited traditional themes and episodes expressed with traditional epithets and formulae. All of the oral forms of the song which came before him inevitably comprised his intertext, which would be "transformed and absorbed" in his own effort.[54] One

---

[50] See Julia Kristeva, *Séméiotikè: Recherches pour une sémanalyse* (Paris: Éditions du Seuil, 1969), 255. On Joyce specifically, see Susan Stanford Friedman, "Weavings: Intertextuality and the (Re)Birth of the Author," in *Influence and Intertextuality in Literary History*, ed. Jay Clayton and Eric Rothstein (Madison: University of Wisconsin Press, 1991), 146-180.

[51] Julia Kristeva, *Desire in Language: A Semiotic Approach to Literature and Art*, ed. L.S. Roudiez (New York: Columbia University Press, 1980), 66; quoted by Arkins (1999), 57.

[52] Joyce was also concerned with the sound of the Greek itself. Not incidentally, Schork reports that "An ear-witness in 1937 reports that Joyce 'quoted long passages [of Homer's *Odyssey*] in his strange pronunciation where modern Greek coalesced with the Erasmus tradition and was flavored by English intonation'" (Schork [1998], 252, and see footnote on 296); see further Johannes Hedberg, "Hans Kraus, Jan Parandowski, and James Joyce," *James Joyce Quarterly* 99 (1996): 441-446. Joyce's fixation with pronunciation is also undeniable in his permutation of the Greek word for enemy, resulting in the word "exthro" (*FW*, 92.1), which produces the necessary aspiration. See Schork for discussion of how Joyce's early spelling error of the word in Notebook VIII.A.4.9 and a 1933 postcard to Paul Ruggiero bear out this learning process (Schork [1998], 256).

[53] Albert Lord, *The Singer of Tales* (Cambridge, Mass.: Harvard University Press, 1960), 95, 102.

[54] W. B. Stanford explains why Homer cannot be considered a totally

can then imagine Homer listening to other bards' versions of his song for the same sort of reliance and inspiration, according to the Parry-Lord theory. As James Redfield characterizes the creative process, "The oral poet, like others, stretches his tradition as he puts it to use."[55] Homer's oral creation of his song therefore emerged in a similar manner as Joyce's written text: both are re-creations of the forms of the story which they inherited.[56] Lord's reflection upon the task of oral poets gives further authority to the idea that despite the written nature of Joyce's text, Joyce has assumed most of the responsibilities and goals of the oral poet as a modern novelist:

> the picture that emerges is not really one of conflict between preserver of tradition and creative artist; it is rather one of the preservation of tradition by the constant re-creation of it.[57]

Homer and Joyce can both be fairly deemed to have revolutionized their inherited traditions and themes with their own insights and innovations, even

---

original storyteller but one who was reacting to his own intertext: "As far as extant literature goes the story of Ulysses begins in the *Iliad* and the *Odyssey*. Earlier records have not revealed any definite references to it, as yet. But Ulysses was apparently not Homer's own invention, and Homer never suggests it. On the contrary he makes it clear by implication that Ulysses was already a familiar figure when he began to write about him" (Stanford [1968], 8).

[55] James Redfield, "The Proem of the *Iliad*: Homer's Art," *Classical Philology* 74 (1979): 95.

[56] Contrasting Rickard's notion of "intertextual memory" (John Rickard, *Joyce's Book of Memory: The Mnemotechnic of Ulysses* [Durham, N.C.: Duke University Press, 1999], 167 ff.) with Ellmann's idea that "while Homer's use of traditional phrases and archaic forms could not be precisely duplicated, Joyce achieved something of the same effect by having his characters quote well known phrases from past authors" (Ellmann [1977], 26) raises the prospect that to some extent, Joyce's cultivation of such intense intertextuality reflects the method of oral composers like Homer. On how Adam Harvey's performance of a memorized monologue of *Finnegans Wake* reflects the methodology of oral poets, see Keri Elizabeth Ames, "Joycean Performance: How the Muse Came to Berkeley," *The James Joyce Literary Supplement* 15, no. 2 (2001): 21-23. Even the now infamous Gabler-Kidd dispute over the proper methodology for editing *Ulysses*, which has led to voluminous scholarly debate and caused David Fuller to aver, "There can be no definitive edition of *Ulysses*" (David Fuller, *James Joyce's Ulysses* [New York: Harvester Wheatsheaf, 1992], i) reflects the elusiveness of Homer's song and the haunting question of when and how it became a text at all. The original Homeric song and an utterly decisive text of *Ulysses* are both equally unattainable to some degree.

[57] Lord (1960), 29.

as they also affirmed and preserved the traditional story which they inherited.[58]

Nonetheless, if one is strictly examining influences in Joyce, one must solely rely upon those texts which we can prove Joyce read. Admittedly, the line between influence and intertextuality is difficult to demarcate, because as Eric Clayton and Jay Rothstein admit, "the shape of intertextuality in turn depends upon the shape of influence."[59] Hence studies on the influence of Homer upon Joyce must include only those translations and classical sources that Joyce actually used. Yet Clayton and Rothstein's observation that Barthes "advances a theory of intertextuality that depends entirely upon the

---

[58] Albert Lord observes how the modern oral singer Avdo Mededovic engages in just this process. Lord marvels at how closely Avdo echoes the version of the song which he has just heard while simultaneously thoroughly appropriating the story in order to reflect his own personal idea of heroism: "...how well Avdo followed his original and yet how superbly he was able to expand it and make it his own...Avdo has not only lengthened the theme from 176 lines to 558, but *he has put on it the stamp of his own understanding of the heroic mind*" (Lord [1960], 78-79; emphasis added). Lord observes how Mededovic uses his traditional language and repeats traditional themes and episodes but still makes his story an original creation of his own.

[59] Eric Clayton and Jay Rothstein, eds., *Influence and Intertextuality in Literary History* (Madison: University of Wisconsin Press, 1991), 3. Mary Reynolds offers a superb study of the influence of Dante on Joyce and describes her aims thusly: "My own attention to theme, style, and form represents an effort to move beyond the merely inferential and implicit, in order to show that Joyce's relation to Dante was not merely appreciative but purposeful... Dante's art takes on a fresh perspective as and instrument in Joyce's work" (Mary Reynolds, *Joyce and Dante: The Shaping Imagination* [Princeton, N.J.: Princeton University Press, 1981], 8). Most recently, Jennifer Margaret Fraser identifies what Zack Bowen calls "a new category of intertextuality, one that she terms *initiatory*" (Jennifer Margaret Fraser, *Rite of Passage in the Narratives of Joyce and Dante* [Gainesville: University Press of Florida, 2002], foreword). Fraser argues, "Joyce seems to battle against an anxiety of origin rather than an anxiety of influence; rather than expressing distress about powerful literary ancestors, Joyce strives to create out of the void an intertextual self that integrates and celebrates influence... Dante was one of a crucial group of guides who led Joyce around the spiritual journey of self-inscription... Dante does not influence Joyce; he teaches Joyce how to harness and yet circumvent authority" (ibid., 2, 8). Demarcating the line between influence and intertextuality is very tenuous and tricky indeed. On how authorial motives and intentions bear upon interpretation, see Quentin Skinner, "Motives, Intentions, and Interpretations of Texts," *New Literary History* 3 (1972): 393-408.

reader as the organizing center of interpretation"[60] enables us to expand that scope in intertextual studies. If the reader is indeed the location of the intertextual process, then any and all translations of Homer (as well as the original poem) known to readers are relevant and valid for comparison with *Ulysses*. Hence, to consider the intertextuality of *Ulysses*, one need not be limited to any single translation of Homer, nor to the Greek poem itself. In fact, the intertextuality that Joyce encouraged with the title *Ulysses* far surpasses the bounds of his own intentions. Michael Riffaterre explains why the intertext transcends authorial intention:

> Intertextuality is a modality of perception, the deciphering of the text by the reader in such a way that he identifies the structures to which the text owes its quality of a work of art... The intertext proper is the corpus of texts the reader may legitimately connect with the one before his eyes, that is, the texts brought to mind by what he is reading. This corpus has loose and flexible limits. Theoretically it can go on developing forever, in accordance with the reader's cultural level...[61]

Joyce's own reading, and his own purposive allusions to other texts, should therefore not limit our consideration of the intertext at all. The *Ulysses* intertext would properly include Homer's Greek poem and any and all translations of Homer, in addition to any other texts called to mind by the reading of *Ulysses*, whether Joyce knew them or not.

One example of how intertextual studies of *Ulysses* can rely most fruitfully upon the Greek text of the *Odyssey*, as well as upon various translations which Joyce read, can be found in the work of Fritz Senn. Senn examines the role of Nausikaa and Gerty MacDowell, asserting that Gerty MacDowell's blushes find their inspiration in Nausikaa's hidden desire and secret shame:

> After her dream the princess Nausicaa gives her father a number of plausible reasons for granting her the use of wagon and mules for the laundrying excursion, all except the main one that Pallas Athene in her dream had pointedly insinuated. Homer comments on what Nausikaa left out: '*aideto gar thaleron gamon exonomenai*' (*Od.* 6:66) (She was ashamed [*aideto*] to speak of her marriage [*gamon*]). Similar shame motivates Gerty MacDowell at times. Much of what moves her is not mentioned (*exomenai*). Pope freely elaborates on the Odyssean line with a gratuitous 'but blushes ill-restrained

---

[60] Clayton and Rothstein (1991), 21; Roland Barthes, "Death of the Author," in *Image-Music-Text*, trans. Stephen Heath. (New York: Hill and Wang, 1974), 142-148.

[61] Michael Riffaterre, "Syllepsis," *Critical Inquiry* (1980): 625 and 627.

betray/Her thoughts intensive on the bridal day.' [Pope, *Od.* 6.79-81] The translation also illustrates the father's simple understanding ('*noei*'): 'The conscious Sire the dawning blush survey'd.' Gerty MacDowell displays many telltale flushes; they betray thoughts, and so do omissions. The reader understands as well as Nausikaa's father does, though perhaps not everything: *panta noei*. Structured elisions or disclosive blushes are ways of conveying what words do not say.[62]

Senn quite rightly presumes that Gerty's blushes do not emerge directly from Homer's Greek but from Pope's interpolation of the shame Nausikaa displays when she neglects to mention to her father that Athena had predicted that her marriage is imminent: "For your marriage is close... and you well know that you will not be a virgin much longer" (*Od.* 6.27). Nausikaa's shame over her possible sexual awakening, betrayed in Homer's Greek poem by her omission of any reference to it in her narration to her father (*Od.* 6.57-65), finds a new form in the blushes that Pope ascribes to her. So, Senn concludes, "Joyce need not have derived Gerty's blushes from Pope's embroidering... An epic technique has been reused, the potency of absence, interdynamically."[63] Homer, Pope, and Joyce employ the technique of omission differently, but its impact for conveying Nausikaa's situation endures.

Senn makes no comment about the breakthrough in methodology that he has accomplished, but here we should pause to assess the implications of his work for future intertextual studies.[64] In Senn's exploration of Nausikaa's portrayal, Joyce's knowledge of Pope from Belvedere would support a claim that Gerty's blush was indeed influenced by Homer's Nausikaa's shame and narrative omission and in Pope's Nausikaa's blush. But whether Joyce was influenced by Pope or not, the intertextual relationship that Senn has exposed is still valid. The dynamic Senn has explored functions on the basis of the intertextuality of three texts: Homer's Greek poem, with which Pope was grappling in the hope of expressing it most accurately and effectively in English and which Joyce summarily read in fragments; Pope's translation,

---

[62] Fritz Senn, "In Classical Idiom: Anthologia Intertextualis," *James Joyce Quarterly* 25 (1987): 46-47.

[63] Ibid., 47.

[64] His only stated desire in his article is to begin to examine the Greek and Roman influences in Joyce's work which he believed had been neglected up to that point: "the multifarious samples that follow are fragmentary, random, arbitrary, a garner of possibilities. No claim is made that the relationships suggested are necessarily conscious adaptations, nor even that they exist. They are merely constructible by intertextual synergism or coactive readers' assiduity... One aim is to discern, provisionally, the diversified modulations in which older texts, techniques, or insights are transposed" (ibid., 31).

which Joyce studied at Belvedere; and finally *Ulysses* itself. As a result, Senn's work begins to redeem the fallacy pervading intertextual Homer and Joyce studies of which Kenner complained almost forty years ago: "That the fundamental correspondence is not between incident and incident but between situation and situation, has never gotten into the critical tradition."[65] Senn's work has opened the door to an exploration of the interdynamic intertextuality of Joyce's texts with each other and with their classical inspirations, and it is the task of future scholars to follow in his footsteps. Had Senn limited his inquiries to the Butcher and Lang translation, scholarship would be much poorer for the restriction.

Furthermore, one suspects that Joyce would not have endorsed such a restriction anyway. Budgen recalls that when he bemoaned his own lack of Greek, Joyce

> thereupon regretted his insufficient knowledge of that language but, as if to underline the difference in our two cases (or so I interpreted it) he said with sudden vehemence: 'But just think: isn't that a world I am peculiarly fitted to enter?'[66]

Budgen does not explicitly clarify when this conversation took place, but *Ulysses* demonstrates Joyce's entrance into that world despite his lack of the proper Greek credentials. The intricacy and resonance of the intertextual echoes in *Ulysses* with the *Odyssey* becomes nothing short of amazing when one knows how little Greek Joyce actually knew.[67] He was indeed peculiarly fitted for his task, qualified by no unusual linguistic proficiency in Greek but by some insight that seems to have defied the problems inherent to reading translations and translating individual words or phrases by themselves. Joyce himself imposed no artificial boundaries on his reading and it cannot be supposed that he would advise his readers to do so, either.

The lack of a single, authoritative translation of the *Odyssey* that guided Joyce's creative exploits justifies the use of any translation of Homer's *Odyssey* in intertextual inquiry. No negative aesthetic guides Joyce's reliance

---

[65] Hugh Kenner, *Dublin's Joyce* (New York: Columbia University Press, 1965), 181.

[66] Budgen (1960), 322-323.

[67] For justification of this claim, I cite my own work: "The Oxymoron of Fidelity in Homer's *Odyssey* and Joyce's *Ulysses*," *Joyce Studies Annual* 2003 (forthcoming), and "The Rebirth of Heroism in Homer's *Odyssey* and Joyce's *Ulysses*," in *Twenty-First Joyce: Essays in Honor of Zack Bowen*, ed. Ellen Carol Jones and Morris Beja (Gainesville: University Press of Florida, 2004 [forthcoming]).

upon Homeric translations whatsoever. Further, the intertextual echoes that Joyce fostered are not circumscribed to those that he intended to create, and so scholars and critics need not limit themselves to those texts that Joyce encountered unless they are focusing only upon direct influences. If we were actually to circumscribe our intertextual inquiries according to Joyce's knowledge, no classical scholar, nor anyone who could read ancient Greek with any degree of technical skill, would be able to apply any of their knowledge of Greek in relation to their interpretation of *Ulysses*. The absurdity of eliminating Greek scholars from valuable investigations regarding *Ulysses* highlights the absurdity of limiting intertextual studies to any single Homeric translator. As scholars of *Ulysses* we should strive to be as greedy as Joyce was in his insatiable reading. As Joyce is one of the most accretive writers in the history of western civilization, so we should strive to be accretive intertextual scholars. The intertextual enterprise lends itself to inclusion rather than exclusion, and one finds good cause to suppose that Joyce, who subscribed at least in part to Yeats' theory of universal mind and memory, would not have objected to this intertextual line of inquiry.[68]

In light of this possibility, it is particularly intriguing that Senn establishes that Stephen's statement in *Ulysses* with which we began, "whose works I enjoy reading in the original", was added to the manuscript "at a late stage, between 19 and 25 August 1921 (*JJA*, 18:196), while " I must teach you. You must read them in the original. *Thalatta! Thalatta!*" "is part of the signature dated '21 juin 21' (*JJA*, 22:7)... The choice adjective 'gorbellied' was a last touch done on the page proofs, in October 1921 (*JJA*, 23:196)."[69] Up to the very last moments, Joyce was still exerting himself to emphasize the Homeric intertext to which his title alludes. Surely if that intertext were of

---

[68] Frank Budgen writes, "It is sometimes forgotten that in his early years in Dublin Joyce lived among the believers and adepts in magic gathered round the poet Yeats. Yeats held that the borders of our minds are always shifting, tending to become part of the universal mind, and that the borders of memory also shift and form part of the universal memory. The universal mind and memory could be evoked by symbols. When telling me this Joyce added that in his own work he never used the recognized symbols, preferring instead to use trivial and quadrivial words and local geographical allusions. The intention of magical evocation, however, remained the same" (Budgen [1960], 325). Lord claims that "the peculiar purpose of oral epic song...was magical and ritual before it became heroic...the poet was sorcerer and seer before he became 'artist'....The roots of traditional oral narrative are not artistic but religious in the broadest sense" (Lord [1960], 66-67). Joyce may even have revitalized that aspect of the oral tradition through his writing.

[69] Senn (1991), 215 and 216.

little use other than as structural scaffolding, such emendations at such a late stage would hardly have been necessary.[70]

Joyce's late addition regarding the enjoyment of "reading in the original" does not emerge out of nowhere. The Rosenbach manuscript of *Ulysses* already contains a reference to how Leopold seeks and finds precisely that pleasure in "Ithaca." The section reads:

> What cerebration accompanied his act?
>
> Concluding that his silent companion was engaged in mental composition he reflected on the pleasures derived from literature of instruction rather than of amusement as he himself had applied to the works of Shakespeare more than once in the solution of difficult problems in imaginary or real life.
>
> Had he found their solution?
>
> In spite of careful and repeated reading of certain passages, aided by a glossary, he had not derived conviction from the text.
> (*Ulysses*, Rosenbach Manuscript, P629-631 L 791-792 N677-678)

The Placard for the passage reads somewhat differently; I italicize the changes:

> What cerebration accompanied his act?

---

[70] The idea that the *Odyssey* is only structural scaffolding for *Ulysses* originated with Ezra Pound (*Literary Essays of Ezra Pound*, ed. T. S. Eliot [New York: New Directions, 1968], 406) and has most recently been endorsed by Morton Levitt, *James Joyce and Modernism: Beyond Dublin* (Lewiston, N.Y.: Edwin Mellen Press, 1999). Thomas Staley deems this stance "the dismissal theory" (Thomas Staley, "Stephen Dedalus and the Temper of the Modern Hero," in *Approaches to Ulysses: Ten Essays*, ed. Thomas F. Staley and Bernard Benstock [Pittsburgh: University of Pittsburgh Press, 1970], 15). Michael Groden quotes Pound's entire comment: "These correspondences are part of Joyce's medievalism and are chiefly his own affair, a scaffold, a means of construction, justified by the result, and justified by it only" (Groden [1979], 76, from Pound's Paris letter of June 1922). Groden claims, "Pound greatly underestimated the importance the parallels and correspondences eventually assumed in Joyce's mind....[Joyce] came to believe that life consists of cyclically recurring forms, always repeating themselves despite altered specific settings... [Bloom] re-enacts a pattern set by many epic heroes before him" (ibid., 76 and 36). Michael Seidel explains why Pound repudiated his position to a certain degree later on, finding the "epic texture of *Ulysses* something more crucial to the novel" (Seidel [1976], xv). For a review of the literature on the subject, see my dissertation, Ames (2003), 1-11.

> Concluding *by inspection but erroneously* thath is [sic; corrected by Joyce to read that his] silent companion was engaged in mental composition he reflected on the pleasures derived from literature of instruction rather than of amusement as he himself had applied to the works of Shakespeare more than once *for* the solution of difficult problems in imaginary or real life.
>
> Had he found their solution?
>
> In spite of careful and repeated reading of certain *classical* passages, aided by a glossary, he had derived *imperfect* conviction from the text, *the answers not bearing in all points*. (*JJA* 21:30-31)

In the page proofs, Joyce adds two more words: Leopold's act of sipping cocoa more quickly that Stephen (which directly precedes this quotation; *U*, 17.377-381) becomes "frequentative" and "William" is inserted before Shakespeare (*JJA*, 27:150). Hence in the genesis of the text, we can witness Joyce emphasizing the use of a glossary to read "classical" passages specifically. While Leopold reads "classical passages" in the original English, which is not a foreign language to him, one might expect others to use lexicons for reading the classics of Greece and Rome, while the term glossary would apply more specifically to superannuated terms used by Shakespeare in Leopold's situation. Still, the adjective "classical" rather than "classic" encourages readers to consider glossaries for English texts and lexicons for texts written in foreign languages as somewhat interchangeable, to be considered in either case as useful resources for explicating textual matters. Joyce clarifies in his revision that Leopold reads "for" the sake of finding solutions to difficult problems, both real and imaginary. For Leopold, the pleasure of reading is not found in its capacity for amusement but its capacity for instruction, for resolving textual problems within the imaginary world as well as others occurring in real life. Joyce thus alludes most subtly to the task he is placing before his own readers. The problems to be solved are not only the infamous obscure puzzles and enigmas which show no sign of failing to keep professors busy but pragmatic ones confronted in daily living.[71] Applying one's attention to "classical passages" results in the solution of some problems confronted in the course of ordinary life, although Joyce's emendations illustrate how he wrestled with the degree to which any text can provide conviction and resolution. In the end, *Ulysses* would seem to imply

---

[71] Most recently, Sebastian Knowles has accepted the task of resolving Joycean enigmas in *The Dublin Helix: The Life of Language in Joyce's Ulysses* (Gainesville: University Press of Florida, 2001).

that only "imperfect" resolution can be reached from reading. But if the answers derived therein do not bear upon all points, readers are still incited to wonder how such classical reading and rereading inspires some degree of resolution, however imperfect. Textual puzzles and real life puzzles are thereby interconnected, and "careful and repeated reading" of classical passages should certainly send readers of *Ulysses* back to Homer again, with glossaries, lexicons, translations, and Greek texts and grammars in hand.

Ellmann establishes that after Joyce died, "On his desk, they [Giorgio and Nora] found two books, a Greek Lexicon and Oliver Gogarty's *I Follow Saint Patrick*" (*JJII,* 742), suggesting that Joyce engaged as long as he lived in the process which "Ithaca" depicts Leopold following. Ellmann does not specify which lexicon, but capitalizes the 'l', perhaps amusingly illustrating that there is really only one lexicon for Greekists, that of Liddell and Scott. Carola Giedion-Welcker, the source of Ellmann's information, does not clarify in her own memoir which Greek lexicon Joyce had in his room when he died, writing only, "Auf seinem Tisch lagen zwei Bücher: ein griechisches Lexikon und daneben das Buch von Oliver St. John Gogarty *I Follow St. Patrick.*"[72] Her footnote identifies the Gogarty book as the 1938 edition published by Rich & Cowan in London, but no further information is offered about the lexicon. Her description of Joyce's "Tisch" is perhaps more accurately described as a little writing table as might be found in the poor Pension Delphin. Further, it seems unlikely that while fleeing through the Nazi controlled borders, Joyce would have carried a huge, heavy volume like Liddell and Scott. Fritz Senn suspects the lexicon might have been one in German which Joyce could have borrowed or picked up somewhere locally without great expense.[73] Joyce's haphazard encounters with Homeric translations certainly lends authority to the notion that Joyce simply relied upon whatever books he could manage to lay his hands on when he wanted them. But none of this is proves that Joyce never used Liddell and Scott. Schork suggests there is "also internal evidence from the *Wake* that Joyce was familiar with the work of Liddell and Scott", arguing that "What had she on, the liddell oud oddity?" (*FW,* 207.26-27) and "liddle giddles" (*FW,* 448.25) are "best understood...as a reference to [Liddell's] daughter Alice Liddell, who was a model for the feature character in Lewis Carroll's *Alice in Wonderland.*"[74] Perhaps Joyce's little Liddell giggle is that he can make allusions to the standard Greek lexicon and the real life Alice simultaneously.

---

[72] Carola Giedion-Welcker, *Schriften 1926-1971* (Cologne: M. Dumont Schauberg, 1973), 73.
[73] Personal conversation, Zürich James Joyce Foundation, 19 May 2003.
[74] Schork (1998), 260 and 261.

In some sense, he used the lexicon as if he was eating Alice's mushroom in so doing! For in a most fanciful sense, when Joyce devoured lexicons and the like "with a meticulosity bordering on the insane" (*FW*, 173.34), he managed to use what he learned alter linguistic reality for his readers just as the mushroom changed Alice's physical reality and perspective.

Aside from my own fanciful suggestion in that regard, unquestionably Joyce consulted lexicons, commentaries, and glossaries as he wrote, hence managing to achieve a "parser's revenge"[75] in his work by incorporating a vast array of Latin and Greek transmogrifications into his writing. Joyce began to toy with the possibilities offered by creating parsing enigmas and neologisms quite early. For example, one such Greek transmogrification appears in the early notes for *Ulysses*: "ichthyophagoi rizophagoi kreophagoi."[76] Further, Joyce's classmate Eugene Sheehy quotes Joyce's conversations in perverted Latin with John Byrne Francis, the inspiration for Cranly in *Portrait*:

> Joyce and he carried on long conversations in Dog Latin, to which each contributed an ingenious quota. 'Ibo crix oppidum', for instance, signified: 'I am going across town': 'ad manum ballum jocabimus' – 'We will play handball'; and 'regnat felices atque canes' – 'it is raining cats and dogs'. And in more correct Latin, another bright effort on the part of 'Cranly' resulted in the aphorism 'Nomina stultorum ubique scribuntur'. It may be that these talks were, on Joyce's part, the first intimations of the vocabulary of *Finnegans Wake*.[77]

Such joking may also have been the precursor of Joyce's exploitation of what Schork deems the parser's revenge.

Evidence of Joyce engaging in his own careful and close reading of Homer, quite likely with a lexicon in hand, can be found in his notes:

> Pen asleep during slaughter...
> Lampus & Phaethon dawnstars stayed in E, not in W...
> Speech of Achilles
> funeral of Ach at sea, his Thetis
> 18 days of mourning, games

---

[75] Schork (1997), 1. For an explanation of what the parser's revenge means in Schork's terms, see my review of his book: "Joyce's Laughter at the Parser's Revenge: Review of R. J. Schork, *Latin and Roman Culture in Joyce* (Gainesville: University Press of Florida, 1997)," *The James Joyce Literary Supplement* 15, no. 2 (2001): 11-12.

[76] Herring (1977), 23.

[77] O'Connor (1967), 22. "crix" [*sic*] = *crux*?

high tomb on peaks....
Dream of 20 geese and eagle
horn &ivory
Pen proposes 12 axe trial...
Pen wakes, prays
Rather die than marry another[78]

These are very direct references to specific lines in the *Odyssey* made for "Penelope." Herring carefully lists many other such references made at this stage with their correlating page numbers in the Butcher-Lang translation.[79] Yet Herring's exhaustive list is slightly deceptive, for we cannot be certain that Joyce read that translation for these particular notes. But such notes demonstrate the extent of Joyce's meticulous reading of Homer's *Odyssey*. The "dawnstars" note finds its inspiration at *Od.* 23.246, while the speech of Achilles and the following comments apply very directly to *Od.* 24.24-95. Penelope's dream is found at *Od.* 19.560-581, while she proposes the contest of the bow at *Od.* 21.69-79 and leaves to go to bed in the middle of it at her son's insistence (*Od.* 21.384-388). Only then does the plan proceed, with Eurykleia barring the doors of the hall and Philoetius escaping the house in silence to bar the gates of the court (*Od.* 21.381-389). Two other notes show equal perspicacity and close reading of this course of events. First, Joyce wrote, "Pen remote. Big Four escape in dark", and Herring's explanation reads: "*Big Four*: Joyce's term for Odysseus and his three companions, Telemachus, Eumaeus, and Philoetius."[80] Joyce would seem to be alluding not only to how the plan is executed but to how these four leave the house after the success of slaughter in order to go to Laertes' farm, for Homer ends Book 23 by announcing that by the point of their victory and departure, the light of dawn has already pervaded the earth but Athena enshrouds them all in darkness to conceal them as they go forth (*Od.* 23.371-72).

Yet another note of Joyce's, "πυλαρτης" (*pulartes*, bunch of keys)/ no fear of anyone getting out"[81] would seem to refer more directly to barring the escape routes during the slaughter yet to come. The only gatekeeper (πυλαρτης) mentioned in the *Odyssey* is at 11.277, in reference to Hades, but surely Eurykleia, Philoetius, and Telemachus serve precisely that function despite not being overtly named as such.[82] Notably, Telemachus fails to

---

[78] Herring (1972), 495-96, lines 43, 48, 57-60, 70-74.
[79] See ibid, 497.
[80] Ibid., 495, line 52, and 497, note 52.
[81] Herring (1977), 27.
[82] No one other than Hades is ever given this epithet by Homer; its only other uses are at *Il.* 8.367 and 13.415. This detail would likely not have perturbed Joyce in

safeguard the door of the store-room properly before the slaughter, so that the suitors are able to take out weapons and attempt to defend themselves, threatening to foil Odysseus' triumph. Telemachus admits his error to his father in leaving the door open and Eumaeus is commanded to go close it, qualifying Eumaeus as a gatekeeper as well (*Od.* 22.132-159). Herring's allusion to "Keys: like Keyes's ad: no fear of anyone getting out" (*U*, 6.741-742) alongside this note identifies another permutation of Joyce's notes and this notion in the novel, but Joyce's note here likely applies quite directly to the course of events leading up to the slaughter of the suitors.

Thus the precision of Joyce's notes shows his very thorough consideration and commentary on the action of Homer's poem, which one certainly suspects would be the result of repeated and frequentative returns to classical passages with a care and attention to detail with which Joyce is not consistently credited. Further evidence in this regard can be found in an early note referring to Hermes: "'great host' ραβδος / Psychopompos".[83] Hermes' *rabdos* is his golden magic wand, with which he wakens mortals or puts them to sleep, and with which he guides the ghosts of the suitors to Hades in his role as *psychopompos* (meaning conductor or guider of souls or ghosts) in what is traditionally called the Second *Nekuia* (meaning the second descent to Hades after the first one by Odysseus and his comrades in Book 11) at *Od.* 24.1-10.[84] Elsewhere, Joyce makes a characteristic error in the spelling of Nekuia: "2nd nekia, Cyllen. Hermes goldrod,"[85] again referring at a different

---

the slightest, and Roscher does mention it (Wilhelm Heinrich Roscher, *Ausführliches Lexikon der griechischen und römischen mythologie*, 6 vols. and 2 suppl. vols. [Leipzig: B. G. Teubner, 1884-1937], vol. I, 1785), as Herring notes.

[83] Herring (1977), 27.

[84] This epithet is not Homeric and enters into Attic Greek usage only later on. Liddell and Scott cite only three instances of its use in extant texts, one referring to Charon in Euripides' *Alcestis* and two others to Hermes in Plutarch and Diodorus Siculus. But because it is so literally a compound of the Homeric words for soul or ghost (ψυχη) and the noun meaning guide or escort (πομπος), it would naturally have appealed to Joyce with his elementary sense of Greek and his delight in coining his own terms by putting words together in precisely this manner. Herring provides the citation for the word in Roscher (Herring [1977], 27, and Roscher [1884-1937], vol. I, 1783), where Joyce may also have encountered it.

[85] Herring (1972), 495, line 53. Another instance of a note in Greek seems to show Joyce making an error which was actually the result of a copying mistake. Herring's note reads: "Hades τη ιδειν / un seen (maker of)" (Herring (1977), 27). I wondered if herein lay another Greek error on Joyce's part. But when Fritz Senn and I returned to the original notes, we found: "α ιδειν" (*JJA*, 12:156; discovered with Fritz Senn, Zürich James Joyce Foundation, 5 May 2003). The alpha is thoroughly legible, seven millimeters wide and seven millimeters tall, and unmistakable. In this instance,

point in his notes to this passage.⁸⁶ Taken together, these examples in Joyce's notes surely reflect his own "careful and repeated reading of certain passages" (*U*, 17.389), in the present case, of the Homeric passage *Od.* 24.1-97.⁸⁷ There is no reason why we, Joyce's readers, should not do the same careful and close reading alluded to in "Ithaca" and demonstrated by Joyce's own note-taking.⁸⁸

Fritz Senn concludes that Joyce's late emendations to *Ulysses* concerning reading in the original suggest why he "may well have been

Joyce got his Greek spelling correct! More Greek words and phrases can be found throughout the early notes in Herring (1977), 12, 13, 15, 16, 22, 23, 30. Direct citations of Homeric passages include "undied heroes /Od.IV.563 /Rhadamanthys /Ae.VI.541" (Herring [1977], 31), "Od. 15.356" (Herring [1977], 30), and "Od. XI.118.130/-XXIII250-275" (Herring [1977], 28). For my analysis of the significance of these passages to the meaning of heroism in *Ulysses* and the *Odyssey*, see my dissertation, Ames (2003), 227-232.

⁸⁶ Hermes first has his wand in his hand when he goes to Ogygia to deliver the divine order to Kalypso that she must send Odysseus on his way home, and Kalypso's first response to his arrival is a question: "Why then, Hermes of the golden wand, have you come to me..." (*Od.* 5.87). Fritz Senn drew my attention to the abruptness of her question (personal conversation, Zürich James Joyce Foundation, 12 May 2003), which is posed right after she seats him without offering him any refreshment. Indeed, various disputes about this issue have arisen in the past, summarized by Alfred Heubeck who states, "Hermes is seated *too soon*" in this encounter (Alfred Heubeck with Stephanie West and J. B. Hainsworth, *A Commentary on Homer's Odyssey* [Oxford: Clarendon Press, 1991], vol. I, 263). See his summary of the scholarly debate surrounding the issue (ibid., 263-264). For the present argument, what is critical is that Joyce notices the golden wand and its relation to Hermes' role in the poem and refers to it in his notes in two different stages of composition. Recent fine work of the importance of Hermes to *Ulysses* includes Robert D. Newman, "Narrative Transgression and Restoration: Hermetic Messengers in *Ulysses*," *James Joyce Quarterly* 29 (1992): 315-337, and Jennifer Fraser, "Intertextual Turnarounds: Joyce's Use of the Homeric 'Hymn to Hermes,'" *James Joyce Quarterly* 36 (1999): 541-557, but neither addresses the issue of the magic wand.

⁸⁷ Joyce even uses the Homeric method of citing different books by using an omega to indicate *Od.* 24.115 and an epsilon to indicate *Od.* 5.215: "πολυδορος (dowery) / not so beautiful as Artemis (e 215)/ω —115 war)" (Herring [1977], 15), providing more evidence that Joyce returned repeatedly to the inception of Book 24.

⁸⁸ Too many other very specific Homeric and Vergilian references to list here pervade Joyce's early notes, including various heroes, heroines, gods, and goddesses mentioned on every page (see Herring [1977], 11-31). One line, *Od.* 2.260, is copied directly: "Τηλεμαχος δ᾽απανευθε επι θινα θαλασσης" (Herring [1977], 13, and *JJA*, 12:134). The line means, "And Telemachus went away along the shore of the sea." Joyce makes a spelling error here, because χιων should properly begin with the letter kappa.

stressing the benefits of reading in the original, particularly when the novel or epic at hand is one which subversively keeps translating its own material and in its title purports to be a metamorphosis of regressively remote origins."[89] Joyce's addition of the word "frequentative" (*U*, 17.382) in the page proofs (*JJA*, 27:150) only intensifies the power of his point, for just as Leopold's sips become "frequentative" during the course of revision, so his reading is stated to occur "more than once" from the Rosenbach manuscript onward. Joyce emphasizes repetition with the selection of "frequentative" as opposed to "frequent"; his chosen adjective accentuates the repetition of the same act at different instances, not just the short intervals between one sustained act. Consequently, our reading of classical passages should be frequentative and habitual as well. In this way, perhaps the cocoa, which William Tindall finds is derived from the tree with the Latin botanical name *Theobroma cacao*, meaning "god's food,"[90] is related to the repeated reading which may provide another kind of sustenance.

Hence *Ulysses* itself presents the arguments for the merits and perils of the process of reading and rereading in which Joyce himself was engaged. Surely he intended for his readers to do the same, so that *Ulysses* stands as an invitation to investigate to what degree any text is an original and how language itself becomes like the mist of Athena, the mist with which she enshrouds Ithaca upon Odysseus' return to Ithaca so that he cannot recognize his own homeland (*Od*. 13.187ff.). Joyce's own use of a wide variety of Homeric translations in English, as well as the use and study of commentaries which his limited Greek permitted him, shows him struggling to identify the incarnations of Odysseus and Homer's *Odyssey* in his own cultural and historical context. Moreover, *Ulysses* provokes its readers to wonder if a hero by any other name may still be the same hero after all. For all of these reasons, future intertextual Joyce scholars must seek to expose how *Ulysses* returns to the texts that came before it and reaffirms their conceptions and values, as well as how it transcends them and redefines them. That return cannot be restricted to any single Homeric translation and should in fact include a return to Homer's original poem in Greek.

At last, intertextual Joyce readers are not obligated to confine themselves to any particular Homeric translation, nor to translations alone. Yet our efforts to understand how Joyce's own lack of restrictions regarding the Homeric translations he relied upon, combined with his oddly undisciplined yet enthusiastic ventures into the Greek language itself, led to

---

[89] Senn (1992), 217.
[90] Don Gifford with Robert J. Seidman, *Ulysses Annotated* (Berkeley: University of California, 1988), 571.

the "usylessly unreadable Blue Book of Eccles" (*FW*, 179.26), should still governed by a negative aesthetic, but not one which restricts our inquiries to the consideration of the Butcher and Lang translation of Homer. Instead, we should embrace the same aesthetic Joyce himself did in his reading, that of the double negative. That aesthetic requires us to accept and to explore the profundity of Fritz Senn's insistence that "nothing linguistic was foreign to Joyce."[91] In exploring the implications of this notion, far more remains to be discovered concerning how and why Homer's *Odyssey* and the Greek flag inspired the original color of the blue book of Eccles.[92] After all, reading voraciously is the beginning of the intertextual odyssey which Joyce himself endorsed in two letters to his Aunt Josephine Murray, instructing her on October 14, 1921: "If you want to read *Ulysses* you had better first get or borrow from a library a translation in prose of the *Odyssey* of Homer" (*Letters I*, 174). Most intriguingly, he specifies no particular translation whatsoever but only that she should read a prose version. In a letter of November 10, 1922 he writes again to her,

> You say there is a lot of it [*Ulysses*] you don't understand. I told you to read the *Odyssey* first. As you have not done so I asked my publisher to send you an article which will throw a little light on it. Then buy at once *The Adventures of Ulysses* (which is Homer's story told in simple English much abbreviated) by Charles Lamb. You can read it in a night and can buy it at Gill's or Browne and Nolan's for a couple of shillings.[93] Then have a try at *Ulysses* again. (*Letters I*, 193)

What article he sent her will unfortunately remain a mystery. Yet his reassurance that Lamb is simple English and can be read in one night exposes Joyce's hope that normal people like his aunt, not only scholars, could still

---

[91] Fritz Senn, The Eighteenth International Joyce Symposium, Trieste, Italy, 18 June 2002.

[92] Padraic Colum recalls visiting Joyce in Paris in 1923, where he "noticed a Greek flag on the wall of the vestibule of his apartment. 'The Greeks have always brought me good luck,' he said when I looked enquiringly at it. The flag, he told me, was a relic of Trieste" (O'Connor [1967], 79). The blue of the Greek flag would then seem to have become a talisman for Joyce, only confirming his earlier claim about Greeks bringing him luck, written to Harriet Shaw Weaver in 1921 (*Letters I*, 167, and *SL*, 284, quoted previously in this essay).

[93] Kevin Sullivan establishes that Joyce was responsible for Lamb's first seven chapters on his Belvedere exams and that Andrew Lang's text published by E. Arnold or John Cooke's text published by Browne and Nolan were used (Sullivan [1957], 237). Joyce's memory of this reading could then account for his advice to go to Browne and Nolan's.

enjoy his book. One wonders if he recommends the prose version only because it is easier to read, more accessible, and less daunting than Pope. But the fact that Joyce did not even find the issue of translation crucial enough at first to specify which translation she should obtain, instead simply urging her to read whichever one she can get her hands on, reveals a great deal about his own method of reading in preparation for writing *Ulysses*.[94] He himself did what he told his aunt to do: read whatever you can find and understand about Homer's *Odyssey* first.

A more overt intertextual invitation for future readers beyond Aunt Josephine can hardly be imagined. The aim that Richard Ellmann ascribes to Joyce makes much more sense in light of Joyce's own advice: "To some extent, Joyce wished his book to be a sequel to the *Odyssey*, to some extent a reenactment of it."[95] Yet to assess David Norris' insistence that "what Joyce is doing here [in *Ulysses*] is nobly in harmony with the spirit of the *Odyssey*,"[96] one must read the way Joyce hoped Aunt Josephine would. *Ulysses* is the intertextual book *par excellence*, whose author advised not only seeking intertextual appreciation but doing so through the sequential reading of the *Odyssey* and *Ulysses*. Had Aunt Josephine been a Greek philologist, one cannot imagine Joyce forbidding her from reading the Greek poem "in the original" but sending her to Lamb instead. Nevertheless, relying upon his own sort of silence and cunning while in exile, Joyce crafts one more little enigma for the professors by enabling Buck Mulligan to give Greek philologists the same advice that Joyce gave ordinary readers like his aunt. In so doing, the intertextual reading of the *Odyssey* in any form in conjunction with *Ulysses* becomes a call to action from the author himself.

Yale University

---

[94] William Fallon recalls Connolly surmising that Joyce bought a secondhand copy of Pope's *Odyssey* along the quays of Dublin, a copy now lost (O'Connor [1967], 42). Joyce's advice to Aunt Josephine demonstrates his habitual inclination to grab copies of whatever books he wanted wherever he could afford them, lending credibility to the possibility that he acquired Pope in the same way.

[95] Ellmann (1977), 30-31.

[96] David Norris, "A Clash of Titans: Joyce, Homer, and the Idea of Epic," in *Studies on Joyce's Ulysses,* ed. Jacqueline Genet and Elisabeth Hellgouarc'h (Caen, France: G. D. R. d'études anglo-irlandaises du C. N. R. S., 1991), 118.

"NICHTSNICHTSUNDNICHTS": BECKETT'S AND JOYCE'S TRANSTEXTUAL UNDOINGS

DIRK VAN HULLE

During the first decade of Beckett's literary career, Fritz Mauthner and Arthur Schopenhauer connected the twin peaks of literary modernism. James Joyce and Marcel Proust represented the world in all its phenomenal abundance (with a respectively zoological and botanical emphasis). By weaving their textual veils they may have created the impression that something "deeper" lurked behind. Beckett suggested to his friend Axel Kaun that whatever "lurked behind" might simply be nothing at all. This insight, however, did not prevent him from writing. The assumption that there is nothing beyond phenomena except their negation is already present in Beckett's first story, appropriately called "Assumption."[1] Its very first sentence implicitly contains what Beckett stated explicitly in an interview with Israel Shenker: that he was working with impotence as an alternative to Joyce's omnipotence. But just as the Schopenhauerian denial of the will is impossible without will and Mauthnerian linguistic skepticism is unthinkable without language, a wide intertextual exploration is necessary in order to illustrate how Beckett rid his work of its initial erudition. He needed words in order to take them back, negating the kinetic energy of artistic achievement to arrive at the potential energy of ineffability. The issue at stake is not nihil, but the enormous surplus value Beckett gave to the infinitesimal, 'the next next to nothing.'[2]

In 1937, Samuel Beckett wrote to Axel Kaun that his language appeared to him like a veil that must be torn apart in order to get at the things behind it.[3] This view seems to reflect the kind of essentialism which Richard Rorty rejects as "the way in which scientists, scholars, critics and philosophers think of themselves as cracking codes, peeling away accidents to reveal

---

[1] Samuel Beckett, "Assumption," in *Samuel Beckett: The Complete Short Prose 1929-1989*, ed. S. E. Gontarski (New York: Grove Press, 1995), 3-7.
[2] Samuel Beckett, letter to A. J. Leventhal, February 3, 1959, quoted in James Knowlson, *Damned to Fame: The Life of Samuel Beckett* (London: Bloomsbury, 1996), 461.
[3] Samuel Beckett, *Disjecta*, ed. Ruby Cohn (London: John Calder, 1983), 52.

essence, stripping away veils of appearance to reveal reality."[4] But to those "things behind it" Beckett subtly added the parenthesis "(oder das dahinterliegende Nichts)". The paradox of his enterprise was that in order to tear apart the veil of language and reach this absence of things behind it, he had to weave it first. He did so with the help of masters in the art of creating the illusion of diversity such as James Joyce, but also Marcel Proust, Arthur Schopenhauer, Fritz Mauthner, and many others. With the advantage of hindsight, it is possible to investigate the first decade of Beckett's literary career in retrograde direction, taking back his words in five steps, in order to arrive at the textual doings undone in the very first sentence of his first story, "Assumption".

5. Mauthner's "Nichtwort"

"In the word was no beginning" is the first note on page 269 of Joyce's notebook VI.B.41, containing several notes on the German philosopher Fritz Mauthner's *Beiträge zu einer Kritik der Sprache*.[5] Mauthner's linguistic scepticism is based on the idea that thought and language are inseparable.[6] Language is a set of metaphors, according to Mauthner, and since words are based on memory,[7] they are unsuited for communication, for everybody has different memories.[8]

While Joyce was reading Mauthner in 1938 (more than a decade after Wyndham Lewis's criticism in *The Art of Being Ruled* and *Time and Western Man*) he found an answer to the Gracehoper's famous question to the Ondt: "*why can't you beat time?*" (*FW*, 419.7-8).[9] The same question was formulated somewhat differently in Mauthner's *Beiträge zu einer Kritik der Sprache*: "Why is our world, the way it represents itself in our language, so extremely spatial? Why do we find our bearings faster in three-dimensional space than in unidimensional time?" Mauthner's answer is simple: "Because our visual faculty also serves as a space organ. Because our sense of hearing

---

[4] Richard Rorty, "The Pragmatist's Progress," in *Interpretation and Overinterpretation*, ed. Stefan Collini (Cambridge: Cambridge University Press, 1992), 89.

[5] Fritz Mauthner, *Beiträge zu einer Kritik der Sprache*, 3 vols. (Leipzig: Felix Meiner, 1923).

[6] Ibid., vol. 1, 176: "Es gibt kein Denken ohne Sprechen."

[7] Ibid., vol. 1, 212.

[8] Ibid., vol. 3, 641.

[9] James Joyce, *Finnegans Wake* (London: Penguin, 1992 [1939]).

does not equally serve as a time organ."[10] Some excerpts among Joyce's Mauthner notes in notebook VI.B.46, made in 1938, are derived from a section in the *Beiträge* concerning adverbs: "Adverbien - Raum und Zeit,"[11] containing a subsection on "Raum, Zeit und Kausalität." Mauthner contends that language cannot create time concepts and therefore spatial terms are needed to qualify time. When a spatial adverb is used to denote time, we often fail to recognize the metaphorical use. Such an adverb can in turn denote causality. Although it is merely a linguistic detail, the metaphorical transition from spatial to temporal to causal notions leads directly to the most fundamental questions of human understanding, according to Mauthner.[12] Joyce noted down "after = because" (notebook VI.B.46, page 50), corresponding to the passage in the *Beiträge* where Mauthner argues that it would be wise to express the idea of cause exclusively with temporal adverbs, at least if Hume and other skeptics were right in saying that the notion of cause is projected onto the concept of time.

In the third chapter of *Ulysses*, Stephen Dedalus already pondered the "ineluctable modalities" of the visible and the audible, echoing Lessing's notions of *Nacheinander* and *Nebeneinander*. During the seventeen years of *Work in Progress* Joyce seems to have developed and trained this "time organ" (notebook VI.B.46, page 50) in order to find a less exclusively spatial form of expression, combining the *Nach-* and *Nebeneinander* to create the impression of simultaneity by means of the linear medium of the written word. In this respect, Samuel Beckett remarked in his German diaries:

> Long discussion about theatre and film, which Eggers condemns, calls at the best intellectualism. Won't hear of possibility of word's inadequacy. The dissonance that has become principle and that the word cannot express, because literature can no more escape from chronologies to simultaneities, from Nebeneinander to Miteinander, that [than] the human voice can sing chords. As I talk and listen I realize suddenly how *Work in Progress* is the only possibility [possible] development from *Ulysses*, the heroic attempt to make literature accomplish what belongs to music—the Miteinander and the simultaneous.[13]

Beckett's own interest in music, however, was not so much in the notes, but in the way a composer can arrange them so as to create silence. In *Dream of*

---

[10] Mauthner, *Beiträge*, vol. 3, 128.
[11] Ibid., vol. 3, 102-131.
[12] Ibid., vol. 3, 128.
[13] Beckett, German diaries, notebook 6, March 26, 1937; quoted in Knowlson, *Damned to Fame*, 258.

Fair to Middling Women, Belacqua refers to Beethoven's "compositions eaten away with terrible silences."[14] In his letter to Axel Kaun (July 9, 1937), Beckett again explicitly refers to the silences in Beethoven's music:

> Is there any reason why that terrible materiality of the word surface should not be capable of being dissolved, like for example the sound surface, torn by enormous pauses, of Beethoven's seventh Symphony, so that through whole pages we can perceive nothing but a path of sounds suspended in giddy heights, linking unfathomable abysses of silence?[15]

Beckett explained to his German friend how it became more and more difficult for him to write official English. The assumption that the text (conceived as a veil) merely gives the impression that there is some essence behind it and that possibly there is nothing to be unveiled at all, is emphasized when Beckett informs his friend about his plan to "bore one hole after another in [language], until what lurks behind it—be it something or nothing—begins to seep through." His ultimate aim was to reach "that silence that underlies All."[16] But "silence is still a word," Mauthner argued, and therefore he suggested the idea of a "Nichtwort."[17] This seems to suggest a link with what Beckett called his "Literatur des Unworts."

4. Beckett's "unword"

It is possible that Beckett had not yet read Mauthner's *Beiträge* when he wrote his letter to Axel Kaun and that "the entries from Mauthner in the commonplace book [MS 3000] date from after the summer of 1938," as Geert Lernout suggested in "James Joyce and Fritz Mauthner and Samuel Beckett".[18] In the meantime, more Mauthner notes have been retraced in Joyce's notebooks VI.B.41 and VI.B.46.[19] The surrounding jottings give an

---

[14] Samuel Beckett, *Dream of Fair to Middling Women*, ed. Eoin O'Brien and Edith Fournier (New York: Arcade Publishing, 1992), 139.

[15] Beckett, *Disjecta*, 172 (German source text page 53).

[16] Ibid.

[17] Mauthner, *Beiträge*, vol. 1, 83: "Zum höchsten Einssein der Vernichtung gelangt man durch das Nichtwort. Schweigen ist noch ein Wort."

[18] Geert Lernout, "James Joyce and Fritz Mauthner and Samuel Beckett," in *In Principle, Beckett Is Joyce*, ed. Friedhelm Rathjen (Edinburgh: Split Pea Press, 1994), 22.

[19] For transcriptions of Mauthner notes in VI.B.46 and VI.B.41 see respectively Dirk Van Hulle, "Beckett–Mauthner–Zimmer–Joyce," in *Joyce Studies Annual* 1999, ed. Thomas F. Staley (Austin: University of Texas Press, 1999), 143-

indication of the period in which these notes were taken: Oliver St John Gogarty's *I follow Saint Patrick*, published in June 1938, is referred to some ninety pages before the first Mauthner notes in VI.B.41, and the Zimmer notes (VI.B.41:288-9, fifteen pages after the Mauthner notes) are most probably not taken before October 8, 1938 (the date of Heinrich Zimmer Jr.'s dedication to Joyce in the copy of Zimmer's book *Maya* in Joyce's personal library). Samuel Beckett told Linda Ben-Zvi that he "had not read Mauthner to Joyce but had, on Joyce's request, taken the volumes and read them himself."[20] Geert Lernout suggests that "Joyce must have talked about Mauthner and lent the three volumes, after he had finished with them, in the second half of 1938, when Beckett was indeed close again to Joyce."[21] In theory, Beckett need not have had to wait until Joyce had finished with the *Beiträge*. Around the time Beckett wrote his letter to Kaun, Joyce asked several friends to read books for him, summarize them, and sometimes even mark important passages in the margins of the text. A famous example is Mark Twain's *Huckleberry Finn*, which David Fleischman was asked to read not *to*, but *for* Joyce. "I never read it and have nobody to read it to me and it takes too much time with all I am doing," Joyce explained in a letter to David Fleischman (August 8, 1937), mentioning that he had sent him a copy of the book.[22] The next day (August 9, 1937), Joyce wrote a letter to Frank Budgen, asking him to make a *"précis"* of J. Sheridan Le Fanu's *The House by the Churchyard*. In the same way, Joyce might have asked Beckett to read Mauthner's *Beiträge* for him, but in that case it seems more likely that he would have done so when Beckett lived in Paris again (after mid-October[23]). Beckett made notes for Joyce, for instance on Zimmer's *Maya*. But while he does not seem to have taken any particular interest in Zimmer's book, the different (more extensive) nature of Beckett's Mauthner excerpts does suggest a personal interest in Mauthner's nominalist view. The letter to Kaun indicates that in July 1937 (and even earlier, as his philosophy notes suggest), Beckett already took an interest in nominalism.

183, and Dirk Van Hulle, "'Out of Metaphor': Mauthner, Richards, and the Development of Wakese," in *James Joyce: The Study of Languages*, ed. D. Van Hulle (*New Comparative Poetics* 6) (Brussels / Bern / New York: Presses Interuniversitaires Européennes PIE-Peter Lang, 2002), 91-118.

[20] Linda Ben-Zvi, "Fritz Mauthner for Company," *Journal of Beckett Studies* 9 (1984): 65.

[21] Lernout, "James Joyce and Fritz Mauthner and Samuel Beckett," 22.

[22] *Letters III*, 401.

[23] See Knowlson, *Damned to Fame,* 274: "He left for Paris in the middle of October [...]."

Chris Ackerley's suggestion that Beckett may have had Mauthner in mind[24] raises the question what went on in *Joyce's* mind if Beckett told him about his quest for "some kind of Nominalist irony."[25] Since the letter to Kaun has the nature of a poetical statement, it is not unlikely that after Beckett's return to Paris, he discussed this topic with Joyce. The interest in nominalism seems to have been mutual.[26] Since Eugene Jolas remembers having read parts of the *Beiträge* to Joyce,[27] it is plausible that Joyce introduced Beckett to Mauthner's work; on the other hand, it may have been Beckett's interest in nominalism that renewed Joyce's interest in Mauthner. For it is indeed remarkable that Joyce decided to make notes on Mauthner at such a late date in the writing process of *Finnegans Wake*.

On October 5, 1938, Joyce wrote to Daniel Brody: "I have come back to put the finishing touches to *Work in Progress* [...]."[28] This partly explains the nature of Joyce's loose Mauthner jottings and the remarkable difference from Beckett's long Mauthner excerpts in MS 3000 (at the Beckett Archive in Reading). Joyce used the *Beiträge* for the finishing touches in Book IV of *Finnegans Wake*, whereas Beckett was developing his own poetics; Joyce was looking for words, Beckett tried to find the "unword". Beckett could easily adopt Joyce's style of making notes, as is evidenced by the Zimmer notes he made for Joyce. As John Pilling's edition of *Beckett's 'Dream' Notebook* shows, Beckett's writing method at the beginning of the thirties was very much inspired by the non-syntagmatic way in which Joyce jotted down words in his notebooks. A good example is the *Dream* passage on Beethoven, mentioned above, based on excerpts from Romain Rolland's *Vie de Beethoven*:

---

[24] See John Pilling, *Beckett Before Godot* (Cambridge: Cambridge University Press, 1997), 165 and 255, n. 41. I wish to thank John Pilling for the stimulating discussions we have had on this subject. His recent examination of MS 3000 suggests that the Mauthner notes probably date from the spring or early summer of 1938.

[25] Beckett, *Disjecta*, 173 (German source text page 53).

[26] See also *JJII*, 648-649.

[27] Eugene Jolas, *Man from Babel* (New Haven and London: Yale University Press, 1998), 166. *Man from Babel* is not the most reliable source for this kind of dating. The context suggests that he read Mauthner to Joyce in Zürich between September 1934 and October 1935 (see also Van Hulle, "Beckett–Mauthner–Zimmer–Joyce," 146). But if Jolas only mentions Mauthner as a general example to illustrate that Joyce not only asked him to write summaries, but also to read aloud ("I remember reading Mauthner's German volume on language to him"), this does not necessarily refer to their stay in Zürich.

[28] *Letters III*, 432.

> His eyes are closed, he smokes a long pipe
> (Beethoven)
> She's another unsterbliche Geliebte
> (Beet.'s *Teresa Brunsvik*)
> The 7th & 8th *aufgeknoepft*
> Poor B! he was very shortsighted.
> 6 melodies *An die ferne Geliebte*
> *Mein Reich ist in der Luft* [29]

Beckett reshaped and merged these notes in a crucial sentence in *Dream of Fair to Middling Women*:

> I think of Beethofen, his eyes are closed, the poor man he was very shortsighted they say, his eyes are closed, he smokes a long pipe, he listens to the Ferne, the unsterbliche Geliebte, he unbuttons himself to Teresa ante rem, I think of his earlier compositions where into the body of the musical statement he incorporates a punctuation of dehiscence, flottements, the coherence gone to pieces, (...) compositions eaten away with terrible silences[30]

Beckett's Mauthner notes, however, are quite different. Unlike his notes for *Dream of Fair to Middling Women*, which resemble Joyce's jottings, Beckett's Mauthner excerpts are much more extensive: he copied whole pages of text and only left out the examples, whereas Joyce was—on the contrary—particularly interested in the concrete examples, leaving out the abstract philosophy.

A section from the second volume of Mauthner's *Beiträge zu einer Kritik der Sprache* may illustrate this difference. Among Beckett's long excerpts from this volume is a passage on metaphors, where Mauthner refers to literary examples such as Shakespeare and Goethe. About the latter's *Dichtung und Wahrheit*, Beckett excerpted a passage that draws attention to the way Goethe uses words in an "ironic" way, suggesting that the German author regrets being obliged to follow linguistic conventions. The only line which Beckett omitted is the concrete reference to the first pages of Goethe's *Dichtung und Wahrheit*.[31] James Joyce also read this section and made a few

---

[29] John Pilling, *Beckett's 'Dream' Notebook* (Reading: Beckett International Foundation, 1999), 157-158.
[30] Beckett, *Dream*, 139.
[31] Mauthner, *Beiträge*, vol. 2, 506-507: "in seiner (Goethes) bewunderungswürdigen Prosa scheint er sich wirklich mehr als irgend ein anderer Schriftsteller vor und nach ihm über alle möglichen Grenzen der Sprache zu erheben, weil er die Worte in einer unnachahmlichen Weise gewissermassen ironisch

notes. But instead of concentrating on Mauthner's commentary, Joyce focused on actual examples, and merely jotted down short notes such as "hand of mouth" (notebook VI.B.41, page 272) corresponding to a passage where Mauthner needs almost a whole page to explain how Shakespeare parodies his predecessors by using mixed metaphors, often referring to Latin phrases such as "manus oris mei" ("the hand of my mouth").[32] Although Mauthner's linguistic scepticism apparently fascinated Joyce to the extent that he read all three volumes of his *Beiträge*, the impact of this work on Joyce was understandably smaller than on Beckett. For Joyce, Mauthner was an interesting collection of linguistic examples, ready to be plundered in order to enrich his own, almost finished work. Beckett was still establishing his poetics. When his long excerpts are interrupted by omissions, these ellipses or "unwords" marked by three dots [...] often correspond to concrete examples with which Mauthner illustrates his theories. In a way, these ellipses already prefigure the elliptic style of Beckett's late prose, in which he systematically eliminated as many references to concrete objects as possible. This tendency toward abstraction fits in with his attempts to find a literary equivalent for Beethoven's "terrible silences" and his admiration for music—the most abstract of arts—which was undoubtedly stimulated by his reading of Schopenhauer.

3. Joyce's "Nichtsnichtsundnichts"

"At the earthsbest schoppinhour" (*FW,* 414.33), when Beckett was introduced to Joyce, the latter was working on his fable of "the Ondt and the Gracehoper" (*FW,* 414.14-419.10). Joyce kept adding more insects to each subsequent version of this fable in order to create a "world of differents"

---

gebraucht, das heisst mit der deutlich verratenen Klage darüber, dass er einfach dem Sprachgebrauche folgen müsse. Nirgends ist selbst bei ihm dieser Stil so ausgebildet wie in 'Dichtung und Wahrheit'. [Gleich die Eingangszeilen mit ihrer Anführung der astronomischen Ereignisse bei seiner Geburt sind typisch für] diese überlegene Art, die Worte als blosse Worte zu gebrauchen." (Beckett omits the passage in brackets.)

[32] Mauthner, *Beiträge*, vol. 2, 504: "Shakespeare war dennoch ein unvergleichbares Genie; das alte Gebrechen der Sprache, ungehörige Bilder zu vermischen, war nur zu seiner Zeit besonders üppig in Mode. Fast wie bei den stärksten Autoren der römischen Spätzeit. Nur daß die antiken Metaphern bei Shakespeare uns aus zweiter Hand kommen. [...] 'Numquid manus mea valet hoc, aut manus oris mei per loquelas agit tam grandem rem?' (Conf. XI, 11) 'Die Hand meines Mundes', es klingt wie ausgestreckte Sehnsucht."

(*FW,* 417.10). According to Schopenhauer, the diversity we perceive in the visible world is our representation, which he refers to as the *principium individuationis*: "We have called time and space the *principium individuationis*, because only through them and in them is multiplicity of the homogeneous possible."[33] With regard to Schopenhauer's philosophical conclusion—the denial of the will to live—it is interesting to note that in the fifth version of "the Ondt and the Gracehoper,"[34] the latter "will beheld a world of differents," whereas two versions later[35] he "will beheld *not* a world of differents," as if he suddenly understands that the diversity he perceives is merely an illusion. This Schopenhauerian vision occurs when the Gracehoper "makes the aquinatance of the Ondt," living in a "windhame" called "Nixnixundnix" (*FW,* 415.29). After a summer of "jigging ajog" the incarnated will-to-live has nothing to eat: "Nichtsnichtsundnichts" (*FW,* 416.17), three times the last word ("Nichts") of the last part of *The World as Will and Representation* (Book IV: "Affirmation and Denial of the Will-to-Live").

If "the world of differents" as it was recreated by Joyce is to be interpreted as a textual veil of Maya (to use Schopenhauer's term), it is not at all clear whether the weaving of the text was inspired by the assumption that there really was some *Ding an sich* to be unveiled or rather by the desire to "be e'er scheining" (*FW,* 528.22): the text may be nothing but a phenomenal *Erscheinung* which merely creates the *impression* that there is something to be unveiled. Joyce was well aware of the fact that no matter how hard one tries to reveal something, the very attempt to do so wraps it up in words again. The textual development is an envelopment: "Admittedly it is an outer husk: its face, in all its featureful perfection of imperfection, is its fortune: it exhibits only the civil or military clothing of whatever passionpallid nudity or plaguepurple nakedness may happen to tuck itself under its flap" (*FW,* 109.08-12). To reveal is to reveil, which raises the question whether there is anything to be revealed in the first place. Even the opposite of "Nixnixundnix," the Gracehoper's house "Tingsomingenting," is Danish for a "thing like nothing."

---

[33] Arthur Schopenhauer, *The World as Will and Representation*, vol. 1, trans. E. F. J. Payne (New York: Dover Publications, 1969), 331.
[34] *JJA,* 57:357; Yale 9.9-18-9.
[35] *JJA,* 57:369; Texas 22-3.

2. Schopenhauer's negativism

If *Finnegans Wake* is "pure Vico, and Vico, applied to the problem of style," as Beckett argued,[36] *À la recherche du temps perdu* may be regarded as applied Schopenhauer. In Beckett's essay, the German philosopher is called in to elucidate the fact that "the individual is a succession of individuals": "the world being a projection of the individual's consciousness (an objectification of the individual's will, Schopenhauer would say), the pact must be continually renewed."[37] The "projection of the individual's consciousness" may be a reference to an image, employed by Schopenhauer as well as by Proust, to illustrate one of "the Essential Imperfections of the Intellect" and to make clear that our poor brain "can know everything only successively" and be conscious of only one thing at a time: "In this our thinking consciousness is like a magic lantern, in the focus of which only one picture can appear at a time; and every picture, even when it depicts the noblest thing, must nevertheless soon vanish to make way for the most different and even most vulgar thing."[38] On the first pages of the *Recherche*, Proust turned this metaphor of the magic lantern into a metaphor of metaphors: the immaterial images of the magic lantern adapt themselves to the shapes of the material objects in the narrator's room, onto which the images are projected.

The magic lantern's projection of a fictitious reality (the figure of Golo) onto the curtain that separates the narrator from outside reality reflects the idea that language is both an obstacle and a medium: words—Mauthner argues—are merely metaphors. About this most important of Proustian tropes, Beckett notes: "The Proustian world is expressed metaphorically by the artisan because it is apprehended metaphorically by the artist: the indirect and comparative expression of indirect and comparative perception."[39] At the very end of the *Recherche*, Proust refers to the same metaphor when he compares Time to a magic lantern that needs objects or bodies to project itself upon: "le Temps qui d'habitude n'est pas visible, pour le devenir cherche des corps et, partout où il les rencontre, s'en empare pour montrer sur eux sa lanterne magique."[40] Beckett, in his turn, projected his

---

[36] Samuel Beckett, "Dante...Bruno..Vico..Joyce," *Our Exagmination Round His Factification for Incamination of Work in Progress* (London: Faber and Faber, 1972 [1929]), 3-22, 54.

[37] Samuel Beckett, *Proust* (London: John Calder, 1965), 19.

[38] Schopenhauer, *World*, vol. 2, 138.

[39] Beckett, *Proust*, 88.

[40] Marcel Proust, *À la recherche du temps perdu,* vol. IV, ed. Jean-Yves Tadié (Paris: Gallimard Pléiade, 1987-1989), 503.

Schopenhauerian negativism onto Proust's work. Later, he admitted to John Pilling: "Perhaps I overstated Proust's pessimism a little."[41]

1. "the itch to make and nothing to say"

Whereas Joyce considered himself "a frightful example of the will to live,"[42] Beckett seems to have focused on its denial. But without will, there is nothing to be denied. If there was anything that the friendship with Beckett yielded for Joyce on a professional level, it was mainly the former's youthful abundance of will and urge to create. Later, Beckett described himself as "a young man with the itch to make and nothing to say."[43] This description also applies to the protagonist of Beckett's first story. "Assumption" does not have a clear narrative structure, but is constructed on the basis of the tension between sound and silence. The nameless protagonist has the "remarkable faculty of whispering the turmoil down."[44] He imposes silence, also on himself, until "the Woman" enters his life. Thanks to her, he utters his cry, which he had imprisoned for so long: "he dreaded lest his prisoner should escape, he longed that it might escape."[45] The voice which tries to find expression, is presented as some kind of primal scream, a "wild rebellious surge that aspired violently toward realization in sound,"[46] not unlike Schopenhauer's will: a desire that causes pain as long as it is not satisfied and crops up again as soon as it is. This scream is suppressed by the protagonist's "involuntary inhibition."[47] It is remarkable that Beckett employs the adjective "involuntary," not to denote something which surfaces involuntarily, such as Proust's "mémoire involontaire," but something that denies or smothers this surge.

What Beckett refers to as "the Woman" is only a meagre version of the Joycean "full amoral fertilisable untrustworthy engaging shrewd limited

---

[41] John Pilling, "Beckett's Proust," in *The Beckett Studies Reader*, ed. S. E. Gontarski (Gainsville: University Press of Florida, 1993), 22.
[42] Mary Colum and Padraic Colum, *Our Friend James Joyce* (Garden City, N.Y.: Doubleday, 1958), 46-47.
[43] Lawrence Harvey, *Samuel Beckett: Poet and Critic* (Princeton, N.J.: Princeton University Press, 1970), 305.
[44] Beckett, *Complete Short Prose*, 3.
[45] Ibid., 5.
[46] Ibid., 4.
[47] Ibid., 5.

prudent indifferent *Weib*"[48] and her Nietzschean *Lebensbejahung* in "the last word (human, all too human)"[49] of *Ulysses*. Beckett's literary attempts to let his prisoner escape resulted in a somewhat contrived, pseudo-Joycean *Wake*olect, for instance in *Text*, published in *New Review* 2 (April 1932) or in the fragment from *Dream of Fair to Middling Women* that appeared in *transition* 21 (March 1932) under the title *Sedendo et Quiesciendo* [sic].

Gradually, Beckett was able to distance himself from Joyce's poetics. The awareness of the metaphorical nature of language, the frequent failures of communication, and the impossibility to know anything beyond language led Beckett to employ words in order to express precisely this impossibility. The resulting bareness contrasts sharply with Joyce's verbal abundance. But these opposites are two sides of the same coin: the assumption that any text possibly only veils the fact that there is nothing to be unveiled; that there is nothing beyond phenomenality save the negation of phenomenality, its hardly imaginable absence.

In the introduction to his *Beiträge*, Mauthner notes that he is well aware of an inescapable paradox: he needs language (almost two thousand pages of text) in order to give expression to his critique of language. This paradoxical situation has more or less become Beckett's trademark, most concisely formulated at the end of *The Unnamable*: "I can't go on, (…) I'll go on, you must say words, as long as there are any."[50] It is remarkable that this Beckettian signature is already present in "Assumption." By linking the suppressed scream (voice, language) to the young artist's sexual desire, Beckett already expresses the fundamentally paradoxical impotence of human communication: in our capacity of chattering mammals, we have—more than any other species—the ability to express ourselves; but this ability inevitably implies the constant urge to prove this potency. Time and again, this means of expression proves to be not quite adequate after all, resulting in a feeling of impotence. Since Beckett worked with impotence as an alternative to Joyce's omnipotence, the modal auxiliary "can" is crucial in Beckett's poetics. Many of his texts (such as *Worstward Ho*) seem to be attempts to undo themselves and reconstruct a moment when the text was still in a state of full potency. But in order to take back one's words, one has to write them down first. Only in retrospect, therefore, can it become clear how the dilemma of the very first sentence of "Assumption" already

---

[48] *JJII*, 501.
[49] Ibid.
[50] Samuel Beckett, *Molloy – Malone Dies – The Unnamable* (London: Calder and Boyars, 1973), 418.

introduces the fundamental paradox underlying Beckett's complete oeuvre: "He could have shouted and could not."[51]

University of Antwerp

---

[51] Beckett, *Complete Short Prose*, 3.

THE UNNAMABLE: DENEGATIVE DIALOGUE

RUSSELL KILBOURN

> I am he who will never be caught, never delivered, who crawls between the thwarts, towards the new day that promises to be glorious, festooned with lifebelts, praying for rack and ruin.
> —Samuel Beckett, *The Unnamable*

> ...even unnamable is a word calculated to enmesh us.
> — George Bataille, "Molloy's Silence"

This paper presents a reading of Beckett's *The Unnamable* as neither modernist nor postmodernist text per se, but rather as poised within the highly productive gap between these categories, insofar as they are shorthand, respectively, for the contest between the ontological and epistemological imperatives. Through the close analysis of the unravelling of its discourse, I read the radically negative and often self-contradictory language of this novel not in terms of dialectic but dialogue. To this extent the logic and function of negation in Beckett's text is revalued and shown to be neither determinate—and therefore somehow recuperative—nor nihilistic, but *determinedly* negative. The dialogue in the text, I argue, is one between self and Other only insofar as both positions are reduced, by the end of the narrative, to functions of the endlessly speaking voice.

The Unnamable, the final third of Beckett's trilogy, is the paradigmatic "anti-novel," and therefore the most typical of modern novels.[1] But in contrast to *Tristram Shandy*, Sterne's flagrantly self-conscious anti-novel from the genre's formative period, Beckett's work is far less obviously "about" being a novel. There is also the book's extreme and distinguishing negativity, which is not as absolute as Beckett makes it out to be. In *The Unnamable*, he claims, there is "complete disintegration. No 'I,' no 'have,' no 'being,' no

---

[1] "The paradigmatic text of Beckettian estrangement is *The Unnamable*, the text of the grammatological moment. It is the musing of the text itself—the world's most self-reflexive text" (Lance St. John Butler, ed., *Rethinking Beckett: A Collection of Critical Essays* [London: Macmillan, 1990], 197).

nominative, no accusative, no verb. There's no way to go on"[2]—a typical self-appraisal in the apophatic mode of ironic denial that nevertheless leaves unexamined the exemplarily non-determinately negative–even "denegative"– text of this novel.[3]

Of the three novels comprising the trilogy, *Molloy* is the account of two different "quests," two different trajectories which may converge into a single body, but the "fact" of this convergence remains undecidable. *Malone Dies*, on the other hand, is a radically negative narrative. How, then, to

---

[2] William Hutchings, "'The Unintelligible Terms of an Incomprehensible Damnation': Samuel Beckett's *The Unnamable*, Sheol, and *St. Erkenwald*," *Twentieth Century Literature* 27, no. 2 (1981): 111.

[3] Adorno, in the *Negative Dialectics*, elaborated one approach to non-determinate negation (a negation that negates to affirm) (see Theodor Adorno, *Negative Dialectics*, trans. E. B. Ashton [New York: Continuum, 1992]). My immediate source for the term "denegation" is Jacques Derrida's 1987 essay, "Comment ne pas parler: Dénégations" (translated in 1989 as "How to Avoid Speaking: Denials," in *Derrida and Negative Theology*, ed. Harold Coward and Toby Foshay [Albany: State University of New York Press, 1992], 73-142). In this key essay (where he addresses the relation of deconstruction to the various negative theologies, whose apophatic discourse provides the heretofore most radical instance of denegative logic), Derrida foregrounds the double capacity of language to occlude as it discloses, to disclose as it occludes. The logic of denegation is, according to Derrida's post-Freudian formulation, something wholly other than the classical logic which has grounded modern thought since the Enlightenment. Nevertheless, Freud's concept of *Verneinung* (unconscious negation) lurks behind Derrida's deconstructive denegation. *Dénégation* is the French for *Verneinung*, whereby "the content of a repressed image or idea can make its way into consciousness, on condition that it is *negated*" (Sigmund Freud, "Negation," in *The Standard Edition of the Complete Psychological Works*, trans. and ed. James Strachey, 6th ed. [London: Hogarth, 1973], vol. 10, 235. See also Sigmund Freud, "Verneinung," in *Gesammelte Werke*, ed. Anna Freud, vol. 14 (1925-31) [London: Imago, 1948], 11-15). Neither the determinate negation of philosophy, nor denial, nor avoidance, yet a combination of all of these, denegation, in direct defiance of the logic of noncontradiction, names a particular counter-logic haunting the Western literary tradition. Derrida's denegation claims to go a step further, to describe neither a negation that affirms nor an affirmation that negates (only to affirm, which amounts to the same thing), but rather a negation whose structure affirms itself as a negation. In the first place, then, he posits what he calls a "pre-Freudian" denegation. Therefore his use of denegation must imply a negation that pre-exists or "extends beyond" "both the predicative structure and the onto-theological or metaphysical presuppositions which sustain the psychoanalytic theorems" (Coward and Foshay, *Derrida and Negative Theology*, 95). Derrida in effect translates Freudian *Verneinung* and reclaims it as non-determinate negation. See Mark C. Taylor, "nO nOt nO," in Coward and Foshay, *Derrida and Negative Theology*, 167-198.

describe *The Unnamable*? The formal questions raised by this third and final novel remain inadequately addressed forty years after its initial publication. This failing may have to do with the fact that the most fundamental of these questions pertain to narrative generally, and Beckett's novel foregrounds them like perhaps no other work. To echo Maurice Blanchot:[4] who (or what) is 'speaking'? Who (or what) is the subject of the narrating, of the *récit*? To put it in slightly different terms: narrative (*histoire*) aside, does the presence of a *narration* (*récit*) necessarily entail or presuppose a narrator? Do these terms have any value for an analysis of *The Unnamable*? Despite the feature of the text one critic calls "a mockery of the presence of voice," the fundamental significance of *speaking*—speech represented, "imaged," in writing—whether to affirm or negate, would seem undeniable.[5]

In *The Unnamable* Beckett employs a peculiarly negative logic to determine a language of a paradoxically expressive density—grounded in both Greek and Christian apophatic and non-apophatic texts, from Plotinus to Augustine to Dionysius to Meister Eckhart.[6] The "name" of "the Unnamable" expresses a kind of apophatic irony in itself: if this name names the narrator/speaker, it/he cannot logically be said to exist outside of or "precede" or exceed language, for, although unnamable, he is nevertheless named, denegatively. *The Unnamable* is paradigmatic of what Shira Wolosky calls "in general…[the] double impulse toward invention and refutation"[7] — or, in the terms of this discussion, 'denegation.'

To see the significance for Beckett scholarship of an enhanced appreciation of the apophatic or denegative dimension of his writing, one need only recall the traditional association of Beckett with the high modernist trope of an "absurd," Godless, even nihilistic, universe. But in no sense is Beckett a mystic, closeted or otherwise. What he achieves is a paradoxical "affirmation" in the form of the dense and prolix, characteristically Beckettian, narrative—a profoundly parodic discursive context—by means of the progressive discursive denial or "apophasis" ("unsaying") of the self in terms of its "attributes." And while the discursive ground of the text is the

---

[4] S. E. Gontarski, ed., *On Beckett: Essays and Criticism* (New York: Grove Press, 1986), 141.

[5] Butler, *Rethinking Beckett*, 197.

[6] "It is as 'Unnamable Name' that God is designated in his utter transcendence of all temporality, multiplicity, exteriority: by Dionysius the Aereopagite [*sic*]; by St. Augustine; and by Thomas Aquinas as well – although each to be sure intends this title quite differently" (Shira Wolosky, "The Negative Way Negated: Samuel Beckett's *Texts for Nothing*," *New Literary History* 22, no. 1 [Winter 1991]: 223).

[7] Ibid., 221.

subject throughout, the final, lingering effect is to throw a strange, reflective light on the relation that nonetheless persists with an "other" whose existence as such may be purely grammatical. Throughout the trilogy, but most markedly in *The Unnamable*, this "unsaying" is predicated upon a passive awareness of memory's failing that modulates into a conscious "unremembering," or apomnesis. In the constitution of the larger narrative level, the deliberate "giving away" or dispersal of mnemonic content—a process recorded in the narration (the "voice") itself—becomes the very opposite: the narrative's de-constitution through a gradual ironic denial or "denegation" of these diegetic fragments, repetitious locutions, figures of speech. This is why it is possible, or even necessary, when this work is finally over, for the voice to say "I can't go on, I'll go on": it can go on, but there is nothing left to say.[8]

The third part of the trilogy, which might well answer for the "long sonata of the dead" invoked by Molloy (*M*, 31)[9] presents a discourse which over and over again states, contradicts and affirms the speaker's inability to speak (*Un*, 291). This is what is referred to at intervals (and in other texts) as 'going on,' which might be thought in Nietzschean terms as a necessary process if only because it is too late not to begin: "The best would be not to begin. But I have to begin. That is to say I have to go on" (*Un*, 292).[10] And that he (the one I have called the speaker, the one who says "I") goes on, continues speaking, is seemingly guaranteed by what he calls "the voice," in this seemingly indispensable metaphor.

The unnamed, unknown speaker begins by asking key narratological questions: "Where now? Who now? When now?" (*Un*, 291). What are the

---

[8] Samuel Beckett, *Three Novels: Molloy, Malone Dies, The Unnamable* (New York: Grove, 1991) [henceforth *M, MD, Un*], 414.

[9] "…And even my sense of identity was wrapped in a namelessness often hard to penetrate, as we have just seen I think. And so on for all the other things which made merry with my senses. Yes, even then, when already all was fading, waves and particles, there could be no things but nameless things, no names but thingless names. I say that now, but after all what do I know now about then, now when the icy words hail down upon me, the icy meanings, and the world dies too, foully named? All I know is what the words know, and the dead things, and that makes a handsome little sum, with a beginning, a middle and an end as in the well-built phrase and the long sonata of the dead (*M*, 31). Cf. *The Unnamable*: "[T]hese nameless images I have, these imageless names" (*Un*, 407).

[10] I refer to the early Nietzsche of the *Birth of Tragedy*, section 3 (Friedrich Nietzsche, *The Birth of Tragedy and the Case of Wagner*, trans. Walter Kaufmann [Toronto: Random House, 1967]).

space, subject, and time of the narrative?[11] The speaker never ceases circling around these questions. Blanchot collapses the three into two questions: 'Where Now?' and 'Who Now?' (Gontarski, *On Beckett*, 141). The first emphasizes the speaker's preoccupation with his environment and "physical" position, but also entails the fact that, for all his concern with establishing a relation to the others (either his avatars or his "masters"), to the extent that this constitutes a memory-work, it is also in the end revealed as a grammatically present-tense project (as the speaker subsequently remarks, "should the notion of time dawn on his darkness....[i]nvolving very naturally that of space, they have taken to going hand in hand, in certain quarters, it's safer" [*Un*, 362-363]).[12] The second question addresses the crucial problem of the "voice," together with that "obligation to express," to speak, to "go on." These questions can be used to establish the poles between which the whole of the following discussion of *The Unnamable* will take place.

"Where Now?"

In a first reading, it appears that the Unnamable "inhabits" (vocally, if not bodily[13]) a kind of otherworldly afterlife space, populated at intervals by the other characters from the trilogy; a sort of infernal space in which each "sinner" occupies his own Dantean pit (*Un*, 293). This effect accords with the infernal-purgatorial space-time established in the first two parts of the

---

[11] "...Edouard Morot-Sir goes beyond the narratological, placing this tripartite interrogative opening into its philosophical context, on the basis of a comparison of the French and English versions of the text" (Harold Bloom, ed., *Samuel Beckett's Molloy, Malone Dies, The Unnamable* [New York : Chelsea House Publishers, 1988], 132). Morot-Sir contends that, in the French, where the second and third questions are transposed—"Où maintenant? Quand maintenant? Qui maintenant?"—"Beckett respected the usual philosophical order of critical philosophy since David Hume and Kant, whose epistemologies go from Space to Time, from Time to Subjectivity. Working on his translation from the French to English it is possible that Beckett became more aware of the problems of writing proper, hidden behind the three philosophical questions" (ibid.). Morot-Sir then relates these three 'problem' areas to their corresponding literary functions: 'description,' 'nomination,' and narration, "i.e., from the possibility of finding a place to the possibility of designating a person and....to the possibilities of telling stories" (ibid.).
[12] "Then at last I can set about saying what I was, and where, during all this long lost time" (*Un*, 331).
[13] "...The speaker engages in the discursive reduction of his 'physical body,' which he at first affirms: "It is well to establish the position of the body from the outset, before passing on to more important matters" (*Un*, 304).

trilogy, where the literary representability of the afterlife as a place of punishment or purgation is exploited. Initially, it appears that *The Unnamable* will take this conceit to its terminus. Almost as rapidly it becomes apparent that things are rather more complex; that it is no longer possible to speak of this text (of what it "means") without first taking into account the nature of the voice, the logic and rhetoric it employs. In the unspooling of the discourse, every statement or supposition is in its turn contradicted or negated, only to be re-affirmed subsequently, as often as not in the same or very next sentence: "About myself I need know nothing. Here all is clear. No, all is not clear. But the discourse must go on" (*Un*, 294). It appears initially that two things can be taken for granted in this radically indeterminate text, insofar as it is determined by them: the voice and its discourse, both in a sense logically "prior" to the "speaker"-narrator, and yet not independent of him or it— although this is taken on his or its own admission, and as a statement about this text it is as subject to doubt and refutation as any other, a situation contingent on the text itself, on what the discourse "says" (what the speaker says when he speaks, not even certain if he is "saying" anything, or just speaking), just as this posited "speaker" is him or itself an "effect" of this discourse, issuing from the voice; a fact the speaker—paradoxically, agonizingly—all but reasons out, by the end.

It is therefore a mistake to take literally or even seriously the mathematically rigorous circular structure the speaker imputes to the place in which he says he finds himself (*Un*, 295). One can at best note in passing the high degree of formalization to which anything resembling a "character" is subjected in this section: it is as though the "psychiatry" and "anthropology"' of *Molloy* and *Malone Dies* had given way to a purer form of schematization reminiscent of Kleist's, a reduction of "human relations" to geometry or, even better, "astronomy," where lesser bodies revolve around greater ones, in determinable orbits.[14] The celestial associations of this constellation of astronomical and other metaphors in no way cancel out the overridingly hellish overtones of the space the speaker conjures out of his interminable flow of words. In fact, a central thematic preoccupation is introduced here, at the beginning, when the intertextual ties with Hell's past (Dante [*Un*, 293]; Milton [*Un*, 295]) are strongest. The speaker's obsessive and highly self-conscious concern with his provenance, present ontological status, and probable destiny opens out into a general interrogation of the metaphysical dimension of the novel's "world" (although this word promises too much),

---

[14] "...The speaker engages in the discursive reduction of his "physical body," which he at first affirms: 'It is well to establish the position of the body from the outset, before passing on to more important matters'" (*Un*, 304).

culminating in a theological inquiry into what higher agency or authority or power, if any, is responsible for his being there. If nothing else, this is a quest for origins, even if the speaker claims he is in what amounts to a hell as a place with all the pain and suffering but not necessarily the attendant moral justification (*Un*, 296). This often self-contradictory inquiry eventually amounts to what might be termed a "negative theodicy"; an attempt to justify an unknown and unknowable and possibly non-existent master's ways to oneself in the face of the suspicion ('knowledge' is too strong a word) that one is "oneself" merely an effect of a system in which every such suspicion is pre-determined, including this one.[15] It is the logic of the liar's paradox, and it is vertiginous and inescapable. The one flash of hope in this discourse comes early on and is soon effaced—along with most everything else, including the epistemological and emotional conditions for hope—and it works for the most part retroactively, in terms of the first two books of the trilogy. It is a possibility, grounded in the geometric reduction of human or ethical relations, for a sort of "deliverance": the closest the text of the trilogy as a whole gets to mentioning something like "redemption" or "salvation," outside of the parodic keying of events in *Malone Dies* to the Easter season (*MD*, 208). "Deliverance," that is to say, cessation of existence, which, from the speaker's point-of-view, remains perhaps the one thing that is never contradicted outright and remains, at the end, as a sort of "absolute value": if it is too late to prevent one's coming-into-being, it is never too late to begin to cease existing.[16]

The Unnamable begins in and upholds throughout the same mode of ironic disavowal with which *Molloy* ends: "It is midnight. The rain is beating on the windows. It was not midnight. It was not raining" (*M*, 176). This narrative "logic" of blatant and even systematic contradiction could be said to be the "rule" of the text—but that logic, system and rule are all tied to a philosophy and ideology of narrative (a meta-narratology) which the text of *The Unnamable* eschews. Examples are legion:

[15] "...Running through the text of *The Unnamable* is a parody of the inescapability of a certain cast of thought, which seems to go hand in hand with the grammatical strictures that are never abandoned outright; the potentially endless, shadowy chain of authority, there and not-there" (*Un*, 364 ff.). He talks of the others, his tormentors, with their own 'master,' who will one day in turn "punish them, or who will spare them, what else is there, up above, for those who lose, punishment, pardon, so they say" (*Un*, 365). But, like everything else in the text, this apparent metaphysical hierarchy proves susceptible to the exigencies of grammar and wordplay, as it tips over into the finite infinitude of an endless discourse.

[16] In this can be seen the lingering effect of Schopenhauer. See, e.g., Bloom, *Samuel Beckett's Molloy, Malone Dies, The Unnamable*, 1-12.

> These things I say, and shall say, if I can, are no longer, or are not yet, or never were, or never will be, or if they were, if they are, if they will be, were not here, are not here, will not be here, but elsewhere. But I am here. So I am obliged to add this. I who am here, who cannot speak, cannot think, and who must speak, and therefore perhaps think a little.... And the simplest therefore is to say that what I say, what I shall say, if I can, relates to the place where I am, to me who am there, in spite of my inability to think of these, or to speak of them, because of the compulsion I am under to speak of them, and therefore perhaps think of them a little. (*Un*, 301-302)

It is apparent from the beginning that the function if this type of negation is more than rhetorical, as it is turned to the elimination of the speaker even as he reiterates his "obligation" to speak: "I greatly fear, since my speech can only be of me and here, that I am once more engaged in putting an end to both. Which would not matter, far from it, but for the obligation, once rid of them, to begin again, to start again from nowhere, from no one and from nothing and win to me again, to me here again, by fresh ways to be sure, or by the ancient ways, unrecognizable at each fresh faring" (*Un*, 302). He speaks then of "a certain confusion in the exordia, long enough to situate the condemned and prepare him for execution" (*Un*, 302). As if to suggest (in a metafictional leap), that the first two novels, the exordia, prepared the way for him to finish speaking, here, in the last book: "I hope this preamble will soon come to an end and the statement begin that will dispose of me. Unfortunately I am afraid, as always, of going on" (*Un*, 302). "To go on" is in many ways the key phrase in this text and the trilogy as a whole. The speaker calls these first pages the "preamble," with its etymological associations of walking or wandering: this is the part that precedes the narrative "journey," an astronomical metaphor[17] which is, with all the other figures, subordinated to the determining metaphor of the voice speaking: "I am not heading anywhere, my adventures are over, my say said, I call that my adventures" (*Un*, 302). This is a purely discursive wandering, and at this point in his itinerary the speaker acknowledges that his "journey" may have been more metaphorical than either of the first two novels suggested, as he speculates that the place in which he finds himself, "the same place as always" (*Un*, 302), "is perhaps merely the inside of my distant skull where once I wandered, now am fixed, lost for tininess, or straining against the walls....ever murmuring my old stories, my old story, as if it were the first time" (*Un*, 303). For the Beckettian subject the "cosmos," far from being an infinite universe, is reduced to the inside of a skull. The translation of

---

[17] A "journey" being a diurnal duration; a day's travel.

metaphors has been taken as far as possible without all sense being lost: from the rational Platonic "closed world" to a Non-Euclidean subjective space-time.[18] The modern subject reaches its apogee as it meets its death in Beckett. But this does not mean that it is finished.

The speaker does not express a desire to stop speaking—this is acknowledged at this point as an impossibility—but to not *say* anything; to say *nothing*: "If I could speak and yet say nothing, really nothing....But it seems impossible to speak and yet say nothing..." (*Un*, 303). To speak without saying, as if to rewrite or go beyond Wittgenstein's dictum that "what we cannot speak about we must pass over in silence—*darüber muss man schweigen.*"[19] Derrida draws attention to the denegative logic required to speak of what is most important by not speaking of it, by avoiding speaking of it; a logic he finds at work in apophatic texts from Plato's *Timaeus* to Eckhart's sermons to Dionysius' hierarchies to Heidegger's late unpublished lectures. *The Unnamable*, too, recognizes that, in speaking, it is always oneself that one is circling around, that one is avoiding, avoids speaking of, by speaking of anything and everything else:

> All these Murphys, Molloys and Malones do not fool me. They have made me waste my time, suffer for nothing, speak of them when, in order to stop speaking, I should have spoken of me and of me alone. But I just said I have spoken of me, am speaking of me. I don't care a curse what I just said. It is now I shall speak of me, for the first time, I thought I was right in enlisting these sufferers of my pains. I was wrong. They never suffered my pains, their pains are nothing, compared to mine, a mere tittle of mine, the tittle I thought I could put from me, in order to witness it ... give me back the pains I lent them and vanish, from my life, my memory, my terrors and shames. There, now there is no one here but me, no one wheels about me, no one comes towards me, no one has ever met anyone before my eyes, these creatures have never been, only I and this black void have ever been. And the sounds? No, all is silent. And the lights, on which I had set such store, must they too go out? Yes, out with them, there is no light here. No grey either, black is what I should have said. Nothing then but me, of which I know nothing, except that I have never uttered, and this black, of which I

---

[18] Cf. Freccero re the medieval analogy between the movement of the mind and the movement of the cosmos (John Freccero, *Dante: The Poetics of Conversion*, ed. Rachel Jacoff [Cambridge, Mass.: Harvard University Press, 1986]).

[19] Ludwig Wittgenstein, *Tractatus Logico-Philosophicus*, trans. D. F. Pears and B. F. McGuiness (London and New York: Routledge, 1995), 74. In the sermon "Renouamini spiritu," Meister Eckhart quotes Augustine: "what man can say that is most beautiful in respect to God is that he knows how to be silent [*swigen*] on account of the wisdom of the internal [divine] wealth" (quoted by Derrida in Coward and Foshay, *Derrida and Negative Theology*, 121).

know nothing either, except that it is black, and empty. That then is what, since I have to speak, I shall speak of, until I need speak no more.....Ah yes, all lies, God and man, nature and the light of day, the heart's outpourings and the means of understanding, all invented, basely, by me alone, with the help of no one, since there is no one, to put off the hour when I must speak of me. There will be no more about them. (*Un*, 303-304)

"Who Now?"

It is obvious that in this text the questions of place and self, or better subject, are inextricable. The second of the trinity of questions—"Who Now?"—modulates into "who is 'the Unnamable'"? Is it the speaker, who divests himself of a succession of names and attributes, or is it the one of whom the speaker speaks, in naming the nameless other who may or may not be the "source" of the *voice*—at once the source and the object of the speaker's ceaseless discourse? Many readers of the trilogy assume the unicity of the narrating voice, and therefore that of an underlying "self," throughout the tripartite text. Wolfgang Iser's work on the trilogy is typical of a reading grounded in the assumption that all three narrators and/or protagonists (Iser never distinguishes between the two basic narratological functions) are identical, mirroring the hypostatic notion of a "self," whether unique to each individual and irreducible, or a common, grounding "selfhood" shared by all.[20] Once again, this approach leaves too much of *The Unnamable*'s discourse unaddressed.

The theme or idea of the paradoxical "obligation to express"—most famously formulated in the dialogue with Georges Duthuit—is reiterated obsessively in this text: "I shall have to speak of things of which I cannot speak, but also, which is even more interesting, but also that I, which is if possible even more interesting, that I shall have to, I forget, no matter. And at the same time I am obliged to speak. I shall never be silent. Never" (*Un*, 291). This problem and that of the "identity" of the Unnamable converge in the repetition of the first-person pronoun. "I, say I": the speaker offers at the outset, as if in answer to his own question, "who now?"; 'who is speaking now?' 'I, say I.' But to whom does the 'I' refer'? On one level, this is the old modernist conceit, Rimbaud's "'je' *est* un autre." In *The Unnamable* Beckett takes it further, foregrounding the apparent link between the one who says 'I' and the 'source' of the voice itself, even as the speaker, who occupies the

---

[20] See Bloom, *Samuel Beckett's Molloy, Malone Dies, The Unnamable*, 71-83.

former position, generally denies any but a passive, subservient relation to the latter:

> It is not mine, I have none, I have no voice and must speak, that is all I know, its round that I must revolve, of that I must speak, with this voice that is not mine, but can only be mine, since there is no one but me, or if there are others, to whom it might belong...Perhaps they are watching me from afar, I have no objection, as long as I don't see them...So it is I who speak, all alone, since I can't do otherwise. No, I am speechless. Talking of speaking, what if I went silent? What would happen to me then? Worse than what is happening?....I think I know what it is, it's to prevent the discourse from coming to an end, this futile discourse which is not credited to me and brings me not a syllable nearer silence...Perhaps I shall be obliged, in order not to peter out, to invent another fairy-tale, yet another, with heads, trunks, arms, legs and all that follows.... (*Un*, 307)

Is the "obligation" to continue speaking (to "go on") also an ethical obligation of a kind? An obligation to another? Or is it merely a tautological obligation to the self, to speak itself—to tell its story, to repeat its lesson, its 'pensum'—in order ultimately to affirm itself, its discursive "being"? It would seem that the provisional answer is that the obligation is to the voice, which the speaker hears, in a manner of speaking, in his "head": "And what it seemed to me I heard then, concerning what I should do, and say, in order to have nothing further to do, nothing further to say, it seemed to me I only barely heard it, because of the noise I was engaged in making elsewhere, in obedience to the unintelligible terms of an incomprehensible damnation" (*Un*, 308).

The speaker speaks of his "master," to whom he bears a relation that initially sounds like Moran's relation to Youdi, but even this is problematic; a false hierarchy: "Moran's boss, I forget his name. Ah yes, certain things, things I invented..." (*Un*, 312). "My master then, assuming he is solitary, in my image, wishes me well, poor devil..." (*Un,* 312). This "master" of which he speaks is nothing more than another functional category, a narratological function, ostensibly invented by the speaker (the "I"), along with all the other "vice-existers," with or without proper names. "But perhaps I malign him unjustly, my good master, perhaps he is not solitary like me, not free like me..." (*Un*, 313). Such mock-theological speculation leads to hopeful talk for some kind of positive outcome of all this talking: "Why don't they wash their hands of me and set me free? That might do me good. I don't know. Perhaps then I could go silent, for good and all. Idle talk, idle talk, I am free, abandoned" (*Un*, 314). Like Kafka's K. in *Das Schloß*, he feels a certain "freedom," but, unlike K. (or Molloy, Moran, Malone, etc.), he sees and understands the fundamentally negative character of this freedom: he is "abandoned," "free" of responsibility to another, but not, curiously, free of this particular "obligation" of which he repeatedly, obsessively, speaks. Epistemologically, he occupies a wholly different echelon than K. and the other Kafkan protagonists; in one sense, he is at a distinct disadvantage, since his enhanced epistemological awareness allows him to question his ontological status so profoundly.

This questioning leads inevitably, circularly, to an undermining of his epistemological status, ad infinitum. He finds himself caught in the vicious circle of discursively constituted "consciousness": which comes first, the speaking self, or the language with or "through" which it expresses itself? Hence Beckett's positing of a prior "obligation" which affords a measure of "consolation" to the self ostensibly caught in this aporia which is concentrated and epitomized in the desire or need to avoid speaking of oneself, coexistent in the text with the (contradictory) obligation to speak of oneself: "Strange notion in any case, and eminently open to suspicion, that of a task to be performed, before one can be at rest. Strange task, which consists in speaking of oneself. Strange hope, turned towards silence and peace. Possessed of nothing but my voice, the voice, it may seem natural, once the idea of obligation has been swallowed, that I should interpret it as an obligation to say something" (*Un*, 311).

The "consolation" of speaking (even of speaking lies) is contrasted with the "deliverance" afforded by an actual, potentially violent, encounter with another (*Un*, 314). Unfortunately, the latter depends on the former. Furthermore, even this hope of consolation is a lie, an invention: "...I invented it all, in the hope it would console me, help me to go on, allow me to think of myself as somewhere on a road, moving, between a beginning and an end, gaining ground, losing ground, getting lost, but somehow in the long run making headway. All lies. I have nothing to do, that is to say nothing in particular. I have to speak, whatever that means. Having nothing to say, no words but the words of others, I have to speak" (*Un*, 314). And then, as if to quash any suspicion of a possible "ethical" cast to this obligation to speak, he insists that "[no] one compels me to, there is no one..." (*Un*, 314).

The foregoing section sets the "pattern" (if that is the right word) for the duration of the novel: it is as though the speaker discourses out of necessity, tells stories, multiplying variations and ironic commentaries interminably, all to the end of eventually being able to stop for good. In the process he spars with the apostrophized Mahood and company, as if it were all their doing, but then he is never sure whether Mahood or the others "exist" in some sense independently of him or whether they are not inventions of his, or whether he is not an invention of theirs, or whether he even "exists" at all.[21] There are only two things that can be taken for granted in this discourse, apart from the materiality of the discourse itself; two forces or "desires"[22] driving the narrative: the need or will to stop, together with the need or obligation to go on. These two drives are not in an oppositional so much as a complementary relation. The various conditions, modes or temporalities—"existence," "death," and so forth—come to be seen not as categories outside or independent of this discourse, but rather as functions of it, just as are the various positions denominated by the pronouns, "I," "he," or "they." These, too, threaten to become purely discursive or grammatical functions, where the "subject"—insofar as it persists—is a grammatical subject (likewise for the other persons). Wolosky, for one, reaches a similar conclusion, when she chiastically observes that Beckett "plays with the grammar of selfhood, with selfhood as itself a grammar."[23] But it would be too easy to stop at this point and allow all of the ontological or even ethical questions to be subsumed by an all-embracing conception of "language." What frustrates this solution is the other, unnamable, other.

---

[21] Basil, Mahood, (Yerk, Worm), are all avatars whose stories the speaker has not yet told; names for different voices which issue from him: "But his voice continued to testify for me, as though woven into mine, preventing me from saying who I was, so as to have done with saying, done with listening. And still today, as he would say, though he plagues me no more his voice is there, in mine, but less, less" (*Un,* 309). But just as "he" denies that he is Mahood or any of the others that are as it were emanations of him, he is not identical with the voice: "Then my voice, the voice, would say, That's an idea, now I'll tell one of Mahood's stories, I need a rest. (...) To make me think I was a free agent." Narratologically speaking, this is the distinction between the "narrator" and "focalizor" (see Mieke Bal, *Narratology: Introduction to the Theory of Narrative,* trans. Christine Van Boheemen [Toronto, Buffalo, and London: University of Toronto Press, 1997], 157-158). The unique feature of Beckett's text, however, is that it is the focalizor (to abuse the optical metaphor) that is speaking about itself and its relation to the narrator.

[22] In the "pre-oedipal" Deleuzian sense (e.g., Gilles Deleuze and Félix Guattari, *Anti-Oedipus: Capitalism and Schizophrenia* [1972], trans. Robert Huxley, Mark Seem, and Helen R. Lane [Minneapolis: University of Minnesota, 1992], 296).

[23] Sanford Budick and Wolfgang Iser, eds., *Languages of the Unsayable: The Play of Negativity in Literature and Literary Theory* (New York: Columbia University Press, 1989), 181.

Speaking of Voices

Like a refrain the speaker repeats: "But it's entirely a matter of voices, no other metaphor is appropriate" (*Un*, 325); "It must not be forgotten, sometimes I forget, that all is a question of voices" (*Un*, 345); "But it is solely a question of voices, no other image is appropriate" (*Un*, 347). The foregoing have almost the quality of "authoritative" statements in a radically "de-authorized" text like *The Unnamable*, particularly with the qualification of "metaphor." It is a frank acknowledgment of the fact that, at bottom, this paradigmatically novelistic text is made up of voices, even of a single voice, and that this use of "voice" is metaphorical, being a thoroughly written voice (the graphic texture, the "grain" of a voice). This is banal but fundamental: what Bakhtin calls the "image" of a voice.[24] Bakhtin's theory of novelistic discourse brings a number of these questions into focus, preeminent among which is the irreducibility, of which Beckett's speaker could be said to be aware, of the voice, or voices—hence, of speech—which is referred to somewhat formally in the novel as a "discourse." To those who would argue that *The Unnamable* is more dramatic monologue than novel, we have Bakhtin's response: "The fundamental condition, that which makes a novel a novel, that which is responsible for its stylistic uniqueness, is the *speaking person and his discourse*" (Bakhtin, *The Dialogic Imagination*, 332). Obviously, with respect to a novel like *The Unnamable*, the most problematic element in this axiomatic statement is "person," already qualified by Bakhtin

---

[24] Michael Holquist and Caryl Emerson gloss "voice" in Bakhtin's theory as "the speaking personality, the speaking consciousness. A voice always has a will or desire behind it, its own timbre and overtones. SINGLE-VOICED DISCOURSE...is the dream of poets; DOUBLE-VOICED DISCOURSE...the realm of the novel. (...) ...both poetic and prose tropes are ambiguous but a poetic trope, while meaning more than one thing, is always only single-voiced. Prose tropes by contrast always contain more than one voice, and are therefore dialogized" (Mikhail Bakhtin, *The Dialogic Imagination: Four Essays*, ed. Michael Holquist, trans. Caryl Emerson and Michael Holquist [Austin: University of Texas Press, 1981], 434). The apparently "logocentric" quality of this notion of voice is dispelled when it is recalled that, as Holquist and Emerson stress, for Bakhtin, as for Derrida and others in different ways, speech and voice are already "like" writing: "Implicit in all this is the notion that all transcription systems—including the speaking voice in a living utterance—are inadequate to the multiplicity of the meanings they seek to convey. (...) (There is in this obsession with voice and speech a parallel with the attempts of two important recent thinkers—both in other ways very different from Bakhtin—to come to grips with the way intimacy with our own voice conduces to the illusion of presence: Husserl in the *Logical Investigations* and Derrida in his 1967 essay 'Speech and Phenomenon')" (Bakhtin, *The Dialogic Imagination*, xx-xxi).

as itself a kind of metaphor: one of the ways in which "heteroglossia" enters novelistic discourse is "in person," assuming "material form within it in the images of speaking persons" (ibid.). Therefore, he continues, "the human being in the novel is first, foremost and always a speaking human being; the novel requires speaking persons bringing with them their own ideological discourse, their own language." Contrast with this Hugh Kenner's virtual lament in an essay on the trilogy. Discussing the closing pages of *Malone Dies*, Kenner remarks of the protagonist: "he has no life, never had; he is simply the person we intuit when a hundred or more pages of highly idiosyncratic words claim that a person is behind them. Where else would they come from, if not from a person?" (Bloom, *Samuel Beckett's Molloy, Malone Dies, The Unnamable*, 38). On the face of it, Kenner's position accords with Bakhtin's idiosyncratic humanism, insofar as the latter insists on a sort of anti-psychological 'presence' of a voice in the *image* of a speaking person, where the person's, or, more properly, the voice's, materiality does not consist in a body but in this image, which is, first and foremost, the image of a voice: "The speaking person and his discourse in the novel is an object of *verbal* artistic representation" (Bakhtin, *The Dialogic Imagination*, 332). This much is easy to understand and accept. Things become both more complicated and more contentious when attention is shifted to the next narratological level, the significance of author and authority and their relation to the level of "speaking person": "a speaking person's discourse in the novel is not merely transmitted or reproduced; it is, precisely, *artistically represented* and thus it is represented *by means of (authorial) discourse*" (ibid.; author's emphasis). Thus, this speaker and his/her discourse become objects of discourse themselves. Two things should be emphasized at this point: first, that the discourse of the speaker does not "originate" with or out of the authorial discourse; second, that the authorial discourse is not to be confused with the "author" as a historical entity. Nor is it the same thing as "authoritative discourse," best exemplified by the Bible (cf. Bakhtin, *The Dialogic Imagination*, 424). These very questions of origin and hierarchy are thematized in *The Unnamable*, as the speaker struggles to "unname" himself by naming himself, negatively:

> First I'll say what I'm not, that's how they taught me to proceed, then what I am, it's already under way, I have only to resume at the point where I let myself be cowed. I am neither, I needn't say, Murphy, nor Watt, nor Mercier, no – no, I can't even bring myself to name them, nor any of the others whose very names I forget....I never desired, never sought, never suffered, never partook in any of that, never knew what it was to have, things, adversaries, mind, senses. But enough of this. There is no use denying, no use harping on the same old thing I know so well, and so easy to say, and which simply amounts in the end to speaking yet again in the

> way they intend me to speak, that is to say about them, even with execration and disbelief....There's no getting rid of them without naming them and their contraptions, that's the thing to keep in mind. (*Un*, 326)

And beyond these names is that *other* other, radically independent of the self, of whose analogue Malone spoke (*MD*, 295, 299): "For beyond them is that other who will not give me quittance until they have abandoned me as inutilizable and restored me to myself. Then at last I can set about saying what I was, and where, during all this long lost time" (*Un*, 331). Coming to terms with this unnamable other is increasingly associated by the speaker with the possibility of a demise beyond a "going on." This is the other to whom the denegative appellation "Unnamable" may be most justifiably applied, if it is denied the speaker himself as he denies those others, in order to

> try and please the other, if that is what I have to do, so that he may be pleased with me, and perhaps leave me in peace at last, and give me quittance, and the right to rest, and silence, if that is in his gift. It's a lot to expect of one creature, it's a lot to ask, that he should first behave as if he were not, then as if he were, before being admitted to that peace where he neither is, nor is not, and where the language dies that permits of such expressions. Two falsehoods, two trappings, to be borne to the end, before I can be let loose, alone, in the unthinkable unspeakable, where I have not ceased to be, where they will not let me be (*Un*, 334).

Over and over he articulates what might be called the two key modes of being and speaking, in this frankly paradoxical relation, in which he acknowledges that one must be in order to speak, and yet one must speak oneself into being, at the behest of the "voice" which, as he also reiterates, precedes him, which is to say precedes either his speaking or his being, since neither takes precedence: "For on the subject of me properly so called, I know what I mean, so far as I know I have received no information up to date. May one speak of a voice, in these conditions? Probably not. And yet I do. The fact is all this business about voices requires to be revised, corrected and then abandoned. Hearing nothing I am none the less a prey to communications. And I speak of voices!....So nothing about me. That is to say no connected statement. Faint calls, at long intervals" (*Un*, 336). These "faint calls," as often as not, take the form of narrative fragments in which he, the speaker, appears as a "character," as if he "existed," the fond hope of which (his "existence") he claims, if he "remember[s] right, has now passed" from him (*Un*, 336). But this begs the question as to the nature of this "being": if the most positive thing to be said about it is that it coincides with his speaking, then it is a very peculiar ontological category, one which there seems no reason to judge as anything other than a "fictional ontology."[25] The shift from "modernism" to "postmodernism" has been described as a shift from an epistemological to an ontological preoccupation,[26] where (at least in Beckett) the "I" of 'how do I know that I am?' asks "what mode of being does this 'I' have that asks how it knows?" This split in the subject throws it *en abîme*, into the bad infinite of a vain attempt to determine identity by means of language; to try to say "I am either this or that," only to find that this "I" keeps slipping off, always eluding the one saying "I." The only possibility is a temporary "fixing" in the form of images, or of complexes of images (of voices) extended into narratives. That is to say, this speaker, his voice, has no "existence" outside of this text in which his discourse runs on in an all but unbroken flow for some 120 pages. What this means is that the whole question of "existence" in any realist psychological terms is entirely beside the point, since to lose sight of the fact that this text represents the *image* of a voice is to abandon any hope of coming to an understanding of the radically negative manner in which this text produces its "meaning."

He (the one who says "I") becomes the "Mahood" of whom he has been speaking, among other things, while the "namable" other becomes "Worm": "But it's time I gave this solitary a name, nothing doing without proper names. I therefore baptise him Worm" (*Un*, 337). It becomes clear that the speaker has no "identity" as such, only this or that proper name, for a time, even if only the space of a sentence ("For if I am Mahood, I am Worm too... Or if I am not yet Worm, I shall be when I cease to be Mahood" [*Un*, 338]).[27] From one sentence to the next he 'baptizes' another other, or gives

---

[25] Cf. Lubomír Doležel, "Mimesis and Possible Worlds," *Poetics Today* 9, no. 3 (1988): 476-496.

[26] "The shift from the typically modernist preoccupation with epistemological uncertainty... to the ontological doubt that results when one radically thinks through what epistemological doubt entails... announces postmodernism" (Bal, *Narratology*, 117). This is as succinct and useful a definition as any of what can only be seen as a problematic distinction. Unfortunately, a work like *The Unnamable* cannot be said to be exclusively preoccupied with either ontology or epistemology, but if anything "dramatizes" the fact of such a distinction. It could be said then that *The Unnamable* is "about" this shift, and that this accounts for the insurmountable difficulty of understanding it in terms of either pole of the critical literature: neither a realist psychological nor a more self-reflexive, *avant garde* reading bears up under the pressure of Beckett's superfluity of words.

[27] A more "narrativistic" example: "How close to me he suddenly seems, squinting up at the medals of the hippophagist Ducroix. It is the hour of the apéritif, already people pause, to read the menu. Charming hour of the day, particularly when, as sometime happens, it is also that of the setting sun whose last rays, raking the street

the same other another name, then attributes to the other the responsibility of having 'formed' him. The first person speaks of himself in the third: "I," "he," "they"—first-person self and third-person other; subject and indirect object. Grammatically, dramatically, there is virtually no mention here of the direct object, second-person accusative "other" valorized by Buber, Levinas, and Bakhtin (the "you/*tu*/*du*" ["thou"]), as if it were almost too intimate a category to admit of these games, this wordplay.[28] But for all this play with the forms and logic of language, Beckett never abandons grammar in the text of *The Unnamable*.[29] The only place this happens with any significance in the whole of the trilogy is in the closing lines of *Malone Dies* (*MD*, 288), and even there it is only the barest anticipation of the formal experimentation in Beckett's subsequent shorter prose.[30] It is because of this adherence to the basic laws of grammar that the speaker (the"' Unnamable") escapes "being," that is, "naming himself as," both Mahood and Worm, or whomever, at precisely the same time.[31] But then in a sense this is immaterial, as these are all but names, words, attributes to be given or taken away by the speaker as "authorized" ultimately by the order of language, independent of any agency, whether human or divine.[32] This brings us back to the provisional conclusion

from end to end, lend to my cenotaph an interminable shadow..." (*Un*, 340). It is easy to miss the first time how close "he" is to "me," suddenly, right before "me" exchanges places with "he" in the seamless shift to the first person.

[28] Which changes in translation. For a very English example: "Worm, I nearly said Watt, Worm, what can I say of Worm, who hasn't the wit to make himself plain, what to still this gnawing of termites in my Punch and Judy box, what that might not just as well be said of the other?" (*Un*, 339).

[29] Even as he struggles to abandon the first-person, he acknowledges the inevitable intrusion of grammar where there is a speaker using language: "But enough of this cursed first person, it is really too red a herring, I'll get out of my depth if I'm not careful. But what then is the subject? Mahood? No, not yet. Worm? Even less. Bah, any old pronoun will do, provided one sees through it. Matter of habit" (*Un*, 343).

[30] The second novel's conclusion could also be read as a "mimesis" of the mental processes of a writer as he dies, as if he were transcribing these last thoughts as he experienced them, a reading to which this entire thesis stands in opposition (*Un*, 288).

[31] Once or twice this nearly happens, as near as language allows: "Of what is it the time to speak? Of Worm, at last. Good. We must first, to begin with, go back to his beginnings and then, to go on with, follow him patiently through the various stages, taking care to show their fatal concatenation, which have made him what I am" (*Un*, 352).

[32] Cf. Wolosky for the most astute version of this reading: "[The] question of linguistic mediation occurs at the border where epistemology and metaphysics meet. In relation to both, the problem it poses is one of representation. But this

reached above, as if the spiralling course of *The Unnamable*'s narrative determined an isomorphic commentary. As Wolosky argues, outside the "multiplicity" of language "there is in fact no self at all" (Budick and Iser, *Languages of the Unsayable*, 181). At the same time, however, there seems to be another authoritative "agency," as it were concealed by the language. Is it some sort of "pure, essential self," as Wolosky suggests,[33] beneath or behind all of these nominal avatars, these "vice-existers"? This is the question the speaker in effect asks himself, when he speculates about his 'masters.' It is easy, in the end, to put everything down to language, and perhaps this is what must be done, finally. The speaker reframes the ontological question, quasi-chiastically, in terms of a different interrogative pronoun: not "who" but *"where"*: "The essential is never to arrive anywhere, never to be anywhere, neither where Mahood is, nor where Worm is, nor where I am, it little matters…" (*Un,* 338). It is as much a question of "where" as "who," but negatively: neither one nor the other, neither here nor there. This emphasis on non-place can also be construed on the level of the sentence, in terms of grammar, in sequence, its temporally ordered *loci* and *topoi*. Therefore, if he is nowhere, then he is nobody: "Nothing to do but stretch out comfortably on the rack, in the blissful knowledge you are nobody for all eternity" (*Un*, 338). And yet he goes on.

As if perversely, the emphasis shifts back and forth, from ontology to epistemology, a radically negative epistemology continually circling around an unknowable being: "Others. One alone, then others. One alone turned towards the all-impotent, all-nescient, that haunts him, then others. Towards him whom he would nourish, he the famished one, and who, having nothing human, has nothing else, has nothing, is nothing. Come into the world unborn, abiding there unliving, with no hope of death…" (*Un*, 346).

problem raises problems of its own. Knowledge beyond all discursiveness is a questionable project, repudiating the very conditions which define and make knowledge possible; stripping away the self in order to return to a truer, more essential Unity may instead simply be a mode of self-destruction. And language may not be a mere instrument toward an understanding beyond its differentiations, but rather may itself constitute an understanding impossible and nonexistent without it; may not represent, in its condition as embodiment and its assertion of otherness and externality, a lesser reality, but may rather provide the modes without which no reality exists—the doing away with which would reveal not an ultimate Unity but nothing at all" (Wolosky, "The Negative Way Negated," 219-220).

[33] In Wolosky's reading, the Unnamable "assumes that somewhere prior to and outside these representations there is a true self, the signified that these representations merely signify, and in so doing distort and betray" (Budick and Iser, *Languages of the Unsayable*, 180). See also Wolosky, "The Negative Way Negated," 221-224.

This is a negative epistemology beginning to verge on a negative "theology" or even "theodicy," an attempt to articulate not just a negative knowledge but a negative justification of both oneself and the other other with whom he is incommensurable—the unnamable other that is anywhere but at the "center" of the text. With the namable "others" he is in a relation of commensurability; he is all of them, which is to say he occupies all of their places at various times, as well as his own, and he is neither another nor himself. He is no one, but he "speaks all the parts," because it is always the same *voice* that speaks as it were 'through' him, instrumentalizing him as it constitutes him (*Un*, 348).

The speaker's obsession with the dichotomy of being and knowing, of ontology and epistemology—ultimately, with their negation—is part of the dualism underpinning the whole text: Platonic, Christian, Cartesian, or Kantian; body and spirit, body and mind, mind and world, world and other world, etc.[34] Beckett's denegative discourse does not accomplish the dialectical negation or transcendence of these classic binaries so much as succeed, through its relentless self-questioning and self-contradiction, in exposing the radically negative grounding of their relation. Their dialectical opposition is superseded by a third term: speaking. The prevailing force of speech is in turn "legitimized" by its intensely self-reflexive awareness of the other that is utterly distinct from the self. Again, one is forced to look to grammar: "I shall not say I again, ever again, it's too farcical. I shall put in its place, whenever I hear it, the third person, if I think of it. Anything to please them. It will make no difference. Where I am there is no one but me, who am not" (*Un*, 355).[35] As Mieke Bal observes, traditional prosodics recognizes two distinct "voices," the first and third person, "I" and "he," which are, in her view, both "I."[36] The first and third person correspond on the narratological level to the narrating and narrated subject, respectively. This says less about why "he" and "I" are related and more about why "you" is

---

[34] Bloom is right to draw attention to the overlooked significance of Schopenhauer in Beckett, but to contrast the 'Schopenhauerian vision' with Cartesian dualism is to gloss over the differently problematic dialectical dualism fundamental to Schopenhauer as follower (and "improver") of Kant (Bloom, *Samuel Beckett's Molloy, Malone Dies, The Unnamable*, 1-12). On the tenacity of dualistic or binaristic thought across Western intellectual history, see Justus George Lawler, *Celestial Pantomime: Structures of Poetic Transcendence* (New York: Continuum, 1994), 217.

[35] In writing *Das Schloß* Kafka switched from first to third person—as if to confirm that the self is limited to the option of first or, in certain circumstances, the third person. The second person is never opted for, except in rare experimental cases, such as Michel Butor's *La Modification* (Bal, *Narratology*, 29-31).

[36] Bal, *Narratology*, 21.

different in its function and significance. In the trilogy, "you," the accusative, designates the grammatical place of the namable other. This is the familiar other, "know'" to the self because (in a text like this) "invented" by the self as speaker. Eventually, the second person is directly addressed: "how can you think and speak at the same time, without a special gift, your thought's [sic] wander, your words too, far apart, no, that's an exaggeration, apart, between them would be the place to be, where you suffer, rejoice, at being bereft of speech, bereft of thought, and feel nothing, hear nothing, know nothing, say nothing, are nothing, that would be a blessed place to be, where you are" (*Un*, 374).[37] This comes between a section addressed to "they" and sections in the third person ("one") followed by the first again: in this text, the three typical modes. And this is where it is possible to posit an other in a sense "beyond" grammar, a "transgrammatical" Other; an other degree of alterity— another other—that escapes this designation, this "case," that is at times very difficult to distinguish from the self.

The speaker tries to fix the voice, to ascribe it to a single third person other, "He...whose voice it is":

> ...I never spoke, I seem to speak, that's because he says I as if he were I, I nearly believed him, do you hear him, as if he were I, I who am far, who can't move, can't be found, but neither can he, he can only talk, if that much, perhaps it's not he, perhaps it's a multitude, one after another, what confusion, someone mentions confusion...it's the fault of the pronouns, there is no name for me, no pronoun for me, all the trouble comes from that, that, it's a kind of pronoun too, it isn't that either, I'm not that either, let us leave all that, forget about all that, it's not difficult, our concern is with someone, or our concern is with something, now we're getting it, someone or something that is not there, or that is not anywhere, or that is there, here, why not, after all, and our concern is with speaking of that, now we've got it, you don't know why, why must you speak of that, but there it is, you can't speak of that, no one can speak of that, you speak of yourself, someone speaks of himself, that's it, in the singular, a single one, the man on duty, he, I, no matter, the man on duty speaks of himself.... (*Un*, 403-404)

---

[37] The second person is explicitly addressed (and queried) as a potentially separate addressee, if not as an interlocutor, and then as a listener and/or reader: "I must say I prefer that, that what, oh you know, who you, oh I suppose the audience, well well, so there's an audience, it's a public show...perhaps...it's a compulsory show, you wait for the compulsory show to begin, it takes time, you hear a voice, perhaps it's a recitation, that's the show, someone reciting... you make the best of it, you try and be reasonable... it's only beginning, it hasn't begun, he's only preluding, clearing his throat, alone in his dressing-room, he'll appear any moment, he'll begin any moment..." (*Un*, 381).

While the first-person is the position of addresser, it is the second-person that confirms the "I" in its subjectivity as speaker (Bal, *Narratology*, 30-31). Beckett's speaker acknowledges that, in this text at least, whether the narration occurs in the first or the third person, it is always what he calls "the man on duty" that speaks, that is speaking of himself, in a strange sort of autobiographical discourse, the written narrative that is always a self speaking of itself through the tacit collusion of the unnamable other. As to the aforementioned "master" and the speaker's speculation about a metaphysical hierarchy: "we don't intend, unless absolutely driven to it, to make the mistake of inquiring into him, he'd turn out to be a mere high official, we'd end up by needing God...there are still certain depths we prefer not to sink to" (*Un*, 374-375). This "master" is, after all, just another "he" and not "you." And even "God is just another proper name, a grammatical category. As in Kafka, this metaphysical "hierarchy" reveals itself to be a potentially infinitely repeating series of false fronts, a bad infinite of "everlasting third part[ies]" allowing not for a revelation of authority but for an infinite deferral of responsibility, as the speaker apostrophizes his tormentors, eventually claiming: "It's all a bubble, we've been told a lot of lies, he's been told a lot of lies, who he, the master, by whom, no one knows, the everlasting third party, he's the one to blame, for this state of affairs, the master's not to blame..." (*Un*, 374-375).

As part of a series of pre-conclusive "resolutions" (beginning *Un*, 389), he offers this affirmation of his being, physical as well as mental, in what is almost a self-reflexive invocation of the text's empirical author: "Equate me, without pity or scruple, with him who exists, somehow, no matter how, no finicking, with him whose story this story had the brief ambition to be. Better, ascribe to me a body. Better still, arrogate to me a mind. Speak of a world of my own, sometimes referred to as the inner, without choking" (*Un*, 390). As this relentless succession of denials and contradictions begins drawing to its end, the emphasis shifts, perversely, to the self paradoxically aware of its own ontological impossibility:

> When I think, that is to say, no, let it stand, when I think of the time I've wasted with these bran-dips, beginning with Murphy, who wasn't even the first, when I had me, on the premises, within easy reach, tottering under my own skin and bones, real ones, rotting with solitude and neglect, till I doubted my own existence, and even still, today, I have no faith in it, none, so that I have to say, when I speak, Who speaks, and seek, and so on and similarly for all the other things that happen to me and for which someone must be found, for things that happen must have someone to happen to, someone must stop them. (*Un*, 390-391)

It is no longer a question of either being or non-being, but of either speaking or not speaking: "I'll speak of me when I speak no more. In any case it's not a question of speaking of me, but of speaking, of speaking no more..." (*Un*, 392). Suspicions are allowed to arise that the voice, seemingly from "outside," utterly alien to the speaker, is in truth his own, as the distinction between inner and outer worlds (and, in a sense, between self and other) threatens to collapse altogether. "Hearing this voice no more, that's what I call going silent": listening hard to hear the voice, his voice, he will perforce go silent (*Un*, 393).

"Perhaps I've said the thing that had to be said, that gives me the right to be done with speech, done with listening, done with hearing, without my knowing it. I'm listening already, I'm going silent" (*Un*, 393-394). If he stops speaking to listen to the voice, there will be silence (not because it is his voice, but because it is him speaking). The voice is that of the other, the one that is inassimilable, irreducible, and utterly absent in the sense of "presence," as in Derrida's logocentric "metaphysics of presence." All the concern with the self or subject amongst critics of Beckett tends to obscure the insistent traces of this other that guarantee the relentless ranting of the "I" not devolve into a monologue of unmitigated self-nescience. It is this other "voice" that prevents the narrative described or inscribed by the speaker's discourse from closing at the end into an infernal circle of self-contradiction and self-annihilation.

It is the voice that "goes on," as it allows him to say he can't go on; the threatened resolution of "I" and "he" never quite arrives. The novel's denegative ending is anticipated: "I can't go on in any case. But I must go on. So I'll go on" (*Un*, 393); "there was never anyone, anyone but me, anything but me, talking to me of me, impossible to stop, impossible to go on, but I must go on, I'll go on..." (*Un*, 394-395).

Apomnesis

Even at this extremity of ontological and epistemological uncertainty, of semantic near-exhaustion, the novel's intertextual moorings resist disappearing altogether: "If I could remember what I have said I could repeat it, if I could learn something by heart I'd be saved... the seconds must be all alike and each one is infernal..." (*Un*, 395). In a denegative allusion,[38] the quasi-Augustinian meditation on the materiality of time (one of several

---

[38] Cf. Wolosky: "avoidance of allusion" is the third category of "figural evasion" (Budick and Iser, *Languages of the Unsayable*, 165).

instances of this parodic style) elides with an ongoing, almost elegiac meditation on memory, which, logically, leads back again to the central preoccupation with the relation between narration and ontology (*Un*, 395). Memory is the crux: never having "existed," each of Mahood and Worm, like the nameless others, is now nevertheless a "memory" (an image, a narrative): "I never saw him, and yet I remember, I remember having talked about him, I must have talked about him, the same words recur and they are your memories. It is I invented him, him and so many others, and the places where they passed, the places where they stayed, in order to speak, since I had to speak, without speaking of me, I couldn't speak of me, I was never told I had to speak of me, I invented my memories, not knowing what I was doing, not one is of me" (*Un*, 395-396). In memory's compass, the difference between speaking and being collapses, since memory, in *The Unnamable*, is itself a function of the discourse.

Formally speaking there is no difference in *The Unnamable*'s discourse between story and memory as narrative constructs. Stories as often as not told in the third person become displaced first person ("autobiographical") memories:[39] "I've told another little story, about me, about the life that might have been mine for all the difference it would have made, which was perhaps mine, perhaps I went through that before being deemed worthy of going through this, who knows towards what high destiny I am heading, unless I am coming from it. But once again the fable must be of another" (*Un*, 398). The narrative continues in this vein to the point where it is impossible to tell the difference between fictional story and memory; the difference no longer signifies, for the speaker is here engaged in divesting himself of these narratives. This is a kind of "forgetting": "to know nothing, to be capable of nothing, and to have to try, you don't try any more, no need to try, it goes on by itself, it drags on by itself, from word to word, a labouring whirl, you are in it somewhere, everywhere, not he, if only I could forget him…" (*Un*, 402). To forget this third-person other is to forget himself; it is the "forgetting" of the self: an "unsaying" or "speaking away" of diegetically constituted memories.[40] In *The Unnamable*, the "obligation to

---

[39] "[A]nd another question, what am I doing in Mahood's story, and in Worm's, or rather what are they doing in mine…" (*Un*, 377); "there's nothing to be got, there was never anything to be got from those stories. I have mine, somewhere, let them tell it to me, they'll see there's nothing to be got from it either, nothing to be got from me, it will be the end, of this hell of stories" (*Un*, 380).

[40] "[A]ll these stories about travellers, these stories about paralytics, all are mine, I must be extremely old, or it's memory playing tricks" (*Un*, 412). He has no memory in which to "store" these stories, no mouth with which to speak them, no ears with which to hear them, etc. ("the old rigmarole") (*Un*, 412-413). And yet he hears,

express," to speak, is tantamount to the need or desire to forget, to "unremember": to divest one's memories of content (mnemonic images or narratives) through the mode of denegative "expression" here referred to as apomnesis. The two activities elide: the only way to stop is to go on; the only way to 'forget' is to recall and recount. This is one of the ways in which *The Unnamable* (and the trilogy as a whole) remains on the near side of the (so-called) modern/postmodern divide: despite its unparalleled negativity, formally and "thematically," it retains to the end an elegiac tone rendered all the more poignant for the speaker's ironic awareness of its provenance in the discourse.

Insofar as the speaker acknowledges his own positive, performative "role" in the text as the narrative focalizor,[41] he presents a way of describing *The Unnamable* as a paradigmatic modern novel. That is, when he is not disavowing or contradicting his own statements, he speaks "self-reflexively" of his speaking as the primary "action" that is "imitated" (in a nod to Aristotle), which is to say it is the only "action" as such in the text: all the various stories recounted in the course of the overall narrative only "depict" "action" in a secondary sense, as the image of action, as the narrative "voice" is an image of a voice, but the primary one, since the text is irreducibly verbal, irreducibly "written." *The Unnamable* is thus typical of a certain type of novel in that every such narrative up to this point corresponds to the general pattern of at least this one principle "level" of narration (the narrative "frame" in more complexly structured works), which is spoken/written/recounted by a narrative subject, in a particular voice, which determines, to use Bal's term, a particular focalization. In the trilogy, and especially in *The Unnamable*, Beckett reduces this paradigmatic format to its basic constituents: a voice, speaking "through" a speaker, who is only distinguished from this voice because he claims to not be identical with the "source" of his own discourse, that this discourse "originates" prior to and outside of the speaker's subjective limits, but still within the order of language. It originates in an outside 'within' language, a radical, otherwise unnamable otherness, other than the familiar, accusative, second-person; an other beyond the reach of pronominal deixis—of "you," "she," "he" or "it"—and therefore outside the circuit of conventionally conceived "communication." It is in this respect that the text of *The Unnamable* comes

---

speaks and remembers them.

[41] See Bal, who defines "focalization" as "the relations between the elements presented and the vision through which they are presented" (Bal, *Narratology*, 100). Further, "[t]he subject of focalization, the *focalizor*, is the point from which the elements are viewed" (ibid., 104).

closer than perhaps any other modern novel to a "replication" of the theological apophatic text.[42]

The final lines of the text are representative of its denegative character, wherein contradiction is subsumed by a general, non-determinate negation: "you must go on, I can't go on, you must go on, I'll go on, you must say words, as long as there are any, until they find me, until they say me, strange pain, strange sin, you must go on, perhaps it's done already, perhaps they have said me already, perhaps they have carried me to the threshold of my story, before the door that opens on my story, that would surprise me, if it opens, it will be I, it will be the silence, where I am, I don't know, I'll never know, in the silence you don't know, you must go on, I can't go on, I'll go on" (*Un*, 414). This inverts the logic of the ending of *Molloy* ("Then I went back to the house and wrote, It is midnight. The rain is beating on the windows. It was not midnight. It was not raining" [*M*, 176]), which was already an inversion or negation of the opening of the second part ("It is midnight. The rain is beating on the windows" [*M*, 92]). The locution "to go on" shows itself here at the end as a response to the obligation to express that sounds across Beckett's œuvre: "to go on" is to go on speaking (or writing), in the light of the knowledge that this "going on" is always shadowed by its negation, which is itself, too (prior to the real death outside the text), a "going on."

This stripping down, this negation, this "laying bare" and consequent exposure of such figures for what they are—figures of speech (itself a figure of speech) —leaves very little of certainty for the reader other than the voice itself. There appears to be a subject at first, to whom certain things can be attributed because he attributes them, he tells stories about himself, he speaks as if he were a "real" fictional character like any other. Soon enough, everything begins to drop away, is spoken away, denied, by the voice. Even this subject, this subjectivity, is seen to be merely an "effect" of the voice, a necessary "feature" of the discourse. It becomes apparent that the voice is neither synonymous with nor dependent upon the subject, or subjectivity. The voice exceeds subjectivity. It is limited to neither the place, time, nor, consequently, the point-of-view of a subject, and therefore it is not confined to the single pronoun "I." Does this mean that in *The Unnamable*, this extremity of the modern novel, we have returned to the myth of the Tower of Babel, the dream of the original, originary voice, "anterior to all names, the voice that does not speak but gives to be spoken as it withdraws

---

[42] Cf. Pseudo-Dionysius, *Mystical Theology*, chapters 4 and 5 (Pseudo-Dionysius, *Complete Works*, trans. Colm Luibhead [New York: Paulist Press, 1987], 140-141).

into the universal cry"?[43] Does this voice speak the "one language...which presents the nonrepresentable cry, the end of all language as its origin in the unnamable name"? (Marin, "On a Tower of Babel in a Painting by Poussin," 183). It is both tempting and, to a certain degree, justifiable to invoke this paradigm, and yet it seems safe to say that the voice in *The Unnamable* does *not* issue out of the lingering promise of a once and future unity and origin. Much of the Beckett criticism contradicts such a conclusion. The question remains: is the text of *The Unnamable* as radical as some make out, or does it covertly articulate a species of "nostalgia" of the kind (according to a certain interpretation of the original story) that prompted the building of the Tower?

McMaster University

---

[43] Louis Marin, "On a Tower of Babel in a Painting by Poussin," in *Of the Sublime: Presence in Question*, trans. Jeffrey S. Librett (Albany: State University of New York Press, 1993), 183.

MINGLED FLESH

ULRIKA MAUDE

All Strange Away, Imagination Dead Imagine, Ping, and *The Lost Ones* figure among the shorter prose fictions Samuel Beckett wrote in the 1960s. Critics have tended to approach this group of texts, which are linked not only in imagery but also through their textual genetics, as allegories of the human condition or as parables of the authorial process. Closer scrutiny of these works reveals that the prose fragments engage in a probing examination of the contradictory nature of perception and the embodied state of subjectivity. Through a systematic set of negations, marked by the abandonment of the first-person narrator, the privileging of gesture and posture over language and hearing and, most prominently, the prioritising of the sense of touch over that of vision, these works question and undermine the primacy of the conceptual order, foregrounding exteriority and surface over interiority and depth. The narrating voice itself, through its application of conflicting and ultimately self-negating registers, becomes the locus merely of further doubt and uncertainty. The same can even be said of the persistently failing mathematics of the narrator. In short, the systematic interrogations and negations in the texts set into motion a vacillating dynamic between subjectivity and its dissolution.

During the 1960s, Samuel Beckett wrote a series of shorter prose fictions that have acquired an enigmatic place in their author's canon. The series begins with *All Strange Away,* which dates from 1963-1964, and *Imagination Dead Imagine,* which appeared a year later in 1965; continues with *Ping,* which appeared in 1966, and concludes with *The Lost Ones,* a novella which has appeared in three different English language versions, the first of which dates from 1971.[1] These short prose works are closely linked with one another, if

---

[1] *Le Dépeupleur,* the French version of the novella, was famously abandoned by Beckett in 1966, published in fragments, then subsequently unabandoned and completed in 1970, when Beckett added a final fifteenth section to the fourteen preceding ones. The novella was first translated into English in 1971 and exists, at present, in three different English language versions: the original and identical British and American editions, both published in 1972 by John Calder and Grove Press respectively; a version published in issue 96 of the *Evergreen Review* in

not intertwined, not only because all four share similar imagery of bodies in austere spaces, geometrical descriptions and fluctuating light, but also because they share a common genetic. *Imagination Dead Imagine* is, as Stan Gontarski has called it, an "evolutionary descendant" of *All Strange Away*, and *Bing* (the French version of *Ping*), as Beckett himself said, "may be regarded as the result or miniaturisation of 'Le Dépeupleur' abandoned because of its intractable complexities."[2] As Leslie Hill observes, "plott[ing] from the working drafts of *Bing*":[3]

> [...] it appears as though *Bing* began as a gloss on *Le Dépeupleur* as well as, to some extent, a part of it. In the initial versions, therefore, *Bing* seems to be devoted to exploring or detailing what it might be possible to say about a body's life in the niches described in *Le Dépeupleur*.[4]

The Lost Ones, which is the longest of the group of texts that have often been referred to as Beckett's prose fragments, describes the life, in a cylinder, of "two hundred bodies in all round numbers" (204). The bodies are divided into four groups, according to their activity and motility: those who are constantly searching; "those who sometimes pause" (204); the sedentary searchers who rarely move and finally the vanquished, who appear motionless. *All Strange Away, Imagination Dead Imagine* and *Ping* are similar, but in them, individual bodies rather than a community become the focus of the narrator's attention.

What has most puzzled critics about these works is the peculiarity of their setting and subject matter, together with the oddity of their linguistic register. In the case of *The Lost Ones*, which to date has received the most critical attention, the abundance of measurement and precise numerical

---

1973, which for its part was published as a Dell paperback in the same year, and finally the most recent version, published in *Samuel Beckett: The Complete Short Prose 1929-1989*, ed. S. E. Gontarski (New York: Grove Press, 1995), which contains features of both of the previous English language versions. See S. E. Gontarski, "Refiguring, Revising, and Reprinting *The Lost Ones*," *Journal of Beckett Studies* 4, no. 2 (Spring 1995): 99-101. All references in the text to Beckett are from *Samuel Beckett: The Complete Short Prose 1929-1989*, unless otherwise stated.

[2] Gontarski's comment is from his introduction to *Samuel Beckett: The Complete Short Prose 1929-1989*, xv. The quotation is from Beckett's personal notebooks which also contain the manuscripts of the two texts, reprinted in Richard Admussen, *The Samuel Beckett Manuscripts: A Study* (Boston: G. K. Hall and Co., 1979), 22.

[3] Leslie Hill, *Beckett's Fiction: In Different Words* (Cambridge: Cambridge University Press, 1990), 149.

[4] Ibid., 150.

information about the space that the bodies inhabit, accompanied by the curious inaccuracy and inconsistency of the information given, has proved baffling enough to arouse discussion about the possible mistakes Beckett made when writing or translating the work.[5]

For some, *The Lost Ones* has functioned as an allegory of the human condition or as a parable of the authorial process, while for others, the realm of science or even science fiction has offered a frame of reference.[6] A closer look at the changing narrative strategies of *The Lost Ones* and the group of works it belongs to, however, suggests a different account. Far from merely "representing the movement of the narrator behind" the works[7] or functioning as simple tropes of the human condition, these stories engage in a probing examination of the nature of perception and the embodied state of subjectivity that is in stark contrast with the affirmative tone of humanist-existentialist readings of Beckett. At stake, therefore, in the re-reading I propose, are more fundamental questions about the contradictory nature of embodiment in Beckett as the very essence of a precarious identity, which is itself repeatedly undermined through an aesthetics of negation.

Even a casual glance at the short texts suffices to call attention to their difference from Beckett's earlier fictional works. Indeed, one might even define them as a series of negations of the rhetorical and dramatic foundations of Beckett's earlier writing. Perhaps the most obvious and yet striking change is the abandonment of the first-person narrator as the texts' principal vehicle, still present in the four novellas (1946), the trilogy (1947-

---

[5] For an exhaustive account of the mathematical errors and inaccuracies in *The Lost Ones,* see Enoch Brater, "Mis-takes, Mathematical and Otherwise, in *The Lost Ones,*" *Modern Fiction Studies* 29, no. 1 (Spring 1983): 93-109. See also, Gontarski, "Refiguring, Revising, and Reprinting *The Lost Ones.*"

[6] For examples of an allegorical reading, see Peter Murphy, "The Nature of Allegory in 'The Lost Ones,' or the Quincunx Realistically Considered," *Journal of Beckett Studies* 7 (Spring 1982): 71-88; Antoni Libera, "The Lost Ones: A Myth of Human History and Destiny," in *Samuel Beckett: Humanistic Perspectives,* ed. Morris Beja, S. E. Gontarski, and Pierre Astier (Columbus: Ohio State University Press, 1983), 145-156; and Lance St. John Butler, *Samuel Beckett and the Meaning of Being: A Study in Ontological Parable* (London: Macmillan, 1984), 171-173. For an account of *The Lost Ones* as a parable of the authorial process, see Eric P. Levy, "Looking for Beckett's Lost Ones," *Mosaic* 12, no. 3 (Spring 1979): 163-170. For a discussion of entropy and the novella, see Sylvie Henning, *Beckett's Critical Complicity: Carnival, Contestation, and Tradition* (Lexington: University Press of Kentucky, 1988), 159-195. Finally, for a reading of the novella as an example of "(self-dismantling) cybernetic fiction," see David Porush, "Beckett's Deconstruction of the Machine in *The Lost Ones,*" *L'esprit créateur* 26, no. 4 (Winter 1986): 87-98.

[7] Levy, "Looking," 165.

1950), the *Texts for Nothing* (1950-1952) and *How It Is* (1964).[8] Closely connected with the shift to second and third-person narratives is a major deconstructive move: instead of trying to penetrate an inner core or nucleus, in a manner typical of Western thought at least since the Renaissance, Beckett is fascinated in these works by the outside, the exterior, the surface of being. The so-called cylinder works, in other words, form a group of narratives that have in common a strikingly discernible quality of surface exploration, in which sense objects only are described and experienced: "None looks within himself where none can be" (211).[9]

Apart from abandoning the first-person narrator, these works also have a shared thematic interest that is worked into the texts through the third-person descriptions, namely, a perceptible questioning and withering of the sense of vision within the narrative environments.[10] In *The Lost Ones*, the nature of the light in the cylinder is such that it obscures rather than aids vision: "[l]ight in a word that not only dims but blurs into the bargain" (214). As Sylvie Henning says, the light has paradoxical effects: "[a]t the same time it enlightens, it also obscures and confuses, by making it difficult for the eye to adapt. The sense of sight is impaired and eventually ruined by the oscillating murky yellow."[11] As the detached narrative voice of *The Lost Ones* puts it:

> It might safely be maintained that the eye grows used to these conditions and in the end adapts to them were it not that just the contrary is to be observed in the slow deterioration of vision ruined by this fiery flickering murk and by the incessant straining for ever vain with concomitant moral distress and its repercussion on the organ. (214)

---

[8] Samuel Beckett, *The Beckett Trilogy: Molloy, Malone Dies, and The Unnamable* (London: Picador, 1979), and *How It Is* (London: John Calder, 1996). Beckett finished *Comment c'est* (Paris: Les Editions de Minuit, 1961), the French version, in 1960. The four novellas and the "Texts for Nothing" are reprinted in *Samuel Beckett: The Complete Short Prose 1929-1989*.

[9] John Pilling refers to the style of Beckett's prose in this group of works as a "notational technique" (John Pilling, *Samuel Beckett* [London: Routledge & Kegan Paul, 1976], 50).

[10] This move is already anticipated in the search for dark, confined spaces that characterized the four novellas and the trilogy, and that is present as early in Beckett's work as *Murphy*, namely in Murphy's fascination with the garret and with the padded cells of the Magdalen Mental Mercyseat (Samuel Beckett, *Murphy* [London: Picador, 1973]).

[11] Henning, *Beckett's Critical Complicity*, 180.

It is in the nature of this light to provide "illumination of the broad surface of things while obscuring the more troublesome irregularities."[12] The problem of vision is replicated in *Ping*, where it is the very whiteness of the illuminated walls and planes that works to undermine the discriminatory nature of sight; to the eye, the surfaces become almost indistinguishable from one another, making the white narrated skin of Ping all but intermingle with its surroundings: "bare white body fixed one yard white on white *invisible*"[13] (193). The body itself becomes reduced to a featureless, indistinguishable blank: "Nose ears white holes mouth white seam like sewn invisible"[14] (194). In *Imagination Dead Imagine*, too, "all shines with the same white shine, ground, wall, vault, bodies, no shadow" (182). The distinguishing markers disappear: "long black hair gone, long black lashes on white cheekbone gone, glare from above for features on this bonewhite undoubted face right profile still hungering for missing lashes [...]" (177). The undifferentiated surfaces threaten selfhood, for "merging in the white ground were it not for the long hair of strangely imperfect whiteness, the white body of a woman finally" (184). There is a sense in which this dissolution of individuality in the works is even oddly pleasurable and compelling.

The mysterious light and its effect upon surfaces constitute only one of the multiple changes that appear in the cylinder texts. Verbal communication, the supreme mode of interaction between interior consciousnesses, is also negated, giving way instead to gesture and posture, while voice is replaced by fluctuations of heat and light, with "[b]rief murmurs only just almost never" (193). We are faced with a question of "sitting, standing, walking, kneeling, crawling, lying, creeping, all any length, no paper, no pins, no candle, no matches [...]" (170), all else being reduced to "silent flesh" (176). Not only, in other words, do these works question vision; there is also a move away from sound. Because of the rubbery surface of the floor and walls,[15] even footfalls cannot be heard:

> The only sounds worthy of the name result from the manipulation of the ladders or the thud of bodies striking against one another or of one against itself as when in sudden fury it beats its breast. Thus flesh and bone subsist. (204)

---

[12] Ibid., 187.
[13] My italics.
[14] The narrator adds, "nails fallen white over" (195).
[15] The ceiling, too, is of the same material: "[d]ash a rung against it and the sound is scarcely heard" (203).

The remaining sounds, in other words, are corporeal, with even the murmur of the fluctuating light reminiscent of regular intakes of breath, "[i]ts restlessness at long intervals suddenly stilled like panting" (202). A kiss, the narrator says, due to the effect of the climate on the mucous membrane, "makes an indescribable sound" (202).

The bodies, in the cylinder of *The Lost Ones,* situate the ladders they carry in the desired location not with the aid of sight but by means of tactile exploration; as the narrator informs us, the bodies "are required to *hug* the wall at all times eddywise"[16] (210), instead of simply finding their way with the help of vision. Eric Levy has suggested that the eye, in *The Lost Ones,* in fact functions more as a symbol of the need to search than as the organ of vision as such, which would explain the recurring references to vision after the faltering eyesight of the bodies in the work is established.[17] For the niches themselves, once the climbers begin to ascend, are found by means of touch.[18] The fact that surfaces, the sense of touch and the skin in general are emphasized in *The Lost Ones* is made clear by the narrator's comments on the "[c]onsequences of this climate to the skin" (202) and on the way the skin performs in the cylinder in comparison to the eye:

> The effect of this climate on the soul is not to be underestimated. But it suffers certainly less than the skin whose entire defensive system from sweat to goose bumps is under constant stress. It continues none the less feebly to resist and indeed honourably compared to the eye which with the best will in the world it is difficult not to consign at the close of all its efforts to nothing short of blindness. (219-220)

Touch, in other words, becomes a "common sense" in the cylinder, not only because the skin, as Didier Anzieu has observed, acts as a "surface containing pockets and cavities where the [other] sense organs [...] are located,"[19] but because when light fluctuations can no longer be seen, the accompanying heat fluctuations can still be felt. Communication itself becomes tactile, with aural messages in *The Lost Ones* replaced by thumps and blows. When one of the climbers that choose to halt on the ladders

---

[16] My italics.

[17] Eric P. Levy, *Beckett and the Voice of Species: A Study of the Prose Fiction* (Totowa, N.J.: Barnes & Noble, 1980), 97. This notion would be supported by the narrator's reference to the three different zones of the cylinder, "invisible to the eye of flesh" (216).

[18] As Sylvie Henning points out, "every climber's moves are made by feel [au jugé]" (Henning, *Beckett's Critical Complicity,* 187).

[19] Didier Anzieu, *Skin Ego,* trans. Chris Turner (New Haven and London: Yale University Press, 1989), 103.

(instead of entering one of the niches) loses track of time, thus violating the "climbers' code":

> It is in order then for him due next for the ladder to climb in the wake of the offender and by means of one or more thumps on the back bring him back to a sense of his surroundings. Upon which he unfailingly hastens to descend preceded by his successor who has then merely to take over the ladder subject to the usual conditions. (209)

In the phenomenologically reduced cylinder world of the Lost Ones, the skin functions as a medium through which the characters perceive the external world, judging time through the oscillating heat fluctuations, and assaying space by means of the skin's visualising ability, achieved through the tactile exploration of surfaces. The importance of touch in *The Lost Ones*, like many of its diverse characteristics, is replicated in the other cylinder works. In *All Strange Away*, the narrator urges, "hands, imagine hands. Imagine hands," and goes on to add, "something in this hand, imagine later, something soft, clench tight, then lax and still any length, then tight again, so on, imagine later" (173). There is a striking emphasis on tactile verbs: "[i]magine him kissing, caressing, licking, sucking, fucking and buggering all this stuff, no sound" (171). The narrator makes several mentions of body parts that *touch* the walls and plains, and much is made of self-touching, and of squeezing, clenching and crushing in the text.[20]

The sedentary searchers in *The Lost Ones* are said to be sensitive to tactile encounters, for "[a] sedentary searcher stepped on instead of over is capable of such an outburst of fury as to throw the entire cylinder into a ferment" (210). There is, in the case of the sedentary searchers, an agonizing nature to touch, for the skin functions as a common sense also because of its inability to reject stimuli. The sedentary searchers may control vision, but the skin "can neither close like the eyes or the mouth, nor be stopped up like the ears or the nose."[21] It remains forever vigilant, never allowing the sedentary searchers to suspend their relationship to the world they inhabit. In the last section of *The Lost Ones,* the narrator again mentions "the horror of contact" of the "withered ones," who are "compelled to brush together without ceasing" (223). The terror of this when the world is not of one's choosing is

---

[20] The narrator says, for instance, "[l]eft hand clinging to right shoulder ball, right more faint loose fist on ground till fingers tighten as though to squeeze [...]" (174); "[l]oose clench any length then crush down most womanly straining knuckles five seconds then back lax any length, all right, now down while fingers loose [...]" (178).
[21] Anzieu, *Skin Ego*, 15.

tremendous, and the Beckettian canon is, as we know, littered with glimpses of this terror.

Although the bodies in the cylinder at first seem almost indistinguishable from one another, or at least from the particular group of searchers they belong to, there are, however, certain identifying markers that receive attention in the text. One of these is hair, for the woman who is described as "mechanically clutching to her breast a mite" is said to have white hair (211), while the woman vanquished, referred to as the "north," has "red hair tarnished by the light" (221). Another distinguishing marker is age, for, somewhat curiously, there are bodies of all age groups, "from old age to infancy," in the cylinder (211). Perhaps the most emphatic form of identification, however, occurs through the (even) closer examination of the skin, for "the skin of a climber alone on his ladder or in the depths of a tunnel glistens all over with the same red-yellow glister and even some of its folds and recesses in so far as the air enters in" (215). There are even times, the narrator tells us, "when a body has to be brought to a stand and disposed in a certain position to permit the inspection at close hand of a particular part or the search for a scar or birthblot for example" (222).

The nudity of the bodies in the cylinder is significant, for there is a distinct obsession with the phenomenology of the skin in the cylinder works. It is, after all, the skin that functions as a register of experience which exposes us to the world. Embryologically, the skin and the nervous system have the same developmental origins, which entails that the "nervous system is [...] a buried part of the skin" or inversely, that the skin functions as the exposed part of our nervous system.[22] The expression *skin-deep*, used to denote shallowness, may therefore in fact be a misguided one, if we see the skin as extending to the innermost centre of our being, "all known without within" (194). The skin not only reveals the age and health of the subject, but also the traumas and worries we believe belong to the secret core of our being. The scars, wrinkles and lines caused by anxiety that bear witness to our mishaps and that are recurring identifying markers virtually throughout the Beckettian canon therefore reinforce the interpretation of the skin as an external nervous system that carries the inscription of life's crises and misgivings. The skin, in other words, is the external nervous system in this aspect, too, that it reflects that degree of past and present well-being or lack of equilibrium that we cannot hide from the world.

---

[22] Ashley Montagu, *Touching: The Human Significance of the Skin,* 3rd ed. (New York: Harper & Row, 1986), 5. Both the brain and the skin develop from the ectoderm (Anzieu, *Skin Ego*, 9).

The skin in *The Lost Ones* therefore functions not only as an organ of perception, but also as the marker or betrayer of identity; as Anzieu says, "[t]he skin shields the equilibrium of our internal functioning from exogenous disruptions, but in its form, texture, colouring, and scars, it preserves the marks of those disruptions."[23] The outer markers of identity, replicated in the case of the cylinder itself, with its shifting measurements, in other words, become more oscillating, complex and determining of identity than any inner ones. The skins of the Lost Ones, due to the climate conditions of the cylinder, are said to change color and texture, for the "desiccation of the envelope robs nudity of much of its charm as pink turns grey and transforms into a rustling of nettles the natural succulence of flesh against flesh" (220). In *Ping*, too, inscriptions appear on the skin: "[w]hite scars invisible same white as flesh torn of old given rose only just" (195). Beckett in summary presents us with an exploded facticity, with thought become flesh. To borrow an opportune quote from Adorno, "forlorn particulars [...] mock the conceptual, a layer composed of minimal utensils, [...] lameness, blindness, and the distasteful bodily functions."[24]

The title of *The Lost Ones* famously originates in Lamartine's *Méditations poétiques*, specifically in the rather moving line "Un seul être vous manque et tout est dépeuplé!"[25] The problem, regardless of its amorous nature in Lamartine, is, in essence, that of restrictive selfhood. There is a sense, in *The Lost Ones*, in which the bodies are trapped *within* surfaces, in the very exteriority of being, whether of the cylinder, from which all but the vanquished are searching to escape,[26] or of their own skins and bodies that "brush together with a rustle of dry leaves" (202).[27] Due to the adverse conditions of the cylinder, "[t]he mucous membrane itself is affected which would not greatly matter were it not for its hampering effect on the work of

---

[23] Ibid., 17.

[24] Theodor W. Adorno, *Notes to Literature*, vol. 1 (New York: Columbia University Press, 1991), 252.

[25] Alphonse de Lamartine, *Méditations poétiques: choix de poèmes*, ed. Suzette Jacrès (Paris: Librairie Larousse, 1968), 28. Vivian Mercier's translation of this passage is "You miss a single being and the whole world is unpeopled" (Vivian Mercier, *Beckett/Beckett* [New York: Oxford University Press, 1977], 226).

[26] "From time immemorial rumour has it or better still the notion is abroad that there exists a way out" (206).

[27] As Anne Fabre-Luce puts it, in *The Lost Ones*, "no one is alone, but everyone is hopelessly solitary" (Anne Fabre-Luce, "The Lost Ones," trans. Larysa Mykyta and Mark Schumacher, reprinted in *Samuel Beckett: The Critical Heritage*, ed. Lawrence Graver and Raymond Federman [London: Routledge & Kegan Paul, 1979], 313-315).

love" (220). Whatever the searchers are after, the narrator however tells us, it is not a question simply of physical love (213).

The only instance at which the bodies are immune from the examinations of the searchers is when queuing for a ladder:

> Obliged for want of space to huddle together over long periods they appear to the observer a mere jumble of mingled flesh. Woe the rash searcher who carried away by his passion dare lay a finger on the least among them. Like a single body the whole queue falls on the offender. Of all the scenes of violence the cylinder has to offer none approaches this. (222)

Mingled through their flesh, the individual bodies become as one, for it is in the nature of the tactile that whenever one touches, one is also oneself necessarily touched, which makes it difficult to define the boundaries between the self and the world.[28] One thinks of Michel Serres's remark:

> Contingency means mutual touching: world and body meet and caress in the skin. I do not like to speak of the place where my body exists as a milieu, preferring rather to say that things mingle among themselves and that I am no exception to this, that I mingle with the world which mingles itself in me. The skin intervenes in the things of the world and brings about their mingling.[29]

Touch, in other words, is inherently reflexive: through it, as Don Ihde puts it, one is "constantly 'in touch' with that" by which one is surrounded.[30] The skin is fundamental in situating us in the world, for it on the one hand procures the distinction between the inside and the outside, but also on the other hand brings the two together in a way which is characteristic of no other part of the body. Although the skin, in other words, is a discriminatory organ, it also collapses boundaries between the self and the world, effecting the release from restrictive selfhood, intermingling us with the world or with the other in a manner that brings us to a state of coexistence which is also a dizzying proximation of nonexistence.[31]

---

[28] Don Ihde, *Sense and Significance* (Pittsburgh: Duquesne University Press, 1973), 99.

[29] Michel Serres, *Les cinq sens* (Paris: Hachette, 1998), 97; see *Michel Serres's Five Senses*, trans. Steven Connor, 4; available online at: http://www.bbk.ac.uk/De...English/skc/5senses.htm.

[30] Ihde, *Sense and Significance*, 99.

[31] For an empirical example of how the tactile can at times collapse the distinction between subject and object, see Ihde, *Sense and Significance*, 96-97. There is also a biological explanation of how the tactile collapses boundaries between the

The idea of intermingling in *The Lost Ones* is reinforced by the sedentary searchers and the vanquished bodies that become themselves topographical features of the landscape within the abode. As the narrator informs us, "[t]here does none the less exist a north in the guise of one of the vanquished or better one of the women vanquished or better still the woman vanquished" (221). The yellow, white and grey monochrome shades of the different cylinder works reinstate the idea of intermingling, making it at times difficult, as we have seen, for the narrator-observer to detect the difference between the surface of the bodies and their world, and hence making vision itself participate in the epidermal intermingling the works evoke. Even the peculiar organic quality of the cylinder functions to undermine the difference between the bodies and their world, for despite the machine connotations of its shape, the cylinder has a distinctly natural constitution. Not only are its heat and light fluctuations reminiscent of the rhythm of heartbeat or of respiration, but the rubbery nature of the surface is itself suggestive of skin, while the cylinder's tunnels and niches bring to mind the orifices and cavities of the body. "A more or less wide mouth," the narrator tells us, gives the inhabitants access to the niches (203-204). The

---

inside and the outside. According to Stanney et al., "the sensations of the skin adapt with exposure to a stimuli [*sic*]. More specifically, the effect of a sensation decreases in sensitivity to a continued stimulus, may disappear completely even though the stimulus is still present, and varies by receptor type" (337). Whereas phasic receptors adapt quickly, tonic ones are slow to adapt and have an "afterimage that persists even once the stimulus is removed" (337) (Ray M. Stanney, Ronald R. Mourant, and Robert S. Kennedy, "Human Factors Issues in Virtual Environments: A Review of the Literature," *Presence* 7, no. 4 [August 1998]: 327-351). It is as if the skin had a short-term memory and a long-term one, just as the mind. Stanney et al. go on to add that the sensation of touch also depends upon the "[s]urface characteristics of the stimulus." Soft surfaces are, somewhat surprisingly, more easily felt after initial contact, whereas in order to feel hard surfaces, "active pressure must be maintained" (ibid., 337). It should be added, however, as Jean-François Lyotard does in the case of vision, that "even the subtlest explanation of the physico-chemical phenomena that 'accompany' vision cannot account for the very fact of seeing" (Jean-François Lyotard, *Phenomenology*, trans. Brian Beakley [Albany: State University of New York Press, 1991], 88). In other words, the explanation of the structure of perception forms a poor substitute for the *understanding* of perception. Our need for tactile communication can also be explained by means of the burden of selfhood and the manner in which touch at least in part collapses our sense of separation from the world. For a philosophical account of the burden of individual subjectivity, see Jonathan Dollimore, "Death and the Self," in *Rewriting the Self: Histories from the Renaissance to the Present*, ed. Roy Porter (London and New York: Routledge, 1997), 249-261.

sense of entrapment the Lost Ones experience only consolidates the corporeal nature of the cylinder, for the characters can no more escape from the confines of their "abode" than they can from the predicament of the body. The word "abode" with which the narrative opens, stems, as Susan Brienza has observed, from the Middle English word *abood*, "meaning 'a waiting, delay, [and most significantly] stay.'"[32]

I suggest, in short, that Beckett turns his focus on the tactile because of the way in which touch collapses the boundaries between the active and the passive, the endogenous and the exogenous, and the concrete and the abstract, hence complicating the preconceived categories and binarisms through which we organize our perceptions and thought patterns. Although touch is a concrete sense that involves physical contact and therefore, on occasion, gives us a stronger sense of "reality" than do the other senses, confirming, as Gabriel Josipovici has observed, not only the presence of the sense object but that of ourselves,[33] there is also a sense in which the tactile is too intimate, too close to our bodily being or to the sensory objects we perceive for us to be able to experience the otherness of our surroundings or of the world through it.[34] In this way, the skin *refuses* the premise of subjectivity as interiority, denying the subject the possibility of a separation from the outside world. The very tension between individuality and its dissolution that functions as the driving force of subjectivity, that

> restless, dissatisfied energy which is the stuff of life [,] is always shadowed by that desire to *become unbound*; that is, the desire for oblivion, for a dissolution of consciousness, the irresistible desire to regress back to a state of zero tension before consciousness, before life, before effort, before lack.[35]

It is perhaps this very tension that explains why the skin, which is also a vehicle of procreation, should so acutely epitomise the complex link between individuality and its loss. There is an anticipation of this loss in the intermingling with the world that touch effects, explaining, in part, the intricate interrelationship between desire and destruction. If interiority, in

---

[32] Susan D. Brienza, "The Lost Ones," *Journal of Modern Literature* 6, no. 1 (February 1977): 148-168.
[33] Gabriel Josipovici, *Touch* (New Haven and London: Yale University Press, 1996), 57.
[34] Walter J. Ong, *The Presence of the Word: Some Prolegomena for Cultural and Religious History* (New Haven and London: Yale University Press, 1967), 139.
[35] Dollimore, "Death and the Self," 256.

other words, is experienced as individuality, then exteriority seems to function as its antithesis, epitomising the very dissolution and betrayal of selfhood. The skin, more than any other organ, is in touch with both these aspects of subjectivity.

The enclosures the Beckettian characters are ceaselessly seeking can partly be explained by the ambiguous dynamics between interiority and exteriority, individuality and its dissolution, that form such a crucial aspect of subjectivity. On the one hand, the Beckettian enclosures function as a second skin of kinds, embodying the characters' need to hide from the world in which one is exposed by one's embodied being, denied autonomous subjectivity and subjected to an interaction with one's surroundings. On the other hand, however, the Beckettian quests themselves, in the very need the characters portray to leave enclosures and hence shed their armours, enact that aspect of subjectivity that is burdened and exhausted by restrictive selfhood, willing to become dissolved in an interaction with the world. Hence, perhaps, too, the oscillating movement of the Lost Ones, torn between wandering within the different zones of the cylinder and disappearing into the solitude of the niches. As the narrator remarks about the latter, "[t]hose whom these entice no longer climb simply to get clear of the ground. [...] To the fugitive fortunate enough to find a ladder free [a niche] offers certain refuge until the clamours subside" (203).

The linguistic counterpart to these tropes of perpetual dissolution is discernible in the shifting registers of *The Lost Ones,* and several critics have paid attention to the peculiarity of the two opposing voices that coexist in the novella.[36] The first voice is a rational, impersonal one, distanced and permeated with irony, while the second register has a poetic and even sensuous quality that is often achieved by the sheer heightening effect of the incongruity of this voice with the former register.[37] David Porush describes the first voice as "a stylistic evocation of technical and mathematical precision" and labels it "machine language," while he describes the second voice as "the language of the flesh, since it [...] is heir to all the ills of flesh: softness, decay, inefficiency, irrational doubt, and inconsistency."[38] Although a rapid glance at the novella would ascertain the coexistence of the two voices within the text, and although the first register, as many critics feel, would initially appear to emit codes of certainty within the discourse, at

---

[36] Among these critics are Steven Connor, Susan Brienza and David Porush.

[37] Steven Connor, *Samuel Beckett: Repetition, Theory and Text* (Oxford: Blackwell, 1988), 107.

[38] Machine language, Porush explains, "is a code which does not permit ambiguity" but rather evokes "images of positive logic, technical efficiency and computer-like order" (Porush, "Beckett's Deconstruction of the Machine," 94).

closer scrutiny, nonetheless, something more complex is at stake in the language of *The Lost Ones*.

The rational voice, which appears to mimic the discourses of law, mathematics and science in general, as Susan Brienza and others have noted, is littered with modifiers such as "more or less" (202), "scarcely" (203), "roughly" (205), "approximately" (206), "thereabouts" (206), and "sometimes" (204), that undermine the assertive tone of the register.[39] Secondly, the discourse, as Leslie Hill has pointed out, is itself permeated with expressions of doubt and reservation, such as "it is doubtful that" (204), "[i]t is as though" (204), "[t]hat is not quite accurate" (204), "in accordance with the notion requiring as long as it holds" (206), and the expression which appears three times in the novella: "if this notion is maintained" (212, 214).[40] Doubt, therefore, is always already built into the register that at first appears so firm in its convictions.

A further striking quality of the "rational" register of *The Lost Ones* is the relative absence of finite verbs or of "active voice or human agency,"[41] together with the clichéd and peculiarly distanced nature of the voice:

> It goes without saying that only the vanquished hide their faces though not all without exception. Standing or sitting with head erect some content themselves with opening their eyes no more. (221)

Not only does the impersonal voice question and undermine subjectivity, whether that of the narrator or of the Lost Ones themselves; the recurring litotes ("not all without exception" and "to open ones eyes no more"), which form one of the most striking linguistic features of the "rational" register of *The Lost Ones*, function in a manner that erases and cancels literal meaning (not all in place of some; not without exception in place of with some exception; open no more in place of keep closed), causing a slippage in which what is signified is never mentioned, and what is mentioned is never signified, hence creating a gaping gap within the linguistic expression and hollowing out the language itself. The distance between signifier and signified, in other words, undermines and negates the unity and identity of the register.

---

[39] David Porush also makes this point and says, in addition, that "[n]ot a single statement or specification or datum is left to stand without some creeping conditional or vagueness or, as statisticians say, 'fudging'" (Porush, "Beckett's Deconstruction of the Machine," 95).

[40] Hill, *Beckett's Fiction*, 153.

[41] Porush, "Beckett's Deconstruction of the Machine," 94.

Something similar is even at stake in the "poetic" register, which appears to negate the "rational" register, while itself being in turn negated by the latter. Although the "poetic" register would first appear to evoke doubt and, in opposition to the "rational" register, proximity, especially in expressions that are suggestive of onomatopoeia, such as "rustling" (220), "thud" (203), and "succulence" (220), all associated with the language of the body in the works, there are also times in which the voice is oddly stiff and distanced from the bodily reality of life in the cylinder. Expressions such as "[w]oe the rash searcher" (222) or "long vigil" (208) bring to mind and perhaps parody the stiffness and pomposity of heroic epic poetry. The use of nouns such as "coign" (204, 212), "vanquished" (211) or "quest" (207), as Steven Connor observes, gives the English text a chivalric and exotic foreignness.[42] In the expression "fain to look away" (220), Connor draws attention to the manner in which the "hint of medievalism [...] both mocks and heightens."[43] Other heightening expressions are "ambient air" (215), "a brief amaze" (220) and "ever and anon" (213), the latter of which Connor refers to as a "literary cliché that seems to sneer in its place in the English, even as it testifies to an impulse to dignify its subject."[44] We are, in other words, at times also dealing with an elevated language that alienates itself from the contingencies of the quotidian rather than bringing us closer to them.

Although, therefore, the "poetic" register can at times be seen to epitomise doubt, uncertainty, and proximity, and although it can be argued that the cylinder's laws of oscillation, fluctuation and negation are reproduced between the two different linguistic registers of *The Lost Ones*, there is, in fact, a *mise-en-abîme* effect. Not only is the oscillation reproduced in the flux between the registers; the laws of negation are replicated *within* the registers themselves, both of which flicker between heightened certainty and its irrevocable undoing. In this way, the unstable conditions of the cylinder recur in the linguistic expression of the work, preventing and negating any attempts toward unproblematic unity.

The Lost Ones, therefore, fundamentally questions the fixity of any register or conceptual stance, be it poetic or other. The immediacy that the text evokes through its persistent emphasis on the material, in other words, is foregrounded by the erratic linguistic fluctuation. It is no coincidence that the corporeal sounds, that like onomatopoeia transgress conceptual categories by moving beyond the closed system of the language of the dictionary, are the

---

[42] Connor, *Samuel Beckett: Repetition, Theory and Text*, 109.
[43] Ibid., 107.
[44] Ibid., 106.

ones that persevere in the cylinder world of the bodies, nor that the sound made by a kiss, in the abode, becomes "indescribable." Onomatopoeia is also a feature of the other cylinder pieces. Beckett first named the English translation of *Bing* "Pfft," but revised it to *Ping*, which is equally onomatopoeic.[45] The alternative title reveals Beckett's insistence on a move beyond dictionary meaning.

Although the thematic and stylistic questions discussed might at first glance seem mere minor issues, derived from works that have sometimes been dismissed as being equally minor moments in Beckett's œuvre, at stake in these apparent minutiae are much larger questions about the arc and significance of Beckett's project. For there is finally a disintegration of the self in the breakdown of registers and in the insistence on the exterior which characterize *The Lost Ones*. The dynamics between interior and surface, individuality and its loss are also epitomized in the French and the English titles of the novella which themselves portray the loss of oneness, the disappearance of self. Even the individual cylinder texts, in their fragmentary nature, function "like parts of an absent whole which ghost one another but do not coincide except in piecemeal fashion," thus participating in the gradual dissolution and negation of fixed identity.[46]

The different variants of *The Lost Ones* themselves operate in a similar manner, undermining the text's coincidence with itself. The differences between the original English language versions concern numbers, and Gontarski's aim, in the third version he has edited, has been to correct what most critics have seen as Beckett's mathematical errors and inaccuracies.[47] What has been noted less often, however, is that the shifts in measurement also figure in *All Strange Away*. The narrator first describes the measurements of the space the two bodies inhabit by saying, "[f]ive foot square, six high" (169), but later says, "[f]or nine and nine eighteen that is four feet and more across in which to kneel" (172). This is further corrected by the comment, "[c]eiling wrong now, down two foot, perfect cube now, three foot every way, always was" (173), and yet later, "place no longer cube but rotunda three foot diameter eighteen inches high supporting a dome semi-circular in section as in the Pantheon in Rome or certain beehive tombs and

---

[45] Gontarski, *Samuel Beckett: The Complete Short Prose 1929-1989*, xv.

[46] Hill, *Beckett's Fiction*, 149.

[47] Enoch Brater, however, acknowledges that, although Beckett had "initially told his English publisher" that a misprint had occurred in the measurements of the cylinder in the English version of the text, "and that the fault was entirely his own, he let it stand" (Enoch Brater, *The Drama in the Text: Beckett's Late Fiction* [New York and Oxford: Oxford University Press, 1994], 104). Beckett, in other words, chose not to correct the faulty mathematics.

consequently three foot from ground to vertex that is at its highest point no lower than before with loss of floor space in the neighbourhood of two square feet or six square inches per lost angle [...]" (176). Still later, the measurements have shifted again: "Rotunda then two foot across and at its highest two foot high [...]" (177). Given the genealogy of the cylinder pieces, the clearly premeditated shifts in measurement that figure in *All Strange Away* cast serious doubt on speculations about Beckett's possible mistakes in *The Lost Ones*. In a paradoxical manner, therefore, the attempt to "correct" the text of *The Lost Ones* in the third English language version, which contains features of both of the previous versions, has only contributed to the dissolution of the text, for it has made it increasingly difficult to identify the "correct" or originary novella, which may have been Beckett's intention in publishing more than one version of the text in the first place. Somewhat strangely, therefore, the dynamics between identity and its dissolution also seem to offer an explanation to the failing mathematics of the narrator, which within the logic of the cylinder pieces, are always doomed to become undone.

The oscillation between individuality and its loss that is produced in *The Lost Ones* through the emphasis on the tactile, through the different linguistic registers and their breakdown, and the textual variants of the novella, itself reproduces its own laws of vacillation. For there is, finally, fluctuation even within the categories of unity and disintegration evoked by the text. While the former signifies separateness and identity, it also simultaneously entails entrapment and confinement, an exploded facticity, qualities that are epitomised in the skin which itself contains the capacity for both pleasure and pain. Similarly, dissolution, while signifying negation, loss and ultimate extinction, concurrently always suggests release, a *"redemption from redemption,"* turning Beckett's strange novella, finally, into an intricate web that vacillates and flickers in its own erratic light.[48]

University of Durham

---

[48] Simon Critchley, *Very Little...Almost Nothing: Death, Philosophy, Literature* (London and New York: Routledge, 1997), 27.

BECKETT'S PURGATORIES

JOHN L. MURPHY

> Examining these texts within the Catholic medieval conception of purgatory as an intermediate state between sin and salvation, we can consider the position of Beckett's characters as trapped in their ambiguous afterlives. Rejecting the original concept of purgatory as a place of cleansing the soul before its heavenly reception, Beckett and his creations deny medieval certainty and confront modern agnosticism. Influenced by traditional perceptions of the place of purging, yet scouring from his depictions the surety of an end to their suffering, Beckett reshapes purgatory into a negative space of spiritual and physical confinement from which escape remains as uncertain as redemption.

Samuel Beckett presents doubt as the perpetual condition of life. In a perverse reflection of our present world, his fiction narrates human inability in death to accept the posthumous verdict of an omnipotent judge upon terrestrial affairs. As a consequence, his characters are trapped. In imagined vestibules of the afterlife, in which none know what lies beyond their urns, Beckett's figures are "partially purged." Defying voices of authority, doubting the veracity of sacred texts and gasping in the vacuum that surrounds their small enclosures, his doubt-filled souls in *Play*, *How It Is*, and *The Lost Ones* dramatize their relation to the theology of purgatory.

While Beckett does not ascribe overt religious motivation to these characters, their skeptical relationship to salvation derives from the medieval longing to encapsulate certainty that lies at the heart of purgatorial theology. From the fourth to the twelfth century, Catholic belief gradually constructed a realm of the afterlife that existed between heaven and hell—purgatory. Purgatory offered the soul a post-mortem second chance to satisfy the debts due its redeemer for its bodily and spiritual sins. Here (wherever "here" might lie), even the most sullied penitent could await salvation. Light, time, temperature, and all sensory and quantitative experience varied in medieval accounts of purgatory, where the waiting game more often punished remnants of the human body rather than refreshed the soul. The conditions of heat, light, warmth and cold that infused medieval speculation about purgatory also infuse Beckett's texts: his agnostics merit neither salvation nor damnation. Bodily discomfort afflicts them; their waiting never ends.

In the conventional idea of purgatory, the torments of hell ease while the soul is purged of its sins and readied for heaven. Beckett's inmates suffer physical agony and remain uncertain of its cessation. As Malone admits, nearing his own death: ". . . I am easily frightened now. I know those little phrases that seem so innocuous and, once you let them in, pollute the whole of speech. *Nothing is more real than nothing.*"[1] Beckett, as he neared his own death, reinforced the literary origins of his own thought—he reread *The Divine Comedy*.[2] In his youth he wrote an essay that critiqued Dante; his mature fiction and drama explored medieval speculation about salvation and damnation; his later narratives continued his quest to uncover the mystery beyond life's end. As Dante shaped Christian eschatology into poetry, so Beckett crafts his words into a challenge to such traditional belief. [3]

---

[1] Samuel Beckett, *Malone Dies*, in *Molloy, Malone Dies, The Unnamable* (London: Calder and Boyars, 1959), 193.

[2] Christopher Ricks, *Beckett's Dying Words* (Oxford: Clarendon Press, 1993), 27.

[3] For Beckett's adaptations of Dante, see Mary Bryson, "Beckett and the Three Dantean Smiles," *Journal of Beckett Studies* 4, no. 2 [n.s.] (1995): 29-33 and "No Stars without Stripes: Beckett and Dante," *Romanic Review* 87, no. 4 (1996): 551-556; Keir Elam, "Dead Heads: Damnation-Narration in the 'Dramaticules,'" in *The Cambridge Companion to Beckett*, ed. John Pilling (New York: Cambridge University Press, 1994), 145-166; Raymond Federman, *Journey to Chaos: Samuel Beckett's Early Fiction* (Berkeley and Los Angeles: University of California Press, 1965), 31-55; John Fletcher, "Beckett's Debt to Dante," *Nottingham French Studies* 4, no. 1 (1965): 41-52; Wallace Fowlie, "Dante and Beckett," in *Dante Among the Moderns*, ed. Stuart Y. McDougal (Chapel Hill: University of North Carolina Press, 1985), 128-152; P. N. Furbank, "Beckett's Purgatory," *Encounter* 22, no. 6 (1964): 69-72; Hugh Haughton, "Purgatory Regained: Dante and Late Beckett," in *Dante's Modern Afterlife: Reception and Response from Blake to Heaney*, ed. Nick Havely (New York: St. Martin's Press, 1998), 140-164; Sighle Murphy, "Dante's 'Schoolboy Copy' of Dante: A Handbook for Liberty," *Dalhousie French Studies* 19 (1990): 11-9; Neal Oxenhandler, "Seeing and Believing in Dante and Beckett," in *Writing in a Modern Temper: Essays on French Literature and Thought in Honor of Henri Peyre*, ed. Mary Ann Caws (Saratoga, Calif.: Anima Libri, 1984), 214-223.; John Pilling, *Samuel Beckett* (London: Routledge & Kegan Paul, 1976); Michael Robinson, *The Long Sonata of the Dead: A Study of Samuel Beckett* (New York: Grove Press, 1969), and "From Purgatory to Inferno," *Journal of Beckett Studies* 5 [o.s.] (1979): 60-83; Rubin Rabinovitz, *Innovation in Samuel Beckett's Fiction* (Urbana: University of Illinois Press, 1992), 106-117; Walter Strauss, "Dante's Belacqua and Beckett's Tramps," *Comparative Literature* 11 (1959): 250-261. Darko Suvin, "Beckett's Purgatory of the Individual, or the Three Laws of Thermodynamics," [*Tulane*]*Drama Review* 11, no. 4 (1967): 23-36. For Beckett's adaptations of medieval Christian motifs, see William Hutchings, "'The Unintelligible Terms of an Incomprehensible

His lifelong interest in the medieval otherworld inspires his own modern revisions of the afterlife. Critics often describe *Play, How It Is,* and *The Lost Ones* as embodying—however fleetingly or even contradictorily—this intermediate realm of waiting. For this essay, I will focus on these three works, christened "purgatorial" by Vivian Mercier, to unearth the human condition encountered in such forsaken inscapes.[4]

Purgatory occupies the most Beckettian position of the three realms assumed in Catholic afterlife. His heaven and hell lie static; purgatory suggests energy and vitality. Yet Beckett's own texts undercut the elements so praised in his essay on Dante and Joyce's purgatorial conceptions. No easy equivalences exist for Beckett's inhabitants of these suspended states. For one of his first novelistic protagonists, Murphy, hell appealed and heaven repulsed; the hellish half-light offered him respite from unchanging opposites. All three of the later texts Mercier cites tempt critics to place their settings in limbo, an intermediate otherworld, a twilight realm. While clearly not desirable locales, given their grey desolation, their muddy plains, or their cylindrical walls, those in these intermittently dazzling/black, drenched/baked, and stifling/freezing prisons seek the middle ground, the retreat from the extremes. Catholics constructed a realm where sinners earned a second chance at salvation. Beckett's Protestant forebears deny such mercy to the backsliders and the mediocre. Beckett himself avers judgment. He creates an agnostic's afterlife.

"What runs through the whole of Dante," Joyce observed to Beckett, "is less the longing for paradise than the nostalgia for being. Everyone in the poem says '*Io fu*'— 'I was, I was.'"[5] Beckett explores this realm where past recollections comfort, confuse, and torment those who are condemned by memory. Unlike Dante's characters, Beckett's must question their existence as mortal and as post-mortal creations of a creator whose existence cannot be proven. In "Dante...Bruno.Vico..Joyce," Beckett's

---

Damnation': Samuel Beckett's *The Unnamable*, Sheol, and *St. Erkenwald*," *Twentieth Century Literature* 27, no. 2 (1981): 97-112; Edith Kern, "Beckett's Modernity and Medieval Affinities," in *Critical Essays on Samuel Beckett,* ed. Patrick A. McCarthy (Boston: G. K. Hall, 1986), 145-151; V. A. Kolve, "Religious Language in *Waiting for Godot,*" *Centennial Review* 11 (1967): 102-127.

[4] Vivian Mercier, *Beckett/Beckett* (1977; reprint ed., London: Souvenir Press, 1990), 179.

[5] James Knowlson, *Damned to Fame: The Life of Samuel Beckett* (New York: Simon & Schuster, 1996), 638, n. 44.

"youthful eulogy of Joyce"[6] concludes by trisecting the treatment of the Last Things within Joyce's *Work in Progress*:

In the absolute absence of the Absolute. Hell is the static lifelessness of unrelieved viciousness. Paradise the static lifelessness of unrelieved immaculation. Purgatory a flood of movement and vitality released by the conjunction of these two elements. There is a continual purgatorial process at work, in the sense that the vicious circle of humanity is being achieved, and this achievement depends on the recurrent predomination of one of two broad qualities. No resistance, no eruption, and it is only in Hell and Paradise that there are no eruptions, that there can be none, need be none. On this earth that is Purgatory, Vice and Virtue—which you may take to mean any pair of large contrary human factors—must in turn be purged down to spirits of rebelliousness. Then the dominant crust of the Vicious or the Virtuous sets, resistance is provided, the explosion duly takes place and the machine proceeds. And no more than this; neither prize nor penalty, simply a series to enable the kitten to catch his tail. And the partially purgatorial agent? The partially purged.

Are humans as doomed as kittens to chase their tails endlessly, trapped in tautologies? Beckett does not provide any assured answers. He refuses to affirm the Catholic tradition of offering a desperate body a final chance for the soul's redemption. He fails to support the Protestant objection that such offering—unsanctioned by Scripture and tainted by paganism—cannot occur for the soul seeking a qualified chance at salvation. Instead, Beckett crafts his own purgatory, envisioned in his conception of Joyce's *Work in Progress*:

In Beckett's "Dante" essay, he contrasts the Florentine's conical model with the spherical nature of his fellow Dubliner's purgatory: In the one, absolute progression and a guaranteed consummation; in the other flux—progression or retrogression, and an apparent consummation. In the one movement is unidirectional, and a step forward represents a net advance: in the other movement is non-directional—or multi-directional, and a step forward is, by definition, a step back... Sin is an impediment to movement up the cone, and a condition of movement round the sphere.[7]

Whether the light that met Dante at each end of each of his three explorations of an intricate cosmology will reward sinners who seek revelation and cessation from such steps forward and backward in *Play*, *How*

---

[6] Ricks, *Beckett's Dying Words* 53; and Samuel Beckett, "Dante... Bruno.Vico..Joyce," in *Disjecta: Miscellaneous Writings and a Dramatic Fragment*, ed. Ruby Cohn (New York: Grove Press, 1984), 33.

[7] Beckett, "Dante," in *Disjecta*, 33.

It Is, or *The Lost Ones* remains uncertain. Examining Beckett's visions of a proving ground within the afterlife, these selected postwar texts will convey this movement around the sphere. They describe a ruined humanity and they inscribe the necessity to insist—in the compulsion to bear witness—upon the compulsion to revive humanity, again resuscitated from rubble. For his fictions, such depictions of the purgatorial desolation encountered by shellshocked survivors appear less tangible than many of his earlier renderings of damaged psyches. For *Play*, the vast scope of the afterlife narrows to an intense interrogation of a trio, but the state of suspension, of uncertainty, of the liminal persists. The "hellish half-light" twice voiced in this dramatic text qualifies the torment endured by the adulterous man, his mistress, and his (presumed) wife. But is this hell or purgatory? Katherine Worth clarifies that the attitude toward pain, not its absence, distinguishes Beckett's two states of post-mortem punishment. In her opinion, inertia and despair are avoided by those in purgatory, but these inmates resist temptations to cruelty and despair which consume their infernal counterparts.[8] Therefore, a half-light closer to purgatory than hell shines upon those in *Play*. Michael Robinson muses how "Beckett's heroes are not in Hell, but Purgatory: a purgatory on the verge of timelessness."[9] An evocative distinction, yet it underscores how far contemporary understandings of purgatory diverge from traditional Catholic accounts. The whole conundrum of situating a time-bound place for rehabilitation within a timeless spatial state eluded even the best medieval minds. Purgatory occupies the pause between the soul's particular judgment immediately after death and the final judgment of all souls at time's end. Most critics of *Play* fudge this distinction, and place the drama within an indeterminate interrogation room. For *Play*, the trio knows both progression and retrogression, but not their own exact post-mortal "apparent consummation." Most critics judge that *Play*'s three figures, trapped within urns up to their necks, must repeat their accounts infinitely. Repetition without redemption, after all, characterizes otherworldly torments.

Is *Play*, then, in purgatory or hell? Dante's triple vision of the afterlife, and Joyce's version of the same, as Beckett delineated in his essay, fixed purgatory as the "absolute absence of the Absolute." Free of the static states of the doomed and the blessed, those in the middle ascend as painfully as they descend. This alternation, as opposed to Dante's version of the more conventionally orthodox representation of the intermediate state,

---

[8] Katherine Worth, *Samuel Beckett's Theatre: Life Journeys* (Oxford: Clarendon Press, 1999), 54.

[9] Robinson, *Long Sonata of the Dead*, 69-70.

characterizes Beckett's modern vision. Unlike Dante's medieval version, Beckett's cosmology depends upon spherical and not conical organization. *Play*'s urns entomb the three humans. The masks of those trapped resemble the surface of their traps. Their cylindrical nature, their identical grey color, their contact as the containers touch each other: these directions open *Play*. Entrapment dominates the play's content. It rehashes stock suburban characters who repeat parlor banalities as they attempt to outwit one another. In so doing they attempt to grasp love that eludes them after the passion fades and the recriminations die.

Beckett's "vicious circle of humanity" triangulates on stage; the Light squares the circle. And such constriction and contortions form *Play*'s content and become the play's form. As Beckett's stage directions indicate: "From each a head protrudes, the neck held fast in the urn's mouth." Restriction confines all people, in this life or the next. But will those in *Play* ever free themselves from this admittedly tight spot? Or will they wither under the interrogative glare that elicits their responses but fails to illuminate their inner anguish? Does this purgatory increase or diminish pain?

Change, Worth argues, occurs incrementally, and by repetition comes redemption. Slowly, W1 opens her heart: her haughty reference to W2 as a "poor creature" prefaces a humbler acknowledgment of them all as "Poor creatures." Beckett differentiates the players' first recitation as "Narrative" and the second as "Meditation"; he dramatizes how contemplation follows action. This understanding, therefore, would be pointless unless it aimed toward transformation within the three characters. Those in hell suffer only added torment from recollection of their past sins. Those in purgatory gain added insight into their sinful state, and in their sorrow earn credit toward their eventual redemption. They move forward without the constant backsliding that Beckett expects of Joyce's purgatorial sphere. They resist the easy temptation to backslide. They must turn their repentance into restitution toward those they have wronged, and their sufferings thus gain merit toward their redemption. So goes the Catholic explanation.

Outside the conventional Catholic model, we may gaze at the sufferings of the possibly-not damned. Augustine inspired *Godot*'s ruminations upon the fate of the thieves hung next to Jesus. Later, Pozzo asks Vladimir and Estragon: "How did you find me? . . . Good? Fair? Middling? Poor? Positively bad?"[10] Such gradations fracture sharp division between Cosmas the saved and Dismas the damned. Early Christian appeals for mercy

---

[10] Samuel Beckett, *Waiting for Godot*, in *The Complete Dramatic Works* (London and Boston: Faber and Faber, 1986), 37-38.

led to the creation of a less severe set of afterlife penalties for those who could not accept the Manichean cleavage of saved and damned. Augustine, who softened such harsh verdicts, distinguished the *non valde boni* from the *non valde mali* among the emerging intermediate categories for post-mortem souls. Later medieval thinkers debated if these "not quite good" merited purgatory's comparatively easier torments; those "not quite bad" souls might gain a reduction in hell's eternal punishments.[11] Such delineations may be compared to those within the three "purgatorial" texts Mercier mentions. Heat, light, movement and their opposites of cold, darkness, and confinement remain prominent features of the eschatological landscapes of the afterlife— from the medieval theologians known to Beckett until his own century. Beckett undermines this Catholic cosmology.

Another model, however, may provide an intriguing comparison to Beckett's void. Developed at the cusp of the modern era, drawing from ideas long before the Christian era, the cabalistic idea of a deity's shrinking away from our universe, once created, can enrich our understanding of *Play*'s predicament. According to Lurianic mysticism, developed by Jewish exiles at the end of the fifteenth century, God contracted the divine presence in order to energize our world out of the resulting primordial vacuum. Out of this self-limitation, creation emanated. But the vessels designed to contain the divine sparks of light, unable to hold such power, shattered. Only scattered sparks remained in the universe occupied by now-incomplete men and women. Human beings long to gather back this dissipated light.[12] Deirdre Bair notes how Beckett's *Play* figures assume characteristic postures: in the dramatized future, the protagonists speak as fixed heroes, their being expressed by voice; they concentrate their speeches upon the past and fluid world; they lament their present situation from a position of confinement.[13] Unable to break their vessels and escape into a realm of future fulfillment, these creatures wither under the relentless scrutiny of a glaring light that brings them not inspiration but interrogation. As the audience, we too can be trapped in this semi-spherical realm of the stage. Worth reminds us that as spectators, we cannot view *Play* the same way as it repeats itself. She insists that we must re-examine our own complacent responses to its clichés as they repeat themselves. Fixed in our chairs, we too must re-examine our own conscience and its endless accusations and recriminations within our own

---

[11] Jacques LeGoff, *The Birth of Purgatory*, trans. Arthur Goldhammer (Chicago: University of Chicago Press, 1984), 69, 220-227.

[12] Gershon Scholem, *Kabbalah* (1974; reprint ed., New York: Dorset Press, 1987), 128-144.

[13] Deirdre Bair, *Samuel Beckett: A Biography* (New York: Harcourt Brace Jovanovich, 1978), 577.

domestic dramas. Such unsparing cross-examinations do not excuse anybody in Beckett's circle. Both audience and actors are implicated in shared guilt. All must wait and endure the Light's interrogations if they are to be freed and finally escape its eye. In Beckett, the eye inspects the writhings of the "not quite good" and the "not quite bad": we as readers, auditors, and spectators assume the roles God abdicates.

Mary Bryson, commenting on the note cards Beckett used to record his early reactions to Dante, notes the medieval poet's "spotlight" quality in illuminating such figures as Belacqua in Ante-Purgatory for a prominent vignette or conversation before the narrative jumps to another figure or locale.[14] For Dante, the poet manages his verse. For Beckett, the playwright manipulates his stage. The Light itself may be a victim, turning on and off, from person to person, as if hesitant, indecisive, and manipulated.[15] Beckett suggested this to *Play*'s debut director, George Levine. Or, perhaps, the Light served as a metaphor for an audience's short attention span, or the role of the playwright—like Dante, shifting perspectives while traversing a forbidding landscape. All these versions of the Light make it an inquirer. Like the play's three figures, viewers respond differently to its energy, and in revisions, Beckett incorporates the Light as a fourth character, enacting its own uncertain nature as it drilled each of the three figures.

Writing to Lawrence Harvey, Beckett, while working on an early version of *Play*, reflected upon *Ulysses'* ending, with Molly's "saying yes to this atrocious affair of life."[16] She may be resigned, but she will awaken later that June seventeenth. Her life will go on. For the trio in *Play*, no such assurance of freedom from night's spells exists. If this afterlife space is neither dream nor oblivion, then no veils of ignorance shield the three inhabitants from their fate. Unlike Stephen, Bloom, and his wife, the three live in a territory far less charted than that of Joycean Dublin. The sheer lack of detail given their otherworldly state forces those in *Play* to confront their human frailty without the distractions of their former comforts. If the three Dubliners eased their own longings with diversions, these three former Londoners rely upon memories of similar play. But reveries fail to assuage their consciences for long.

Individually, they are trapped within their inner vessels, unable to break out and embrace—or escape—as these souls may prefer—the Light. To end another "atrocious affair of life," the three sides of this love triangle

---

[14] Bryson, "No Stars without Stripes," 550.

[15] Knowlson, in James Knowlson and John Pilling, *Frescoes of the Skull: The Recent Prose and Drama of Samuel Beckett* (1979; reprint ed., New York: Grove Press, 1980), 113-114.

[16] Knowlson, *Damned to Fame,* 445.

must recapitulate their versions of the situation. In *Ulysses*, the three main characters may not fully understand each other, but they do attempt to communicate. Here, the lines of communication are ruptured. Each appears unaware of the other, despite their close proximity. All face forward and do not—or cannot—turn aside. In such fixity, there is no eluding the Light. If this impasse deserves an end, then the unresolved, circular movement of the play must avoid the repetitive circling of the kitten chasing its tail, of the sphere traversed by steps forward only to fall back upon the pilgrim defeated again. The Cone of heaven, of forward travel that brings redemption closer, must be gained. To do this, the urns must be broken, the Light shifted, and the realizations gained by repetition acted upon. Otherwise, movement and vitality will explode but the machine will proceed as "just play," nothing more, eternally. Whether or not Beckett allows his characters such a departure remains, characteristically, uncertain. Ambiguity characterizes all of his depictions of humans caught in such liminal enclosures.

Trapped within a larger cylinder, hundreds of bodies contemplate escape. A few refuse to search. Some climb ladders and crawl into crevices. Others wait their turn near the walls, perhaps unsure if to climb for themselves. The remainder wander and speculate as they pace about the container's floor. They ponder climbing, freedom, inaction. Belacqua's slouch of submission is reproduced by the sitters; Dante's conception of starlight rewarding those who persisted to the end of their ascent entices an ever-dwindling band of climbers. *The Lost Ones* continues Beckett's inversion of Dante.

Light and darkness, heat and cold alternate, as they do in many literary versions of the afterlife. One of the earliest recorded accounts in Britain, Bede's report of Drythelm, tells of that Northumbrian layman's encounter with whirling ice on one side of a mountain and sizzling heat on its other slope. This valley, as in many such visions, trapped those caught between such extremes.[17] But the "ethical yo-yo"—as ex-theology student Murphy puts it in his rejection of easy comparisons between hot and cold, of good light and evil dark—complicates Beckett's version. Murphy in his own "Belacqua fantasy" procrastinates in his rocker rather than undertaking the arduous climb upwards to Paradise. Like Dante's indolent character in the *Purgatorio*, he would rather think than act. For the light offers "the same kick, but corrected as to direction." This "dog's life" he rejects, not for the "Belacqua bliss" of the intermediate realm of half-light but rather the "matrix

---

[17] *Historia*, book 5, chapter 12. See *Bede: A History of the English Church and People*, trans. Leo Sherley-Price, rev. R. E. Latham (Harmondsworth, Middlesex: Penguin Books, 1968), 289-294.

of surds," the ceaseless passing away of identity and form within the flow of "absolute freedom" within darkness.[18] In *The Lost Ones*, as the title indicates, freedom comes along to its inhabitants with the lack of any absolutes save that of absolute freedom: to climb, to wait, to search, to sulk. Purgatory requires a surrender of absolute freedom as the human bargain made with the divine power. Hell offers the lack of such abasement, for there humans assert freedom from any capitulation to the divine. But is the world of *The Lost Ones*, then, truly purgatorial?

The circular structure of *The Lost Ones* incorporates a feature popular in Christian accounts of hell, that of the *refrigerium*. This "cooling-off" period often took place on Sundays and holy days, and was attributed to an arrangement made by the apostle Paul in the third century *Apocalypse of Paul*. The damned from Saturday night until Monday morning gained relief from their torments; *Molloy*'s Moran in #15 of his mental catechism wonders: "Is it true that Judas' torments are suspended on Saturday?"[19] The medieval vision's alternating hot-and-cold motif exists in Drythelm's testimony recorded by Bede, in St. Bernard's preaching, and in the Latin *St. Patrick's Purgatory* recorded by an Irish monk in Germany—which has been claimed as a direct influence upon Dante's own versions of infernal and purgatorial punishment.[20] Yet for Beckett, such a common eschatological

---

[18] Samuel Beckett, *Murphy* (1957; reprint ed., New York: Grove Press, 1970), 76, 110-112.

[19] LeGoff, *The Birth of Purgatory*, 37; and Beckett, *Molloy*, in *Molloy, Malone Dies, The Unnamable*, 168.

[20] For the *refrigerium* in *Apocalypse of Paul*, see Le Goff, *The Birth of Purgatory*, 37 and 197. For early Christian contexts, see Alan E. Bernstein, *The Formation of Hell: Death and Retribution in the Ancient and Early Christian Worlds* (Ithaca and London: Cornell University Press, 1993); Martha Himmelfarb, *Tours of Hell: An Apocalyptic Form in Jewish and Christian Literature* (Philadelphia: University of Pennsylvania Press, 1983); and Carol Zaleski, *Otherworld Journeys: Accounts of Near-Death Experience in Medieval and Modern Times* (New York and London: Oxford University Press, 1987). For *St. Patrick's Purgatory*, see Robert Easting, ed., *Saint Patrick's Purgatory*, EETS [o.s.] 298 (Oxford: Oxford University Press for the Early English Text Society, 1991); Jean-Michel Picard and Yolande dePontfarcy, trans., *Saint Patrick's Purgatory: A Twelfth Century Tale of a Journey to the Other World* (Dublin: Four Courts Press, 1985). For medieval contexts, see Eileen Gardiner, *Visions of Heaven and Hell before Dante* (New York: Italica Press, 1989) and *Medieval Visions of Heaven and Hell: A Sourcebook*, Garland Medieval Bibliographies, vol. 11 (New York: Garland, 1993); Stephen Greenblatt, *Hamlet in Purgatory* (Princeton, N.J.: Princeton University Press, 2001); Michael Haren and Yolande dePontfarcy, eds., *The Medieval Pilgrimage to St. Patrick's Purgatory: Lough Derg and the European Tradition* (Enniskillen, Co. Fermanagh: Clogher

feature, like the inquiring Light of *Play*, serves not to further the justice of a divine judge but rather the interrogation of a jailer—and one who may be in thrall to a higher tribunal under which the jailer itself may be an unwitting captive. The Light remains moored to a level face-to-face with those it illuminates; rooted upon the stage along with the trio entombed alive, the Light too cannot reach transcendence, and it cannot escape. Similarly, those within the walled circle must endure this ever-changing, precisely calibrated thermostat.

The narrator of *The Lost Ones* applies a system of mensuration calculated to appeal to an audience wanting facts and figures rather than seeking repentance and reward from Beckett's modern reworking of the afterlife's architecture. A possible distant precursor of the Hell sermon heard by Stephen Dedalus, the *Elucidarium*—the most popular medieval treatise on the otherworld's penalties and bonuses—systematized its balance sheets of saved and damned into precise categories.[21] Like Joyce, Beckett's later Irish vision expands upon this insular tradition of offering the earthly sinner a terrifying glimpse into the eternal consequences of failure. After a page of deliberative expansion upon the cylindrical space's climate control, we are told: "Out of the eight seconds therefore required for a single rise and fall it is only during a bare six and a half that the bodies suffer the maximum increment of heat and cold which with the help of a little addition or better still division works out nevertheless at some twenty years respite per century in this domain."[22] Is there any permanent release from this predicament? Are the two hundred-odd inhabitants condemned to these alternating currents of energy and entropy forever?

Historical Society, 1988); Shane Leslie, *Saint Patrick's Purgatory: A Record From History and Literature* (London: Burns, Oates & Washbourne, 1932); Takami Matsuda, *Death and Purgatory in Middle English Didactic Poetry* (Woodbridge, Suffolk and Rochester, N.Y.: D. S. Brewer for Boydell & Brewer, 1997); Alison Morgan, *Dante and the Medieval Other World* (Cambridge and New York: Cambridge University Press, 1990); and John Lancaster Murphy, "The Idea of Purgatory in Middle English Literature" (Ph.D. dissertation, University of California, Los Angeles, 1995), 63-120.

[21] Aron Gurevich, *Medieval Popular Culture: Problems of Belief and Perception*, trans. Janos M. Bak and Paul A. Hollingsworth (Cambridge and New York: Cambridge University Press, 1988), 160; see 249, n. 48, for Joyce *Portrait* remark.

[22] Samuel Beckett, *The Lost Ones*, in *Samuel Beckett: The Complete Short Prose, 1929-1989*, ed. S.E. Gontarski (New York: Grove Press, 1995), 215.

If this is, as Hugh Kenner suggests for *Krapp* and *Play*,[23] another of Beckett's sketches of a "Protestant hell," then perhaps the trapdoor that entices those within *The Lost Ones* with the rumor of starlight beyond is as illusory as the other rumor that a passage burrows into a natural Eden beyond the walls of this circular prison. No paradise awaits those willingly incarcerated within this purgatory. An opticon without a visible Light watching, this absence of an Absolute may then portend another Beckettian version of Joyce's purgatories. Yet this spherical quality has been flattened. If Murphy saw his mind as an immense sphere when he contemplated the three realms of his inner immensity, at least he had a more expansive model to inspire his own innerbound quests. Even these interior visions fail to comfort; he takes the madhouse job. These Lost Ones occupy their own asylum, but their keeper refuses to appear.

The trapdoor above the jailed remains a door that will not open skyward. Inmates bicker. None will cooperate to place a ladder in the location where the door can be reached by a straining upraised hand of one climber. On their own, none can reach the trapdoor through an isolated ascent. Forays into the cylinder's crevices remain brief. Ladders regularly shift among those who await their own lonely climbs. Entropy expands as fewer believe that the trapdoor raised will bring them to freedom. Beckett's cylinder encloses a hellish more than a purgatorial regimen. A dwindling band of seekers waver between one time-honored conception and the other for an escape route.

If this was a purgatory and not a Protestant hell, the inmates would eventually leave climbing and pacing to arrive at the roof. Their common selfishness foils the whole group's jailbreak plans. Waiting on a deliverer as they do, they attest to the vanity of their own efforts to be saved. For, as Beckett as shown in many of his works, characters' actions, if done without an underlying belief, doom the inhabitants of such ghost-forsaken haunts to everlasting isolation. The trapdoor may be a skylight, but they—and we as readers of this unfinished work—will never know.

With *How It Is*, Mercier's classification of this late prose narrative as "purgatorial" appears even less likely than that for *The Lost Ones*. Death cannot be attained in the realm of mud in which its characters crawl ever eastward. If Joyce sought to attack temporal identity in his modernist assault upon the sureties of external representation of reality, then Beckett's

---

[23] Hugh Kenner, *A Reader's Guide to Samuel Beckett* (1973; reprint ed., Syracuse, N.Y.: Syracuse University Press, 1996), 134 and 153.

narrative destroys even the confidence that we can hear what the voice dominating the recital tells us. Who relates this quest? Self in space and time breaks down, as not only objects collapse but subjects surrender. The "verbal gasps," as Anthony Cronin interprets them—or "verbal panic," as John Calder[24] proposes—of the fits and starts that convey the steps forward and back as the protagonist makes his journey to and with and away from Pim around always the churning sludge—do advance sinners round the circle. Yet, in a lower state than before, below the light, the protagonist does not edge near any skylight, any trapdoor, any repetition that reveals to him redemption or purpose in his travels.

If so, has hell become truly the place of ultimate and permanent isolation–in which all identity sinks into the mire? Without direction, regression and steps backward overcome the painful progress forward which the protagonist seems to have made in the three stages of his journey.

As with Beckett's model of Joyce's spherical purgatory, here the pilgrim's path ends full circle. In Play, the imprisoned cannot—at least for now—leave their constricted confines. In The Lost Ones, the trapped can—at least momentarily—leave the floor by the ladder for the crevices. But illumination never comforts those in the urns. Light and dark endlessly switch over those in the cylinder, so how can any body adjust to take advantage of a second-and-a-half "respite" every eight seconds of torment? And for those envisioned in the slime of *How It Is*, even the light has faded into the memory of a life above, for now darkness visible seems to shroud them. In a 1959 letter to Jack Schwartz, Beckett admitted that this latest prose narrative describes a "bottomless pit" seemingly "as dumb of light as the Fifth Canto of Hell."[25] As Kenner observes of Krapp and Hamm, Beckett's characters make the Great Refusal.[26] Having rejected love, they must expiate their ignorance uncomprehending that they might nearly touch those beside them that they deceived; or they must find loneliness as they doubt and pace and climb without any support even from their spouses; or they must be hacked and raped and abused as they seek to answer pain afflicted with pain inflicted. But all lack the ability to change, to learn, and to improve. Even if the characters in *Play* do attain this transformation, such a consummation will happen inestimably by degrees beyond an actor or audience's endurance to enact (more than twice).

---

[24] Anthony Cronin, *Samuel Beckett: The Last Modernist* (New York: Harper Collins, 1997), 537; John Calder, *The Philosophy of Samuel Beckett* (London: Calder Books and Edison, N.J.: Riverrun Press, 2001), 100.

[25] Richard Kearney, *Transitions: Narratives in Modern Irish Culture* (Manchester: Manchester University Press, 1988), 73 and 294, n. 13.

[26] Kenner, *Reader's Guide,* 133-134.

Cronin suggests that *Play* and other works assumed to take place in a "sort of eternal after-life" may rather record Beckett's early interest in Bergsonian concepts of time. Spatial time, measured by clocks, conflicts with duration—time as experienced by us.[27] Given our own human limitations, we make our forays into interior realms hampered by the rules of space and time. In *Play, How It Is,* and *The Lost Ones,* the Light and energy seek rest. Rather than salvation, cessation impels the inhabitants of Beckett's limbos, semi-purgatories, hellish half-lights. Unlike the characters in a Beckett narrative, we lack the length of eternity to change, as earthly time—intersecting with that of an entrance to eternity—marks the pilgrim's slow ascent of a conical purgatory. The urns of *Play*, the walls of *The Lost Ones*, the plains of *How It Is*: all lack true heights; all sketch a topographical tautology—kittens endlessly chasing their own tails.

In Beckett's revision of the intermediate state, the categories confidently delineated by Dante themselves clash, as Beckett no longer follows the paths of ascent charted in the *Divine Comedy* and so many medieval journeys. Kenner wonders too where Krapp and Hamm linger: "It is a hell, or perhaps a purgatory without promise of issue. No, not a purgatory; a purgatory without issue is a Protestant hell."[28] According to such a reformulation, Mercier's description of the three "purgatorial" texts we have examined may be more accurate. The Catholic tradition—dissected in Joyce—for Beckett becomes another intellectual construction to be mined. While both resurrect Christian models, they reshape and refigure them to suit the needs of not a believer but an agnostic, one who, centuries after Dante, propagates a refurbished purgatorial vision.

Inspired by the two main Protestant spiritual traditions, that of personal testimony and of an "issueless confrontation with conscience," Kenner continues, Beckett offers a "confession without absolution or hope of absolution, because no man can absolve, and touch with God has not been lost or not initiated." Beckett's demolishes familiar Christian paths into the next world. These ways too often mislead the modern wayfarer. Centuries of Moran's catechism result in hallowed words turned hollow. From such confusion comes the ambiguously "time-honoured conceptions of humanity in ruins."[29] Of the three works Vivian Mercier classifies as purgatorial, *Play* most closely explores purgatorial expiation as one of many such venerable representations of the unilluminated way to enlightenment, the *via negativa*

---

[27] Cronin, *Samuel Beckett: The Last Modernist*, 127 and 593.

[28] Kenner, *Reader's Guide,* 134.

[29] Beckett, "The Capital of the Ruins," in *Complete Short Prose,* 278. See also Phyllis Gaffney, *Healing Amid the Ruins: The Irish Hospital at Saint Lô (1945-46)* (Dublin: A. & A. Farmar, 1999), 75-77.

of the path through darkness. In these three texts, light rarely comforts his wanderers. They may gain awareness along the journey into the soul's dark night, the *noche oscura*, but such a revelation may only verify their own inability to convey the mystery of existence. Pilgrims rely upon their faith as they trudge across muddy bogs, endure fiery tortures, and await ransom from grey confines. Beckett's figures rely upon nothing but themselves. They long for negative termination, the end of contemplation rather than an eternal encounter with the source of all-knowing. They claw upwards, but for them trapdoors await them far more often than skylights.

For those who cannot crawl or climb about the spherical purgatory, the internal path through the negative, the absence, and the void itself may be reconfigured. Whether or not this alternative to the traditional Beckett presentations aligns with the approaches into the liminal realm surveyed in this essay, such imaginings of familiar texts revive debate. Anthony Minghella's recent adaptation of *Play* within the "Beckett in Film" series establishes the funereal setting of three trapped figures differently than Beckett's stage directions allow. The vision of a purgatorial prison encompasses now a plain of other figures enclosed alongside and behind the trio. Although the Beckett estate required fidelity to the author's plays, Minghella here seems to use the camera instead of the Light. He explains: "You are forced to feel the presence of the camera, like you would feel the stage light that shines on them when they speak in a theatrical production."[30] The prompting remains: the interrogating eye, itself under an unseen manipulator's detached control. By bringing into the trio's surroundings more urns, more faces, and more sinners, the scope of *Play* widens. Not only must the three characters enact their story again. In Minghella's version, mute trapped neighbors join them. The circular narrative reifies. Over a mossy, dank stage, *Play*'s plot ripples out to surround other silent souls. *Play* awaits yet another recital. The *via negativa* ends in a cul-de-sac. Neither prize nor penalty rewards their trapped souls.

Beckett shrouds his characters in their nostalgia, as Joyce noted in Dante, for reveries—a girl courted on a swaying punt, a departed parent, the promises of kisses from a younger age, the warmth of a light now faded. In purgatory, such memories torment until the memorialists can detach themselves from these reminders of their terrestrial frailty and begin to attach themselves to the only Cause of all of their losses and gains. Having earned full salvation, these souls grasp the ladder and ascend to heaven without a

---

[30] "Beckett Goes to Hollywood," *The Observer* (November 19, 2000). Minghella has set the three principals in a semi-hallucinatory landscape that could be either post-apocalyptic or purgatorial.

backward glance. But, like Lot's wife, Beckett's characters look back. Although all they may see are seared cities of the scorched plain, their tormenting visions console them. For the characters see in their mind's eye what the detached narrator cannot view. They revive reminders of a lost past, and—like Proust about whom Beckett had began his critical explorations, and like Dante with whom he left them behind as his own life closed—the characters Beckett lives through manage to outlast their own end. In some "hellish half-light" they keep telling their stories. Like Belacqua and Murphy, their indolent refusal to look beyond the trapdoor to the skylight suspends them between annihilation and salvation. Their voices echo in the intermediate state of a suspension of belief so familiar to Beckett's earthbound readers and listeners, who share his own tales as—and about— "humanity in ruins."

De Vry University

THE UNCANNY IN BECKETT

LOIS OPPENHEIM

> "There are more things in heaven and earth than are dreamed of in your philosophy."
> — *Hamlet*

In much of his writing Beckett's primary purpose would appear to be the depiction of creative energy or force. The continual unwriting characteristic of his narrative and dramatic art, and the delineation of the negative impulse that provokes it, are the means to this end. As such, they may be considered not only within the philosophic and aesthetic contexts commonly associated with the critical studies of his work, but within the psychoanalytic context of Freud's notion of the uncanny. After tracing the kinds of uncanniness Freud considers in his celebrated essay on the subject and relating them to several Beckett texts, Oppenheim outlines a three-stage process through which the author achieves his objective. The representation of absence (with its uncanny effect), the negation of the representation of absence, and the overcoming of both are shown to result in the concrete expression of psychic drive. It is thus in the reflection of its own epistemological origin that the Beckett text, in the simultaneous display of uncanniness and its undoing, reveals creative function.

Elisabeth Roudinesco has written recently of our "depressive society" and worse—our "contemporary nihilism."[1] Similarly, Bennett Simon has called ours "the age of the schizoid" and situated the characteristic features of Samuel Beckett's writing—depersonalization, ego fragmentation, blocked affect, and communicative dysfunction—well within it.[2] In the effort to come to terms with tramps who do nothing for two acts or with heads conversing from within garbage cans or urns, Beckett's earliest critics sought to enframe his writings in the philosophic tradition of twentieth-century continental thought. Lately, it has become more fashionable to speak of the writer's high,

---

[1] Elisabeth Roudinesco, *Pourquoi la psychanalyse?* (Paris: Fayard, 1999), 192-195.
[2] Bennett Simon, *Tragic Drama and the Family: From Aeschylus to Beckett* (New Haven, Conn.: Yale University Press, 1988), 235-247.

late, or post modernist practice. However contextualized—psychosocially, philosophically, or aesthetically—it is Beckett's fictive and dramatic *un*writing of narrative,[3] and his depiction of the erasure or negative impulse itself, that we are continually seeking to name.

It made good sense in 1961 for Martin Esslin to write a propos of *Waiting for Godot* that "There is here a truly astonishing parallel between the Existentialist philosophy of Jean-Paul Sartre and the creative intuition of Beckett [...]."[4] It made good sense in 1963 for Alain Robbe-Grillet to relate that intuition to Heidegger's notion of *l'être-là* or Dasein. Indeed, it seemed undeniable that, when Beckett's novels and plays were read as parables, as allegorical equivalents of philosophic theses very much in the air at the time, sense could be made of a literary œuvre seemingly devoted to its denial. Hegel conceived of a pure being and a pure non-being, two opposing abstractions whose unification was the basis of a concrete reality. Sartre brought to bear on Hegel's thinking a temporal adjustment: Dismissing any presupposition of the simultaneity of these abstractions, he affirmed the existence of nothingness in Being's emptying it of something. Nothingness was thus to be viewed as necessarily posterior to Being insofar as Being renders it what it *is*. Heidegger carried the correction further: The existence of nothingness was established by anxiety, the affective manifestation of its apprehension by Dasein. What better critical handle for viewing Beckett than this increasingly refined philosophical proof of the reality of absence? After all, his 1969 play *Breath*, to cite but one, gave us only synchronized light and recorded breath controlled by two identical cries of a newborn—that was all that was left of the dialogue, character, and action that normally made up the theater event.

A decade later, Jean-François Lyotard, Jürgen Habermas, and Gianni Vattimo debated the "end of modernity" and Beckett's critics quickly fell in step. Was Beckett a modernist? Was he rather neo or post? As the twentieth century neared its close, a kind of desperate attempt to locate his work on a spectrum ill-defined from the start was felt. Porter Abbott, one of the smartest writers on Beckett around, gave us "Late Modernism: Samuel Beckett and the Art of the Œuvre." Breon Mitchell offered "Samuel Beckett and the Postmodern Controversy." Nicholas Zurbrugg jumped in with the astute "Seven Types of Postmodernity: Several Types of Samuel Beckett." And books by Steven Connor, Leslie Hill, Thomas Trezise, and Richard

---

[3] This process is intelligently explored by Porter Abbott in "Narratricide: Samuel Beckett as Autographer," *Romance Studies* 11 (1987): 35-46, and in the first chapter of *Beckett Writing Beckett* (Ithaca, N.Y.: Cornell University Press, 1996).

[4] Martin Esslin, *The Theatre of the Absurd* (New York: Doubleday, 1961), 26.

Begam all tackled the question of Beckett's subversive projecting of nothing in one form or another.[5] The circumscription of Beckett's perpetually slippery writing and staging of nothingness had found a new critical forum.

Concomitantly, though, Richard Rorty was calling for an end to the postmodern; Umberto Eco was claiming that the confusion surrounding the terms 'modern' and 'postmodern' was postmodern in and of itself; and Bruno Latour went so far as to argue that "No one has ever been modern," that "Modernity has never begun."[6] Perhaps they had good cause to deflate the dichotomy. Perhaps not. But in the belief that the preoccupation with the either/or, like the delimiting of Beckett's work as the literary counterpart of philosophical theses, is reductive, I aimed to rethink Beckett's place on the cultural horizon of the twentieth century in very different terms. That Beckett's thinking is predominantly visual, that the paradigm of the Beckettian creative effort is fundamentally specular and generically linked, thereby, to painting and the other visual arts irrespective of era or style, was the option I chose.[7] I now propose to extend that thesis as follows: Insofar as the work of art for Beckett is revealed not as object or thing, but *agent* of both artist and spectator's seeing, the representation of absence, endemic to

---

[5] Porter Abbott, "Late Modernism: Samuel Beckett and the Art of the Oeuvre," in *Around the Absurd*, ed. Enoch Brater and Ruby Cohn (Ann Arbor: University of Michigan Press, 1990); Breon Mitchell, "Samuel Beckett and the Postmodern Controversy," in *Exploring Postmodernism*, ed. Matei Calinescu and Douwe Fokkeme (Amsterdam and Philadelphia: John Benjamins, 1990); Nicholas Zurbrugg, "Seven Types of Postmodernity: Several Types of Samuel Beckett," in *The World of Samuel Beckett*, ed. Joseph H. Smith (Baltimore: The Johns Hopkins University Press, 1991); Steven Connor, *Samuel Beckett: Repetition, Theory and Text* (Oxford: Basil Blackwell, 1988); Leslie Hill, *Beckett's Fiction: In Different Words* (Cambridge: Cambridge University Press, 1990); Thomas Trezise, *Into the Breach: Samuel Beckett and the Ends of Literature* (Princeton, N.J.: Princeton University Press, 1990); and Richard Begam, *Samuel Beckett and the End of Modernity* (Stanford, Calif.: Stanford University Press, 1996).

[6] Richard Rorty, *New York Times* (November 1, 1997): B13; Umberto Eco in Stefano Rosso, "A Correspondence with Umberto Eco," *Boundary* 2, no. 12: 5; cited in Breon Mitchell, "Samuel Beckett and the Postmodern Controversy," in *Exploring Postmodernism*, ed. Matei Calinescu and Douwe Fokkeme (Amsterdam and Philadelphia: John Benjamins, 1990), 109; Bruno Latour, *We Have Never Been Modern*, trans. Catherine Porter (Cambridge, Mass.: Harvard University Press, 1993), 47.

[7] See my *The Painted Word: Samuel Beckett's Dialogue with Art* (Ann Arbor: University of Michigan Press, 2000).

the relation of seeing to seen,[8] produces a profoundly uncanny effect. And it is precisely Beckett's continual effort to arrive at its creative core, his persistent attempt to unveil the epistemological process that achieves the uncanny result, which defies the taxonomical impulse referred to above. In what, though, does the uncanny effect consist?[9]

***

In *Being and Time* the uncanny is located in the facticity of Dasein's encounter with the 'nothing' of the world. "[A]nxiety," writes Heidegger, "brings [Dasein] back from its absorption in the 'world'" and, as "[e]veryday familiarity collapses" and Dasein is individualized, it enters "the existential 'mode' of the '*not-at-home*.'"[10] Similarly, in his 1919 paper on the subject, Freud focuses on the horrifying quality of that which is unhomelike or unhomely, on the "un" of the *unheimlich* that serves not to oppose it to the *heimlich*, but to reveal its origin within it: "[T]he 'uncanny' is that class of the terrifying which leads back to something long known to us, once very familiar."[11] In a word, then, the uncanny originates in an emergence of the negated or repressed.

A number of circumstances are described by Freud in which the familiar becomes frightening[12] and uncanny. These include confusion between inanimate and animate objects; the doubling arising from primary narcissism or critical self-observation; involuntary or random repetition (as in the recurrence of the same number in several events of close succession); the projection of envy onto others that is betrayed in the fear of the evil eye; and, finally, the overestimation of the power of one's thinking or the belief in the omnipotence of one's mental processes. What is remarkable is the

---

[8] I refer here to the Merleau-Pontyian notion of the inscription of the visible and invisible within each other, the idea of their intertwining, as demonstrated most notably in *Le Visible et l'Invisible* (Paris: Gallimard, 1964).

[9] I would like to express my very deep gratitude to Sidney Feshbach for our numerous discussions of and his rich insights into the notion of the uncanny in Beckett.

[10] Martin Heidegger, *Being and Time*, trans. John Macquarrie and Edward Robinson (New York: Harper & Row, 1962), 321and 233.

[11] Sigmund Freud, "The 'Uncanny,'" in *On Creativity and the Unconscious: Papers on the Psychology of Art, Literature, Love, Religion* (New York: Harper & Row, 1958), 123-124.

[12] The word "inquiétante" of the French title, "L'Inquiétante Etrangeté," more accurately conveys Freud's meaning.

consistency with which these circumstances are traceable in Beckett and the regularity of their uncanny effect.

While what Freud had in mind with regard to confusion between living and lifeless objects was more on the order of a child's treatment of a doll as a person, Beckett's characters (to the extent they can be termed that) relate to inanimate objects as though they were extensions of themselves. And to the extent that crutches and bicycles, bowler hats and tattered garments, are not quite separable in Beckett's writings from their owner, they muddle the animate/inanimate boundary to elicit a similarly uncanny effect. Lucky, in *Godot*, can think only while wearing his hat. The narrator of *How It Is* holds steadfastly to his sack as he makes his way, belly down, in the mud because it is equated with his life. More extreme is Molloy who, in the novel of the same name, conceives of himself only in relation to the infinite parameters of the universe with which he is fused. The uncanny derives, then, from instances where psychic and physical demarcation, like those of ego and world or self and other, is blurred.

Doubling is so frequently employed by Beckett as to have become a platitude in the critical analyses of his work. Self-awareness, splitting, and twinning (such as we have in Vladimir/Estragon, Mercier/Camier, and Reader/Listener, for example) lend a palpable fragility to the Beckettian speaking subject. Indeed, it is the precariousness of the ego and the need for self-preservation that provoke the defense: Voices replicated on tape (*Krapp's Last Tape, Rockaby*); perceptions of being watched, as by a theatrical audience (*Endgame, Not I*); the craving to be seen (*Murphy, Endgame, Play, Happy Days*); and the flow of identities from one self to another *(Molloy, Malone Dies, The Unnamable, Footfalls, Rockaby)* harbor a terror of extinction. Beckett's penultimate work, *Stirrings Still*—where the lone image is of one who sees himself seeing his previous comings and goings—is also a case in point. In focusing the character's (mental) eyes on himself and, specifically, on a self whose only real activity is (mentally) visual, the narrative makes doubling a means of triumphing over ego dissolution or death:

> One night as he sat at his table head on hands
> he saw himself rise and go. One night or day.
> For when his own light went out he was not left
> in the dark.[13]

---

[13] Samuel Beckett, *Stirrings Still* (New York: Blue Moon Books and London: John Calder, 1989), 1. Moreover, as I have shown in *The Painted Word: Samuel Beckett's Dialogue with Art*, doubling is akin in this narrative to visual art itself insofar as the text is so reduced as to exist only in function of the character's

Using "The Sandman" as the focus of his study, Freud concludes that the quality of uncanniness in E. T. A. Hoffmann's tale is directly linked to the central figure and, thereby, to the fear of "being robbed of one's eyes."[14] This, in turn, is evidence for Freud of something psychologically more profound, namely, castration anxiety, a concern seemingly represented in the doubling (not to be equated with symbolizing) of genitalia, such as we find in *Not I* and, perhaps, even in the reliance on the visual paradigm referred to earlier. Indeed, Beckett's other deep preoccupations that relate to the mastering of visual perception—in addition to vision as the prototype of creativity, there is the failure of art to represent and, also, an anxiety of visual remembrance thematically pervasive in the drama and prose[15]—may reflect the dread of castration as well.

Doubling takes still other forms in Beckett: the 'ghosting' (the term is Ruby Cohn's), for example—all the ghostly presences, ghostly lighting and decors, and ghostly language that run throughout the fictive and dramatic texts.[16] I will return shortly to the negation of such uncanny objects, to the representation of absence that counters narrativity everywhere in Beckett's oeuvre. My point here is simply that doubling, a rich motif in Beckett, extends from ego-splitting to revenants and beyond, and that it not only serves a self-preservational purpose but can become, as Freud notes in his essay, "the ghastly harbinger of death."[17]

It goes without saying that repetition is an important aesthetic strategy in Beckett that is neither involuntary nor random. His play on the (*ad nauseam*) repetition of night and day, for example, continually unveils the passage of time (the *sine qua non* of his texts) as something familiar yet

seeing that comprises it. *Stirrings Still,* in other words, recounts the animation of all art by reader or viewer and *is,* in fact, the visual act displayed 'within' it.

[14] Freud, "The 'Uncanny,'" 136.

[15] This is an obsession that I have previously noted to be entirely incongruent with the author's own photographic memory: See my "A Preoccupation with Object Representation: The Beckett-Bion Case Revisited," *International Journal of Psychoanalysis* 8, pt. 4 (August 2001). While my interest in that essay was a possible connection between the preoccupation with visual memory in Beckett's work and the inconstancy of object relations, the link between visual function and the fear of castration or, more generally, the oedipal predicament from which it ensues is also worthy of investigation. I hasten to add, however, that I would oppose too narrow a focus on the psychohistorical for what we have before us is a creative corpus and nothing more.

[16] See Ruby Cohn, "Ghosting Through Beckett," in *Beckett in the 1990s,* ed. Marius Buning and Lois Oppenheim (Amsterdam: Rodopi, 1993), 1-11.

[17] Freud, "The 'Uncanny,'" 141.

new or foreign, eerie even, to lend an uncanny effect. So, too, the "repetition by distortion" or "misremembering" (to cite Porter Abbott) that is Beckett's means of creating—or, more accurately, decreating, insofar as it is a dismantling of previously used material—is deliberate. Beyond tropic variations and re-adaptations of narrative themes and dramatic concepts, though, less determined philosophic and artistic leitmotifs also unleash the uncanny effect: The manias for measuring and symmetry—as seen in *Watt* and *The Lost Ones*, for instance—may be noted in this regard.[18] In their subtle reminiscence of the compulsive nature of instincts common to early childhood and certain pathologies, these repetitions are perceived as uncanny to the extent that they recall what Freud considered powerful enough to override the pleasure-principle, the repetition-compulsion of the unconscious mind.[19] Molloy's obsessive repositioning in his pockets of his sixteen sucking stones is an obvious example. And, as Samuel Weber reminds us, such repetitive patterns are also a form of doubling since they duplicate the Doppelgänger itself.[20]

One has only to consider "From an Abandoned Work" or Beckett's aptly titled *Film* to know just how nefarious the dreaded gaze or evil eye can be. Thoughts of uniting with mother in the short story are impeded by a paternalized roadman who sends the narrator a petrifying "look." Having gone "in terror of him as a child," the narrator exclaims "Now he is dead and

---

[18] See William Thomas McBride, "The Mania for Symmetry: Beckett's *Homo Mensura*," *Romance Studies* (Winter 1987): 77-85.

[19] Freud does not name the compulsion to repeat as uncanny in and of itself, though he does indicate that "whatever reminds us of this inner *repetition-compulsion* is perceived as uncanny" ("The 'Uncanny,'" 145). I am struck by the inattention to this distinction on the part of some scholars writing on Freud's essay. Adam Bresnick, for instance, in "Prosopoetic Compulsion: Reading the *Uncanny* in Freud and Hoffmann," asserts that Freud is working in "The 'Uncanny'" toward the repetition compulsion, a notion formulated in "Beyond the Pleasure Principle," though he qualifies this by citing the latter as "virtually contemporaneous" with the former (*Germanic Review* 71, no. 2 [1996]; 19 pages). In fact, there was nothing "virtual" about the timing: Freud had already completed "Beyond the Pleasure Principle" in 1919 and he distinctly refers in "The 'Uncanny'" to its readiness for publication. Hence, not only was he not working toward the concept of the compulsion to repeat, insofar as he had already formulated it, but he was explicit in not evoking it as an actual cause of the uncanny effect. Rather, it is the similarity of coincidental recurrences to the repetition compulsion that provokes the sense of *das Unheimliche*.

[20] Samuel Weber, "The Sideshow, or: Remarks on a Canny Moment," *Modern Language Notes* 88 (1973): 1106.

I resemble him."[21] As Michel Bernard has noted, "[T]he son has interiorized the threat, and what the narrator now fears is punishment by his superego as a byproduct of castration."[22] More explicit, the disturbing quality of *Film* stems from the indulgence of O (object) in the agony of being visually perceived and from the extreme measures taken by him to avoid the scrutiny of E (eye). Freud explains the projective mechanism from which the ocular anxiety derives: "Whoever possesses something at once valuable and fragile is afraid of the envy of others, in that he projects on to them the envy he would have felt in their place."[23] The connection to the threat of castration is evident; so, too, is the link to the last instance of the uncanny Freud describes—the narcissistic overestimation of the power of subjective thought. For such fearful intensity can only stem from a belief in the synonymy of intention and act, a belief in the magical powers of self and others comparable to the animistic notion of world that the maturing mind, with its increased faculty of judgment, comes to reject. In the "curiously carved headrest" of the rocking-chair in *Film*, an image on which the camera repeatedly insists, what appears to O as two "evil" eyes neatly combines several of the instances of uncanniness named by Freud. Not least of these is the risk posed by one's mental potency with respect to the external world.

Freud distinguishes this type of uncanniness, the reversion to a primitive belief system previously surmounted by the child's developing psyche, from one in which something hidden by repression re-emerges. Space prevents a closer examination of these (often indistinguishable) origins of uncanniness in Beckett and of the moments when *das Heimliche* extends into and becomes *das Unheimliche*. My purpose thus far has been simply to establish ground for the observation that the uncanny may be said to account better than philosophic and aesthetic framings for the frequently cited primary conundrum of Beckett's writing—namely, that his creative process results from a continual *un*writing of narrative and dramatic art. For the confusion between inanimate and animate, the doubling, repetition, fear of the look, and omnipotent thinking that characterize his work all display an eerie familiarity within the strange *non-assumption of identity* and *non-occurrence of event*, within the representation of absence, that is the Beckett

---

[21] Samuel Beckett, "From an Abandoned Work," in *Samuel Beckett: The Complete Short Prose 1929-1989*, ed. S. E. Gontarski (New York: Grove Press, 1995), 163.

[22] Michel Bernard, "The Hysterico-Obsessional Structure of 'From an Abandoned Work,'" *Journal of Beckett Studies* 4 (1994): 95.

[23] Freud, "The 'Uncanny," 147.

text.[24] Having referred, however, to the negative impulse in Beckett that aims precisely at undoing the uncanny object—or, more precisely, at revealing the epistemological process in which it originates—I turn now to this higher order of negativity, so to speak, and to the function it may be said to serve.

***

At the risk of Hegelianizing—in the negation of a negation—an author resistant to such a maneuver, I will outline a three-stage process that achieves Beckett's primary aesthetic purpose, the depiction of creative energy or force. The first is the representation of absence that I have already qualified in terms of the uncanny effect. We have seen that the uncanny is linked, in its unhomeliness, to anxiety (the source, following Freud's revised theory of 1926, of repression[25]) and to a re-emergence of what was repressed in familiar guise. The representation of this anxiety-laden repression, the imaging of absence as an uncanny form, is what Sidney Feshbach has called the "projection in a visual image such that the image seems to take on a life of its own."[26] From where, though, does it come?

To the extent that Freud's theory of the uncanny, as demonstrated in the analysis of the Hoffmann tale, is based on the fear of castration, the relation of the uncanny to representation becomes clear: As Freud shows in the context of the literary text in question, the threat signaled by the aperception of the female's so-called missing phallus to the child's own narcissistic self-image is transformed into a terror of losing his eyes.[27] The ocular anxiety, in turn, is potentially manifested in dream, fantasy, and aesthetic figuration, primarily in the uncanny ghosts and doublings, in other words, that are the visible rendering of the very object of dread.

Uncanny figuration in Beckett is indeed autonomously, if indelibly, implanted within our minds. As in *Footfalls* and *Rockaby*, one image of repression in *Film* is that of the (absent) generic mother, of the formidable

---

[24] In "Narratricide, Samuel Beckett as Autographer," Abbott refers to the "not-taking-on of an identity" and the "not-taking-place" or "textual non-event" (41-43).

[25] When Freud wrote "The 'Uncanny,'" he saw anxiety as the result, rather than the origin, of repression. The reversal was initially worked out in his 1926 paper "Inhibitions, Symptoms and Anxiety."

[26] E-mail correspondence (June 2, 2000).

[27] Weber gives a good summary of the relation of ocular anxiety to the negative perception that is the discovery of the "incomplete" female body in his paper, "The Sideshow, or: Remarks on a Canny Moment."

threat of engulfment by her, despite her missing persona. As Feshbach has perceptively noted, objects in the filmed room project the undepicted mother in all her phantom glory.[28] Like other, more subtle, instances of uncanniness—the ghostly recurrence of names (and the celebrated repetition of certain letters), the phantomesque lighting, and all the "Ghost nights. Ghost rooms. Ghost graves," and "Ghost loved ones" that Ruby Cohn calls "*a mise en abyme* not only of *A Piece of Monologue*, but of Beckett's whole oeuvre"[29]—the mother in *Film* is a memorable representation of ghostly absence.

Similarly, in *First Love*, the oedipal title by no means gratuitous, it is the mother's undelineated presence (she is no more conspicuous than the generic mother of *Footfalls, Rockaby*, or *Film*) and her wifely reincarnation (as ghost of an already ghosted mother) that render the narrator-son's response (or, rather, lack thereof) to her abandonment of him all the more profound. This is to say that his affective unresponsiveness (which he humorously refers to as "anxiety constipation") is a protective mechanism and that the ghosting of the maternal imago is undertaken in self-defense. The birth of the child that ultimately sends the narrator fleeing at the close of the story, however, repeats the process insofar as the protagonist-son ignores the ghosted maternal figure—now his own infant's mother—erasing her in much the same way as he had erased his own, which brings us to the second of the three stages I wish to outline: the negation of the representation of absence.

I return for a moment to *Film*. Avoiding the gaze of people, animals, and objects alike, O demonstrates an overpowering need to "unlink" (to borrow Feshbach's term) from the uncanny projection of mother onto the objects that fill the room. Of this his additional need to disengage from E—the camera filming him, but also his own paranoid self-consciousness—is proof, insofar as it is the consequence of his having internalized the maternal ghost.[30] In a rather poignant if desperate tearing up of photos of O with mother and father at various points in his life, the effort is to obliterate the parental "ghosts." It is interesting, in fact, to note how consistently strong is the need in Beckett to erase such uncanny effects.

Though I would not go so far as to claim with Abbott that the Oedipal conflict in its entirety undergoes erasure in Beckett, for identity is not sought outside the parent-self dialectic but very much within it, I would

---

[28] E-mail correspondence (June 2, 2000).

[29] Cohn, "Ghosting Through Beckett," 1.

[30] E-mail correspondence (June 2, 2000). It should also be noted that, as the object of perception, O himself objectifies the non-objective or absent E, yet another kind of ghost.

venture that Beckett's impersonal characterizations (however oxymoronic the concept) reveal struggles for identity embedded in obliteration: If affect is flat and numbness prevails, it is not that such structures of familial conflict are denied, but rather that a kind of massive decathexis, what psychoanalyst André Green describes as "a striving towards the zero state," is revealed as a powerful affective defense against them.[31] Indeed, the notion of negative hallucination—which Green defines not as the absence of representation, such as a non-reflected mirror image, but as the representation of the absence of representation[32]—is precisely what Beckett's dissociative and decathected writing continually projects.

Abbott's notion of "narratricide," the "disassembling [of] narrative,"[33] describes well the author's means of unwriting phantom or uncanny effects. For characteristic of Beckett is not only the aborted happening or non-event, but a discourse that self-reflectively focuses on its own undoing of narrative, its *un*writing of writing—in writing. The white on white of *Ping*, like the blueless sea and sky, greenless grass, and colorless flowers that lie "beyond the unknown" in *Ill Seen Ill Said*, and the immeasurable dark of certain of the *Fizzles* and *Company,* visually work against a narrative mode already doomed to fail for its inherent incapacity to re-present. As in Beckett's decreative process (his re-writing, revising, and subsequent reducing of previous texts), the imagining of the unimaginable that this colorlessness evokes is evidence that, as Feshbach puts it, "The negation of the original becomes the representation of the act of negating [itself]."[34]

The third and final stage in Beckett's depiction of creative energy or force is a surmounting of the absence both the uncanny object and its erasure represent. We have seen that the relation of *das Heimliche* to *das Unheimliche* is not oppositional to the extent that uncanniness originates in an emergence of the negated or repressed. This dialectic, the representation of absence and the denial of that representation, is maintained in the ultimate triumph over the denial wherein the aesthetic operation itself is revealed.

In "Negation," a short paper of 1925, Freud refers to the "lifting" of repression that occurs when a repressed image or idea, a re-presentation or ideation of something absent or lost, is negated. Though not an acceptance of the content that the conscious mind has repudiated, the negation serves as "a

---

[31] André Green, *On Private Madness* (Guilford, Conn.: International Universities Press, 1986), 59.

[32] André Green, *Le Travail du Négatif* (Paris: Editions de Minuit, 1993), 376.

[33] Abbott, "Narratricide: Samuel Beckett as Autographer," 43.

[34] E-mail correspondence (May 26, 2000).

way of taking cognizance of what is repressed [...]."[35] Already in "Beyond the Pleasure Principle," the process was illustrated in Freud's recounting of the famous "fort-da" game played by his eighteen-month-old grandson. With the child's exclamations of *fort* and *da* ('gone' and 'there') as he made a wooden reel disappear and return, he mastered absence, which is to say he mastered the anxiety produced by the prospect of his mother's departure. More important for our present purposes, however, with the disappearance and reappearance the play with the toy afforded, the repression to which the anxiety over the potential loss of mother had given rise was itself removed: In being elevated to the higher level of the game, in other words, subliminal awareness of the repressed content (separation from mother) was achieved.

As Paul Ricoeur has noted, "The work of art is also a *fort-da*, a disappearing of the archaic object as fantasy and its reappearing as a cultural object."[36] This aesthetic *Aufhebung*, the term used by both Freud and Hegel, is particularly evident in Beckett. Indeed, it is the epistemological core that he strove to unveil. His so-called second trilogy—the late short novels *Company*, *Ill Seen Ill Said*, and *Worstward Ho*—perhaps most clearly illustrates the interplay of negation and reconstitution that is the creative process: *Company* plays on (imaginary) visions perceptible only in the dark. Only with closed eyes, in "his little void," does the narrator see and hear, for the company of *Company* is a fable, "the fable of one fabling of one with you in the dark." Similarly, *Ill Seen Ill Said* plays on the unwording and wording of the inexpressible void: "Suddenly the look. [...] Look? Too weak a word. Too wrong. Its absence? No better. Unspeakable globe. Unbearable."[37] With *Worstward Ho* we are even closer to the "literature of the unword" necessitated by the impediment of words to seeing. These textual "assault[s] against words" of which Beckett wrote in 1937 to his acquaintance Axel Kaun are the culmination of the following reflection: "[M]ore and more my own language appears to me like a veil that must be torn apart in order to get at the things (or the Nothingness) behind it."[38] The paradox, of course, is that the potential for such destruction lies solely within the province of articulation, a reality responsible for Beckett's oft-cited, oft-misunderstood notion of the failure of art. What Ricoeur has called the "denying-

---

[35] Sigmund Freud, "Negation," in *The Freud Reader*, ed. Peter Gay (New York: W. W. Norton, 1989), 667.

[36] Paul Ricoeur, *Freud and Philosophy: An Essay on Interpretation*, trans. Denis Savage (New Haven, Conn.: Yale University Press, 1970), 314.

[37] Samuel Beckett, *Nohow On* (London: Calder Publications, 1992), 51-52 and 95.

[38] Samuel Beckett, "Letter to Axel Kaun," in *Disjecta*, ed. Ruby Cohn (New York: Grove Press, 1984), 173 and 171.

overcoming of esthetic creation," comparable to the "disappearing-reappearing" of the *fort-da* game,[39] in sum, is precisely the negation, but also the simultaneous retaining and surpassing, of a given reality—the creative *Aufhebung* unacknowledged by theorists of semiotic or formalist inspiration. Thus, as Freud theorized, is the uncanny, in the return of something repressed, produced; thus, as Beckett demonstrated, is the uncanny, in the triumph over the repression, itself erased and the aesthetic process revealed.

***

The connection I have aimed to establish between Beckett and Freud is unrelated to the pathography practiced by psychoanalytically-oriented critics seeking access through artistic content to an artist's psyche. Rather, it is a point of convergence not terribly surprising when traced historically to its source: Both men were profoundly interested in philosophy. The impression made on Beckett by Descartes, Geulincx, Sartre, Kant, and Schopenhauer is well documented. And phenomenology was very much in the air when Beckett was in his most productive period in Paris following the war, the German influence of Hegel, Husserl, and Heidegger having been brought there (directly) by Sartre and (indirectly) by Merleau-Ponty. Like Husserl, Freud was a student in Vienna of Franz Brentano, the philosopher/psychologist for whose "fruitful influence," as Freud himself referred to it, the analyst was exceedingly grateful. A "remarkable man," a "damned clever fellow, a genius in fact," "in many respects, an ideal human being" is how Freud described Brentano to a friend.[40] Recounting a visit to his professor, Freud wrote of Brentano's application of the scientific method to philosophy and psychology and of his merciless taking to task those who "had picked up the wrong end of Descartes' philosophy, his complete separation of body and soul."[41] The significance of the correlation of mind and body for Freud's development of psychoanalysis is hardly worth mentioning. But the influence of Brentano on the evolution of Freud's thought should not be overlooked. An 1875 letter from Freud to Eduard Silberstein reveals the provisional result of his teacher's inspiration: "I have arrived at the decision to take my Ph.D. in philosophy and zoology, further negotiations about my admission to the philosophical faculty either next term

---

[39] Ricoeur, *Freud and Philosophy*, 316.

[40] Walter Boehlich, ed., *The Letters of Sigmund Freud to Eduard Silberstein 1871-1881*, trans. Arnold J. Pomerans (Cambridge, Mass.: Harvard University Press, 1990), 95.

[41] Ibid., 102-103.

or next year are in progress."[42] So, too, the impact of phenomenology on the origin of Beckett's preoccupation with subject and object in his fictive and dramatic writing, its bearing on his simultaneous insistence upon and resistance to the dualistic thinking of Descartes (the binary concept of man as *res cogitans*), is exceedingly important.

My point is this: Both Beckett and Freud struggled with radical dualities (those of the primary/secondary psychic processes and the pleasure/reality principles most important to Freud; those of subject/object and mind/body of greatest consequence to Beckett). Each found in negation the means to overcome the impasse which the Cartesian legacy had bestowed upon modern thought. As Harold Bloom has maintained with regard to the Freudian *Verneinung*, "Few insights, even in Freud, are so profound as this vision of negation, for no other theoretical statement at once succeeds as well in tracing the epistemological faculty convincingly to so primitive an origin [...]."[43] The same could be said of Beckett's creative praxis wherein negation unveils the epistemological core of the relation of reality to art.

The question remains as to what Beckett's depiction of this epistemological core—the creative energy or force—consists in. What do we have when the negation that is the representation of absence (the uncanny as resurfaced repression) has itself been negated? In a word, we have a 'theatrereality' (Ruby Cohn's term) and a 'prosereality' (its narrative counterpart) that reflect an utterly non-conceptual and primarily visual thinking.[44] In his paper Freud claimed that the uncanny effect is "often and easily produced by effacing the distinction between imagination and reality [...]."[45] The congruence of dramatic and real time in a play such as *Godot,* of dramatic and real sound in *Not I,* and of narrative and real imagery in both the early and late fiction is proof. In fact, Beckett's privileging of sight alone—the unifying force of all his work—is given to uncanniness from the start: No other sense removes as definitively the imagination/reality distinction as that which serves as the quintessential ontological metaphor and the paradigm of aesthetic creation as well.

Indeed, this is why Freud's metapsychology aimed, first topologically and then structurally, to figure the mind. Even the more recent

---

[42] Ibid., 95.

[43] Harold Bloom, ed., *Sigmund Freud* (New York: Chelsea House Publishers, 1985), 160.

[44] In *The Painted Word: Samuel Beckett's Dialogue with Art,* I discuss this in terms of a *reaesthetization of art,* the continuance of art after its mid-twentieth century 'end' (as employed by Arthur Danto) in Pop and Beckettian minimalism. See, in particular, chapters 2 and 5.

[45] Freud, "The 'Uncanny,'" 152.

theorists of psychoanalytic theory, those of the object relations school, were compelled to construct a model—intersubjectivity being no less apprehensible by the mind's eye—for the figurative handle is a necessary point of departure. I need not review here the many instances of Beckett's own psychic figurations, in *Murphy* and *Watt* most notably, to be found both in the prose and in the plays. But I do want to emphasize that Beckett goes beyond symbolic representation (*Watt*'s "no symbols where none intended" is a caveat not to be ignored) to delineate the empirical, imaging not only the mind but its energy too. This, then, is precisely where Beckett's double negation leaves us—before the dynamic discharge of psychic activity that Freud termed the id.

Already in *Murphy* (1938) representation *in* (as opposed to *of*) the id is Beckett's primary concern: The only certainty to which the protagonist subscribes is the "partial congruence of the world of his mind with the world of his body,"[46] a consonance that sets the stage for all the works to come. In the short narratives of the mid to late 1960s—specifically, "Imagination Dead Imagine," "Enough," "Ping," "Lessness," and "The Lost Ones"—through a cosmic negation of earthly existence the flow of energy from soma to psyche is distilled. In *Ill Seen Ill Said* (1981) Beckett renders the "silence at the eye of the scream"[47] at least as successfully as Edvard Munch. Projecting the bodily source of psychic function, the late plays further depict the constellation wherein ideation is negated and fantasy is the concrete manifestation of somatically rooted drive. *Not I* (1972) and *...but the clouds...* (1976), for example, go so far as to reduce to a mouth in the former and a mouth and eyes in the latter the organic origin of the affective imaginary.[48]

---

[46] Samuel Beckett, *Murphy* (New York: Grove Weidenfeld, 1957), 109.

[47] Samuel Beckett, *Ill Seen Ill Said, Nohow On* (London: Calder Publications, 1992), 73.

[48] I am inspired in this however brief consideration of the notion of representation in the id by a discussion between a number of psychoanalysts published in *The Hartmann Era*, ed. Martin S. Bergmann (New York: Other Press, 2000). Following the assertion by André Green that Freud did not subscribe to such a concept, Otto Kernberg refutes the claim and defines the id accordingly: "The id is a constellation of primitive wishes that take the form of unconscious fantasies that contain a powerful affect, a self representation, and object representation" (ibid., 259). Peter Neubauer perhaps best clarifies the point when he says that "The somatic source of the drive aims at discharge and is on different levels of representation and on a different level of discharge. This puts the drive, except for the source, in the realm of psychic function and not in between the somatic and the psychological. Only the source is in between the two" (ibid., 261). It is, in part, Neubauer's description of the integration of soma and psyche in an organic impetus manifested affectively in id

In summary, a double negation occurs in Beckett resulting in a three-stage process depicting psychic energy or creative force. The unwriting that we associate with the non-assumption of identity and the non-occurrence of event in his texts, a narrative deconstruction seen by some as characteristic of what Roudinesco and Simon refer to as the nihilist or schizoid age, is describable in terms of the interplay between the representation of absence and of the re-emergence of what has been negated or repressed. The consequence of this uncanniness and its undoing is a focus on psychic function, a visualization projectioning at once fantasy and actuality, both the concrete expression of drive and the reflection of its own epistemological core. It is this that promotes the perception of Beckett's work as exceedingly complex and yet simple—beyond words.

Montclair State University

representation that impels my thinking on the resolution of the double negation in Beckett.

DEATH SENTENCES: SILENCE, COLONIAL MEMORY AND THE VOICE OF THE DEAD IN *DUBLINERS*

NELS PEARSON

> Behove this sound of Irish sense.... Here English might be seen....
> One sovereign punned to petery pence.... The silence speaks the scene.
> —*Finnegans Wake* 13.1-3

> Estragon: All the dead voices
> . . .
> Vladimir: What do they say?
> Estragon: They talk about their lives.
> Vladimir: To have lived is not enough for them.
> Estragon: They have to talk about it.
> Vladimir: To be dead is not enough for them.
> Estragon: It is not sufficient.
> — *Waiting for Godot*

While the topic of silence in *Dubliners* has drawn considerable attention over the years, the majority of critics, especially in recent studies of Joyce, tend to rely on poststructural interpretations of negation that overlook the specific historical and political importance of absence in the text. By focusing on how the collection's narrative gaps subvert or deconstruct either Ireland's "provincial" religious and institutional mores or more universal forms of ideology, critics have missed a crucial dimension of the *Dubliners* stories: their profound engagement with the problem of narrating colonial memory and identity, especially with regard to women and the dead, the two most deeply silenced, symbolically de-voiced, and overwritten subjects of the contested Irish past. As a corrective to these oversights, I argue that Joyce's deployment of the negative points not only to the disturbing liminality of subaltern representation, but also to a potential site of agency wherein, rather than speaking or being spoken for, the subjects of Irish colonial memory resist the manufactured occasion for speaking (in a manner that subtly anticipates the shifting and waking narrative voices of Joyce's later fiction) and seriously problematize the attempt to represent otherness without altering the politically encoded terms and conditions of representation itself. By bringing structural and deconstructive analysis of *Dubliners* into dialogue with both postcolonial theory and Irish history, my larger objective is to encourage further connections between the formal and cultural/historical dimensions of Joyce's works—between Joyce the evolving modernist and Joyce the evolving postcolonial writer.

In Joyce's "The Sisters," the closest we can get to hearing the voice of the dead—which would require Father Flynn telling his own story—is the boy narrator's recollection of a dream in which he hears the "murmuring voice" of the priest trying to confess to him:

> the grey face still followed me. It murmured; and I understood that it desired to confess something. I felt my soul receding into some pleasant and vicious region; and there again I found it waiting for me. It began to confess to me in a murmuring voice and I wondered why it smiled continually and why the lips were so moist with spittle. But then I remembered that it had died of paralysis . . . . (*D*, 11)

As several critics have pointed out, the young narrator's control over the explicit details of his story becomes noticeably strained when he tries to represent, or recall from his dream, the confessing voice of the recently deceased priest.[1] The boy's strange attraction to the ineffable, an important corollary to his otherwise scrupulous concern for the explicit representation of events, seems most noticeable—and, some would argue, most typically western and modern—when, in a later attempt to remember the dream, he tries to place it "in Persia" or "some land where the customs were strange" (*D*, 13, 14). There are clearly political as well as psychological dimensions to this act of "orienting" the unspeakable, but they may run significantly deeper than a Victorian adolescent's equation between the mysteries of sin and death (or an attempt to master them) and a fantasy of the East. While the

---

[1] See, for example, Jean-Michel Rabaté, "Silence in *Dubliners*," in *James Joyce: New Perspectives*, ed. Colin MacCabe (Bloomington: Indiana University Press, 1982), 45-72, in particular 48-57. According to Rabaté, "the child is not a narrator, but an interpreter, who also believes that [the others know] more than he does, while constantly suspecting the validity of his information. . . . [As he recalls his dream], it becomes obvious that the symbolic realm of interpretation exhibits its gaps which are soon filled by imaginary fantasies [that] contaminate the interpretive process" (ibid., 49). For a psychoanalytic analysis of the boy's "obsessive concern" for precise, objective language, see Garry Leonard, "The Free Man's Journal: The Making of Hi[S]tory in 'The Sisters,'" in *Reading Dubliners Again* (Syracuse, N.Y.: Syracuse University Press, 1993), 24-55.

West's ineffable *is* here projected onto the East, the dream, and the larger struggle against the inadequacy of available language of which it is a part, are also deeply related to the fact that the boy is attempting to tell stories of Ireland—and, more specifically, attempting to speak for the Irish dead—in a late-colonial environment dominated, in both private and public spheres, by an immediate concern over the political and historical implications of language. When we further consider it in relation to the eight centuries of language dispossession, the paradox of de-Anglicizing cultural forms in Ireland, and Joyce's decision to go into exile to write about Ireland, we realize that the boy narrator's limited access to language and forms of storytelling is just as much a colonial phenomenon as is the fact that he fills a gap in his knowledge with an orientalist reverie. Indeed, especially insofar as they foreshadow Stephen Dedalus's battles against the "language" of "an accustomed world" (*P*, 156) the "acquired speech" of the English language (*P*, 189), and the "ineluctable modalit[ies] of the visible" and "audible" (*U*, 3.1, 3.13) forms of representation, the boy's struggle within and against the explicitness of language and consciousness—and the questions of silence and absence in *Dubliners* that that struggle introduces—must also be read in an Irish colonial context.

For many an aspiring Irish storyteller, as the deep and enduring relationship between artistic expression and exile in Irish literature attests, the dream of the "east" also includes, and in some senses begins with, the continent of Europe and the cosmopolitan forms of identity and expression that it presumably represents. Seen in this light, the association that "The Sisters" draws between the dream of escape to the east, the desire to confess on behalf of the dead, and the compulsion to access forms, languages or audiences beyond Ireland to do so, may be telling of the problems inherent in Joyce's own effort to write "a chapter of the moral history" of Ireland, and in his (perhaps cunningly hyperbolic) conviction to do so with the "scrupulous" techniques and "looking glass" aims of realist narrative. It certainly anticipates the pivotal (but unrealized) dream of "going east" in the Joyce canon: Stephen Dedalus's desire to escape to an imaginary "Europe of strange tongues . . . out there beyond the Irish Sea" (*P*, 167) where he believes he will be able to "express [his spirit] in unfettered freedom" (*P*, 246), but also "forge, in the smithy of [his] soul, the uncreated conscious of [his] race" (*P*, 253). Just as understanding the concept of going into "exile" to "forge" in the "soul" an "*uncreated* conscience" of a "race" involves the difficult task of envisioning a simultaneous motion toward and away from a cultural history, understanding the silences of *Dubliners* requires us to consider how the unspoken may be suspended between literary objectives that usually strike us as antithetical—the need or desire to access the voices of the dead (or the past) and the supposedly "cosmopolitan" dream of escape from prior conditions of belonging, and its related quest for new forms of expression.

In this essay, I explore the political and historical importance of "suspended" silences in *Dubliners*, and argue that they are not ends in themselves, but devices that Joyce employs, in tandem with a theme of death and occluded voices, to expose the various limitations and biases that are inherent in the scrupulously controlled (and often imperially and patriarchally encoded) forms, perspectives, and languages in which his stories are being told. I conclude that Joyce's use of silence indicates not only a profound and disturbing liminality relative to the problem of the subaltern speaking, but also a site of potential agency wherein, rather than speaking or being spoken for, the subjects of Irish colonial memory resist the manufactured occasion for speaking and, in a manner that subtly anticipates the shifting and waking voices of Joyce's later fiction, suggest the impossibility of representing the occluded voices of the past without altering the terms and conditions of representation itself.

While the topic of silence and absence in *Dubliners* has drawn the attention of many critics, and while most of these critics point out the challenges to ideology that silence represents, their analysis tends to rely on poststructural models that underestimate the "local," or Irish historical and political, significance of their own conclusions. In his seminal essay "Silence in *Dubliners*," Jean-Michel Rabaté argues that the narrative gaps of the collection, following a pattern laid out in "The Sisters," suggest "a perversion at work in the signifiers of the text" that serves to undermine both the symbolic order of the dominant religious and patriarchal discourses of Dublin and our own readerly desire for interpretive certainty. For Rabaté, silence demonstrates, at the same time that it enacts, an "emptying of the symbolic power" of Catholic dogma that graduates to a general "denegation of the locus of the Other."[2] The "blocked gestures" of speech and understanding in the first part of the collection lead to an "endless circulation"[3] of "the problematics of enunciation" in the stories of public life, where "the bankrupt petty-bourgeois of Dublin" become terminally linked "to the doomed circularity of confession."[4] Thus *Dubliners*, "which constantly hesitates between the status of a cure, a diagnosis, and that of a

---

[2] Rabaté, "Silence in *Dubliners*," 59. Rabaté clarifies in a footnote that by "the Other" he essentially means Lacan's "Big Other," or the social and institutional hegemonies or master discourses against which the subject measures himself or herself, and in relation to which s/he qualifies his/her desires.

[3] Ibid., 59.

[4] Ibid., 63.

symptom, produced by the same causes it attempts to heal,"[5] aptly deconstructs, by "scrupulously" depicting, a "city of paralysis" that is "corrupted at its very core by an absent and mute center."[6]

For Laurent Milesi, who similarly reduces the colonial dimensions of the text to Joyce's attempt to depict "an Irish symptomatology,"[7] the key to understanding the affect of absence in *Dubliners* lies in recognizing the relationship between the "anamorphic" dissolution of the subject that takes place in "The Sisters" (which in turn becomes a type for the one experienced by Gabriel at the end of "The Dead"), the "unstable narrative status" of the boy narrator's dream episode and the closing lines of "The Dead," and the general deconstructive self-representation that the "gnomic vision" of *Dubliners* forces its (presumably Irish) readers to undergo.[8] According to Milesi,

> Joyce's "nicely polished looking glass" offers the writer's fellow citizens [the] opportunity to cross anew the mirror stage, where the subject experiences its radical alterity by way of the gaze, in order to realize the emptiness of imaginary desires and narcissistic identifications, and some of the short stories culminate with such a silencing vision of horror, the epiphanic moment when the subjects nullity is apocalyptically revealed to him/her, thereby opening up a gap between his/her desire and what s/he actually is. This point of dissolution or aphanisis to which the subject is reluctantly brought can only be conceived in such a fugitive, self-abolishing trance, in the silent performative recesses of the text or in the blank on which it closes.[9]

Echoing Rabaté's contention that "interpretation [in or of *Dubliners*] abolishes itself in a moment of silence,"[10] Milesi concludes that

> [Joyce's] characters remain mired in a circular structure, full of iterative dead ends. If it wants to reach [the mirror stage] effect, the epiphanic writing must "condemn" itself to a silent gesture of monstration... [Thus, the text's] gaps, overlaps, repetitions, occulted vistas and imaginary visions call for an articulation as well as, at the same time, frustrate it ... and it is

---

[5] Ibid., 47.
[6] Ibid., 63.
[7] Laurent Milesi, "Joyce's Anamorphic Mirror in 'The Sisters,'" in *New Perspectives on Dubliners*, ed. Mary Power and Ulrich Schneider (Atlanta: Rodopi, 1997), 91-113; see 96.
[8] Ibid., 103.
[9] Ibid., 110.
[10] Rabaté, "Silence in *Dubliners*," 65.

this gaping disjunction, in all its parallactic instability, which can arguably be seen as the ultimate problematic of *Dubliners*.[11]

Thus, while both Milesi and Rabaté point to the fissures in ideology and subjective epistemology that silence represents (Milesi even claims that the silences "call for an articulation"), both assume that the textual gaps are "self-abolishing," or ultimately designed to collapse on themselves, in a manner that "reflects" the perpetual, internal paralysis of the city. As Rabaté puts it, Joyce's silences suggest a "vanishing point of all assertion [that] exhibits the empty space [within religious and phallologocentric symbolic orders] which the writing of the text constantly re-covers and recovers, in its multiplication."[12]

I wish to point out two substantial, and related, problems with these readings: first, they rely heavily, if implicitly, on uncomplicated and largely evanescent assumptions about Joyce's detachment from "national" or specific imperial/colonial concerns, especially those involving language and historical narrative; second, by focusing most of their attention on the "irreducible" dissolution of male, or presumably dominant, institutional symbolic systems, they distract us from equally irreducible questions of *silencing* and breaking silence—of the many subjects and potential voices in *Dubliners* that do *not* speak, or *for* whom Joyce, within the confines of the scrupulous narrative modes he so frequently calls our attention to, has elected not to speak. As to the first problem, it is often where Rabaté's and Milesi's readings are most theoretically progressive that their fundamental assumptions about Joyce's politics are not. Both arguments seem to harbor, in their own silences, tired assumptions about the cold, diagnostic detachment that writing from exile represents—that is, they rely heavily on the traditional concept of Joyce the aloof, Flaubertian craftsman, scrupulously composing a "symptomatology" of a "doomed" "city of paralysis" so that "his fellow citizens" can see themselves. They pay far less attention to the Joyce who is equally concerned with the problems of "giv[ing] [Ireland] to the world," (*JJII*, 111) who speaks to a Triestine audience about an oppressed Ireland that has been "deaf and dumb . . . at the bar of public opinion" (*CW*, 174), and who is alertly engaged with both the general problem of speaking for the unrepresented and dispossessed, and the more specific, deeply Irish, problem of the space able to be claimed by genuine Irish voices within the interdependent discourses of cultural

---

[11] Milesi, "Joyce's Anamorphic Mirror in 'The Sisters,'" 112.
[12] Rabaté, "Silence in *Dubliners*," 68.

imperialism and nationalism.[13] Thus, important as their analysis is for demonstrating the decentering and potentially subversive effects of silence, it loses a necessary immediacy by failing to account for Joyce's awareness of the degree to which language itself has been a consistent conspirator in the paralysis of his Irish subjects.

Related to this oversight is the second problem of a deconstructive reading, which is its tendency to overlook the double-voicing of the unspoken, wherein silence involves acts of *silencing*, or occlusions of voice, that simultaneously suggest a will *toward* speech, and a need for unstigmatized modes of expression in which to represent that willed speech, from subjects relegated to the "other" side of silence. Most problematic, and certainly an exacerbation of the latter problem, is the fact that these readings, which focus on the masculine or collective social crossing of the mirror stage, fail to alert readers to the fact that the problematics of absence in *Dubliners* is often tied to the two most deeply silenced, symbolically devoiced, and overwritten subjects of Irish colonial history—its women and its dead.

Given these problems, it is imperative that we look again at the problem of speech and silence in the pivotal dream episode of "The Sisters," and realize that the boy narrator's strained recollection actually introduces two important images of muted attempts to speak that will appear, with strong postcolonial implications, in Joyce's later work. The inability to "confess," as we know from Stephen's struggle with prayer and confession in *A Portrait* and *Ulysses*, is often Joyce's metaphor for the complications of artistic self-expression, a complication Stephen more than once relates to the Irish population's inability to confess what he sees as their most notable historical sin—"allow[ing] a handful of foreigners to subject them" and "thr[owing] off their language and t[a]k[ing] another" (*P*, 203).[14] The image

---

[13] In the same letters to Grant Richards that Milesi and Rabaté rely on for the purely diagnostic aims of *Dubliners*, Joyce, who is of course angered deeply (and inclined toward his characteristic thematics of betrayal) by Richards and Irish publishers in general, makes the far more ambiguous claim that *Dubliners* has "taken the first step towards the spiritual liberation of my country." He also connects this "liberation" to the crisis of cultural nationalism: "Reflect for a moment on the history of the literature of Ireland written in the English language before you condemn this genial allusion of mine which, after all, has at least served me in the office of a candlestick during the writing of this book" (*JJII*, 62-63).

[14] Joyce himself referred to Ireland's transformation from a Gaelic to an English speaking culture as a decisive historical transformation, after which "Ireland ceased to be an intellectual force in Europe... and the sacred and profane culture fell into disuse" (*CW*, 161).

of Father Flynn's "lips moist with spittle," meanwhile, anticipates Joyce's later use of moist lips, or spitting in place of speech, as metaphors for the paralysis of speech and the difficulty of the narrative act.

Of particular importance to an Irish reading of "The Sisters," and the *Dubliners* stories in general, are the images of spitting and silence in Stephen's own (rare) attempt at a public narrative performance in the "Aeolus" episode of *Ulysses* (*U*, 7.923-1027).[15] In the apparently symbolic story that he titles "*A Pisgah Sight of Palestine* or *The Parable of the Plums*," Stephen tells (or attempts to tell, but is continually interrupted and misinterpreted) a story about "two Dublin vestals" who buy a bag of plums and climb Nelson's Pillar, the most prominent (and undeniably phallic) symbol of Ireland under British rule, to eat the plums and chat. The women climb to the base of the statue, but become dizzy when they look up at the figure of Nelson. Like Moses, who looked out over the promised land of Palestine from mount Pisgah, the elderly women gaze upon Dublin from their perch. But rather than speak, they eat their plums and spit the stones through the railings onto the infertile "pavingstones" of the street below. Not unlike the boy narrator, Stephen has created a framework for a story, and introduced two female narrators who seem to harbor the interior, and larger portion, of the story he is trying to tell. But his would-be narrators remain silent, not even able to engage in brief dialogue, and merely spit seeds of their potential voice onto barren ground. Perhaps the message in Stephen's version of the holy sighting is not only that Dublin (under the long dominion of outside rule) is no longer the promised land it once was, but also that its representative figures (the virgins in the story are most likely the two elderly vestals on the crest of Dublin) are too confined by the patriarchal and imperial languages available to them to speak about it.

Unlike their counterparts in *Finnegans Wake*, the two elderly washerwomen who reconstruct the story of ALP and whose flowing, but linguistically decentered, retelling of that story is interrupted by the voice of ALP, Stephen's two old women seem to lack not the voice, but the *language* necessary to tell their story. Both of these moments, where Joyce's poetics are either on the verge ("Aeolus")[16] or in the process (the ALP chapter of the

---

[15] See also *P*, 100-101, where Stephen, during his encounter with a prostitute at the end of the second chapter, senses the "dark presence" of some "other" world, and some "other" form of consciousness: "Its murmur besieged his ears like the murmur of some multitude in sleep; its subtle streams penetrated his being. . . . He was in another world: he had awakened from a slumber of centuries. ... and his lips parted though they would not speak."

[16] Many critics have commented that "Aeolus" is the chapter in which Joyce's breakdown of language begins in earnest. See W. J. McCormack, "James

Wake) of representing multiple voices and erasing the limited perspective of a male narrator, are prefigured by the boy narrator's fixation upon Father Flynn's "desire to confess something" and his "lips moist with spittle." It is the first of many Joycean images combining silence with the desire to speak, and it powerfully conveys the idea of a story, and a storyteller, that are confined within the lacunae of available forms.

Looking ahead to the political and cultural dimensions of style in *Ulysses* and *Finnegans Wake*, it is also important to recognize the subtle connection that "The Sisters" already suggests between women, the dead, and the *breaking* of silence. At the end of the story, after the Priest's sister and the boy's aunt have washed and dressed the corpse, the women begin to explain, in their low-Dublin accents, and through a less formally mediated connection with the past, what the men in the story could not:

> [Eliza] stopped, as if she were communing with the past and then she said shrewdly:
> —Mind you, I noticed there was something queer coming over him latterly. Whenever I'd bring in his soup to him there I'd find him with his breviary fallen to the floor, lying back in the chair and his mouth open.... He was too scrupulous always, she said. The duties of the priesthood was too much for him. And then his life was, you might say, crossed. ...
> A silence took possession of the little room.... Eliza seemed to have fallen into a deep revery. We waited respectfully for her to break the silence: and after a long pause she said slowly:
> —It was that chalice he broke. ... That was the beginning of it. Of course they say it was all right, that it contained nothing, I mean. But still. . . . (*D*, 17; last two ellipses Joyce's)

Curiously, an ellipsis breaks off Eliza's narrative communion with the past. But *within* that silence is the suggestion that cannot be suppressed of an audible voice of the dead. Immediately following the ellipsis, each of the sisters seems to experience the slight sensation of hearing the voice of the Priest, but the boy narrator, apparently, does not:

> She stopped suddenly as if to listen. I too listened; but there was no sound in the house: and I knew that the old priest was lying still in his coffin as we had seen him, solemn and truculent in death, an idle chalice on his breast. (*D*, 18)

Joyce, Cliche, and the Irish Language," in *James Joyce: The Augmented Ninth, Proceedings of the Ninth International James Joyce Symposium*, ed. Bernard Benstock (Syracuse, N.Y.: Syracuse University Press, 1988), 323-336.

This haunted tableau, especially insofar as it suggests a voice of the dead that speaks but cannot be heard, foreshadows Gabriel's epiphany at the end of "The Dead." There, as Gabriel's "soul ... approache[s] that region where dwell the vast hosts of the dead," Gabriel feels "his own identity fading out into a grey impalpable world" while the "solid world" around him "dissolve[s] and dwindl[es]" (*D*, 223). But here the boy narrator will not relinquish his identity or his obsessive narrative control over the exact details of what he sees and hears, thus we get only silence.

As far as we can tell from the boy's limited perspective, all three characters dismiss the possibility that the Priest is trying to communicate with them, and Eliza resumes her telling of the Priest's story. Again, however, the ellipsis mutes the information necessary to solve the mystery of the dead:

> Eliza resumed:
> —Wide-awake and laughing-like to himself. . . . So then, of course, when they saw that, that made them think that there was something gone wrong with him. . . . (*D*, 18)

The story ends with an ellipses that, perhaps more than any other silence in the Joyce canon, reads like a precisely placed rest in an elaborate musical score. The last note Joyce plays for us in "The Sisters" is a lingering, audible silence wherein the possibility that Priest has indeed spoken, or that the dead and the living have engaged in any sort of metalinguistic communion, remains forever suspended in the realm, or perhaps the language, of the indecipherable past.

The untold story of Father Flynn, poised as it is in the "grey, impalpable" realm between the spoken and the written, between past and present, dead and living, in many ways occupies the liminal space of creative expression gained at the threshold of cultural and historical emergence—a space in which both a loss of the past and the potential for new forms of accessing and articulating an identity become mingled. As in the dream sequence and Stephen's parable, it is possible that the boy, as an unyielding controller of the narrative who is also controlled by conventional notions of language and storytelling, has not so much faithfully recorded or experienced an absence as he has failed to translate one. In fact, we might even argue that somewhere "beneath" the confined narrative perspective of "The Sisters" is an Irish priest confessing his unspeakable sin and speaking, if you will, in the language of the dead—a language that Joyce's more or less conventional narrative method cannot, or more likely will not, yet accommodate. Thus instead of reading the final ellipsis as a moment in which all potential for speech is abolished in an endless and thus "victorious silence"[17] of recognition, we might read it as a pivotal, and forward-looking, moment in (post)colonial Anglo-Irish literature: a moment when the form and language in which the tale has been told (realistic narrative in English) is exposed as incapable of communicating the reality of its subject (the Irish dead).

Indeed, while "The Sisters" does seem to "call for an articulation and, at the same time, frustrate it," the most important historical and political implications of this fact may lie *between* those two options, rather than in how they appear to collapse on one another. As Gayatri Spivak cautions us, it is precisely the silent moment suspended between a potential "articulation" and its "frustration" that we must fix upon and "measure" if we wish to expose the silencing mechanisms of "the codifying [language] of imperialism" and consider a "consciousness of the subaltern" that the text cannot, or will not, articulate.[18] In *The Location of Culture*, Homi Bhabha makes a similar general assertion about the historical significance of the unspoken. According to Bhabha,

> the critic must attempt to fully realize, and take responsibility for, the unspoken, unrepresented pasts that haunt the historical present. . . . It is not simply what the house of fiction contains or 'controls' *as content*. What is just as important is the metaphor[ic or metonymic significance of] . . . those subjects of the narrative that mutter or mumble . . . or keep a still silence.[19]

While a clumsy application of larger postcolonial models is no doubt inadequate to grasp the complexity of Joyce's use of silence, the arguments of Bhabha and Spivak, insofar as they are concerned with the critic's obligation to hear the colonial or minority (as opposed to the broader psychological, aesthetic or ideological) implications of the unspoken, provide a meaningful framework in which to think about *Dubliners'* occluded voices. Their insistence on an *active* speech of the other that may be locked beneath the silences of a text seem especially important when consider the sense of *audible presence* that, not only in "The Sisters" but also throughout the collection, so often attends Joyce's depictions of absence.

---

[17] Rabaté, "Silence in *Dubliners*," 51.
[18] Gayatri Spivak, "Can the Subaltern Speak?" in *Marxism and the Interpretation of Culture*, ed. Cary Nelson and Lawrence Grossberg (Urbana: University of Illinois Press, 1988), 271-313; see 278.
[19] Homi Bhabha, *The Location of Culture* (London: Routledge, 1994), 13-15.

Perhaps the single most politically charged example of this audible presence comes at the climactic moment of "Eveline," where Joyce's stark prose momentarily erupts, or threatens to erupt, with a dead voice from Ireland's traumatic past. Not unlike the boy narrator's dream of the "murmuring voice" of the dead Priest, but with more emphasis on the audible presence of the dead, Eveline's hallucinatory memory of "the final craziness" of her domestically confined mother suggests a powerful, though barely accessible, voice of the past speaking through the confining language of the present:

> As she mused the pitiful vision of her mother's life laid its spell on the very quick of her being—that life of commonplace sacrifices closing in final craziness. She trembled as she heard again her mother's voice saying constantly with foolish insistence:
> —Derevaun Seraun! Derevaun Seraun!
> She stood up in a sudden impulse of terror. Escape! She must escape! (*D*, 40)

The "insane" words of Eveline's mother, which are most likely a garbled or severe dialectical variant of Irish Gaelic (but which, stylistically speaking, sound curiously Wakean), suggest the traumatic history of the west of Ireland, during and after the famine, "which disproportionately affected Gaelic-speaking areas in the south and west," where Eveline's mother most likely grew up.[20] In *James Joyce and the Question of History*, James Fairhall cites this uncharacteristic reference to rural Ireland as an example of why it is "instructive to try to fill in the gaps in [the 'curious rootless[ness]' of Joyce's characters] history."[21] "[W]hatever they denote," claims Fairhall,

> the point of these words may be that they are [a reference to the displacement of Gaelic by English, and hence to] the central trauma of rural nineteenth-century Ireland, famine, especially the hunger of the 1840's ... In this light we may see Eveline's mother as deliriously exclaiming words half remembered from her parents' or grandparents' native Gaelic, a language displaced by English when the family moved from country to city in response to socioeconomic forces including the periodic threat of famine. Hence the cry 'Derevaun Seraun!' reflects a traumatic history repressed by Joyce's Dubliners, who barely acknowledge the site of the trauma.[22]

---

[20] James Fairhall, *James Joyce and the Question of History* (Cambridge: Cambridge University Press, 1993), 75.
[21] Ibid.
[22] Ibid., 76-77.

There may be more to this "gap" in the family history than the "repression" of "a" past that "it is instructive to fill," with Fairhall's essentially anthropological approach. To imply repression is, more or less, to imply an essence or truth that has been forgotten or suppressed, but I think the point of historical occlusion in "Eveline" runs significantly deeper than one of repressed truth. I would argue that Joyce's point here is that to be *faithful* to the story, and especially to the massive cultural losses of Gaelic's demise and the overwritten story of rural Irish women through which cultural nationalism often attempted to reconcile that loss, requires a certain power of silence, or an indication of a silencing that we can not externally rectify. What Joyce suggests by offering, through the extra filter of memory, a woman's cry of anguish in a "garbled" version of the lost native language is that there are certain gaps in history that *cannot* simply "be filled" with accurate "re"-historicizing.[23] This is not only the case because of the original violence or inhumanity of the historical trauma to which those gaps relate, but because that trauma itself has been too often recycled, too frequently combined with the history of narrative claimings and reclaimings identities in the imperial/colonial legacy of Ireland itself, for us to return to or reestablish a legitimate sign for its experience. Silence, or an unfilled absence that is at once palpably present (a presence further emphasized by an occluded voice speaking a garbled form of its "original" language), thus results not exactly from the forgetting of a rural Irish history, but from its disputatious remembering. In "Bogland" (1969), Seamus Heaney speaks powerfully of this crisis by attributing an absence at the would-be "centre" of Irish memory not to a repression or suppression of historical identity, but to the incessant mapping and re-mapping of its cultural geography: "every layer they strip / Seems camped on before, / . . . The wet centre is bottomless."[24]

In the untranslated death of Emily Sinico in "A Painful Case," Joyce drives home a similar, and perhaps ultimately more powerful, point about silence, presence, and narrative inaccessibility. At the end of the story, where James Duffy, the detached, would-be Irish writer and intellectual, tries to come to terms with the death of Emily, who had "become his confessor" but whose own history he never tried to learn, Joyce saturates his prose with images suggesting the physical, and *vocal*, presence of the dead:

---

[23] As W. J. McCormack has argued, "the reader has no access to the formal alternative of further information retrieved from the past" ("James Joyce's 'Eveline' and a Problem in Modernism," in *Irland: Gesellschaft und Kultur III*, ed. Dorothea Siegmund-Schultze [Halle: Martin Luther Universität, 1982], 252-264; see 260).

[24] Seamus Heaney, *New Selected Poems, 1966-1987* (Boston: Faber and Faber, 1990), 18.

> She seemed to be near him in the darkness. At moments he seemed to feel her voice touch his ear, her hand touch his. He stood still to listen. Why had he withheld life from her? Why had he sentenced her to death? ... One human being had seemed to love him and he had denied her life's happiness: he had sentenced her to ignominy, a death of shame. ... He began to doubt the reality of what memory told him. He halted under a tree and allowed the rhythm to die away. He could not feel her near him in the darkness nor her voice touch his ear. He waited for some minutes listening. He could hear nothing: the night was perfectly silent. He listened again: perfectly silent. He felt that he was alone. (*D*, 117)

The images of silence and listening, which are very similar to those at the end of "The Sisters" and thematically resonant of those in "Eveline," clearly demonstrate a preoccupation with the living attempting to hear the dead. Here, however, the silencing mechanisms of a seamless, "objective" narrative perspective are even more visible (via Joyce's repetitive fixation on the limited third person form that reflects Duffy's constrained perspective), and have in fact become inseparable from the story's theme of loss.

Throughout "A Painful Case," Joyce essentially calls us to witness the process of a narrative conscience creating itself and simultaneously transforming that which it does not comprehend into its indecipherable, mysteriously silent "other." From the moment James Duffy begins his first conversation with Mrs. Sinico and "tries to fix her permanently in his memory" (*D*, 109), Joyce exactingly depicts the manner in which a restricted, self-preoccupied mind can literally erase the history it is attempting to construct with every word that it writes. At the beginning of the story, we learn that the intellectually detached Duffy "had an odd autobiographical habit which led him to compose in his mind from time to time a short sentence about himself containing a subject in the third person and a predicate in the past tense. He never gave alms to beggars and walked firmly, carrying a stout hazel" (*D*, 108). The sentence beginning "He never gave alms to beggars" is a formal manifestation of the limited, narratologically constructed consciousness of Duffy, as are most of the sentences in the story. Most notable are the last sentences of the story, which I have quoted above: "He began . . ."; "He halted . . ."; "He could not . . ."; "He waited . . ."; "He felt . . . ." I would argue that James Duffy feels "alone," and fails to "hear" anything but the "perfectly silent" night, not simply because Joyce wants to depict the "pure repetition" of empty words and sounds that "is identified with the silence of death,"[25] but because he aims to expose Duffy, as the repeated sentence structure implies, for his inability to think outside of the

---

[25] Rabaté, "Silence in *Dubliners*," 61.

limited, male-centered, and self-preoccupied language in which that silence occurs. Like "The Sisters" and "Eveline" (which ends not with Eveline's perspective, but her suitor's, who fails to interpret the "sign" [*D*, 41] of her silence) the narrative ends by suggesting the muted presence of a story that the narrative perspective—a perspective reflecting the obsessive concern of a male mind that "abhor[s] ... disorder" (*D*, 108)—cannot, or will not, convey.

Duffy's anxiety over having "sentenced her to death" (*D*, 117) refers to his (justifiable) concern that, in breaking off their love affair, he has been in part responsible for Emily's emotional breakdown and eventual death. But it also suggests the possibility that language itself, whether it be in the form of the ordered, factually obsessed sentences of Duffy's self-centered narrative conscience, or the starkly "factual" and "objective" language of the newspaper's account of Emily's "painful case," is what has forced her ("sentenced her") into the position she now occupies, which is that of absence. As with "The Sisters," the final epiphany is not so much a revelation about the indecipherable phenomenon of death as it is an awareness of the sheer killing power of language itself, especially when "language" is assumed to be a universal or objective phenomenon.

Thus the *history* of "A Painful Case" lies in the story that it does *not* tell—the *possible* story, or stories, about Emily Sinico that the narrator's ruthless and inexorable subjective fixation, and the newspaper's dialectically opposed language of objective verifibililily, do not permit us to hear.[26] Perhaps the most obviously, and narratologically, silenced figure in *Dubliners*, Emily not only combines the theme of the muted woman and the muted dead, but also suggests a drastically different story of womanhood in Ireland than any narrative mired in the tropes and biases of imperial or cultural nationalism would care to convey. Her story, were we permitted to hear it, would include a possible immigration *to* Ireland, a defeated marriage to a man involved in international trade, the possibly pre-marital birth of a "child" (we are not even told the sex of the child), and a potentially vibrant intellectual life that most certainly did not begin with Duffy "provid[ing] her with ideas" (*D*, 110). Suitably for *Dubliners*, however, the only recorded

---

[26] A great deal might be said about exactly what or who, in the person of Emily Sinico, is being occluded by the restricted forms of storytelling that operate in "A Painful Case," if there were any sure information about who she is. While autobiographical arguments might propose that she is based on one of the women Joyce knew in Trieste, we know very little about her. What little we do know comes only from what Duffy troubles to learn about her husband, whose "great-great-grandfather had come from [the Tuscan city of] Leghorn," and who himself "was captain of a mercantile boat plying between Dublin and Holland" (*D*, 110).

version of her story is the bleak newspaper report of the details of her bizarre death. Central to an understanding of how Joyce subtly links this silencing to the pervasive colonial infestation of language as medium for "accurate" representation is the fact that the newspaper that reports Emily's death, the *Dublin Evening Mail*, is a *Unionist* newspaper—one whose ideological bias would of course tend towards the exclusion of British or imperial "culpability" in Irish affairs. Thus when the newspaper blurb frankly explains that she was struck by "the ten o'clock slow train from Kingstown," but ends with the disturbing fragment "No blame attached to anyone" (*D*, 113-115), Joyce delivers a sweeping blow of irony and a seething denunciation of imperial modernity's ideologically self-serving indifference to Emily's presence, and history, that is hard to miss.

The important thing is that Joyce drives this point home not by "filling in" the mystery of her death (which, as the newspaper's dominant presence in the story reminds us, has long since been banished from the possibility of a "real" reclaiming) but by exposing the limitations of the discursive forces that conspire to cause it and make it impenetrable. Even more disturbing, therefore, is the irony embedded in the title: the story of Emily Sinico is *not* just an isolated "case." As we begin to recognize when we think of the title in relation to the other stories in the collection, she is only one of many such Dublin "cases." Like Father Flynn and Eveline's mother, she is "one of those . . . peculiar cases," cases of unarticulated history, that make up the larger, unreifiable "story" of late-colonial Dublin—a panoramic, temporally-extending story that Joyce, in what may be his ultimate deployment of absence (he gives us, as he claimed, only "a *chapter* of the moral history of my country") does not consent to tell.

In "A Little Cloud," Joyce provides a more direct, somewhat autobiographical, commentary on the inaccessible voices of the dead that haunt, and force new modes of expression upon, the would-be authors of Irish identity. By introducing Little Chandler, a would-be poet of Ireland who is also the first in a series of male Irish literary figures (Chandler, James Duffy, Gabriel Conroy, Stephen Dedalus) that Joyce satirically portrays, although with increasing empathy, as being stifled by their difficulties or false-successes in trying to write both of and out of Ireland, Joyce also introduces (for the first time in full) the figure of the aspiring postcolonial author into his work. Chandler, whose poetic ambitions are reminiscent of the "Celtic school" of poets whose works Joyce criticized as being emotionless, sentimentalized and self-consciously Irish, receives the harshest condemnation from Joyce, and is portrayed as the most immature and artistically paralyzed member of the group. But he is also involved in one of Joyce's most penetrating depictions of the conflict between the aspiring Irish artist and the English language and literary forms that are available to him.

As Chandler walks across Grattan Bridge, he looks down upon a row of "poor stunted houses" and thinks about composing a poem to capture the moment, but both his intentions for his poetry—"Perhaps Gallaher could get it into some London paper for him"—and his impressions of the scene resemble the defeated spirit of Irish romanticism—a movement that essentially pandered to English audiences thirsty for the intoxicating melancholy of "Celtic" verse. Later on, as he sits in a pub with Ignatius Gallaher (the journalist who has effectively sold out Ireland to gain a European audience), Little Chandler listens with childish awe as Gallaher spins arrogant yarns of fast living in Paris. As the drinking and storytelling intensify, Gallaher begins to contrast "dear dirty Dublin" to the "beautiful" city of Paris, but he breaks off his hollow praise of the city, at least as far as we know, in mid-sentence: "of course it is beautiful ... But it's the life of Paris; that's the thing. Ah, there's no city like Paris for gaiety, movement, excitement ..." (*D*, 76). Immediately following the ellipsis, Little Chandler, who had told Gallaher minutes before that "I drink very little as a rule" (*D*, 75), gulps down a shot of whisky and then quickly orders another. The ellipses cut off Gallaher's arrogant narrative where a competing voice of Irish identity might create a site of verbal confrontation, if it could find a present voice to speak through. However, Chandler quite literally drowns out this voice by drinking instead of speaking, and we are left with a paralyzing silence akin to the one at the end of "Ivy Day in the Committee Room," where the election canvassers respond to Joe Hynes's romantic ode to Parnell by "dr[inking] from their bottles in silence" (*D*, 135). A possible reading of this moment is that Chandler feels some resentment waking within him, perhaps even the kind of emotional but intelligent defense of Ireland that would require new, as opposed to cliché, forms of expression, but he becomes afraid of voice and action, and opts instead—as will Freddy Malins in "The Dead" —for the comfort of an inebriated silence.

Chandler's story does not end here. Like Gabriel and Stephen, Chandler eventually has an encounter with "inaudible . . . insistent voices" (*P*, 152) that deny him the ability to express himself in tired, exhausted forms and ultimately refuse him the comfortable paralysis of silence. Throughout his formally evolving narrative of static Dublin, Joyce bequeaths the same artistic burden to any truly sentient, aspiring Irish poet or author that he creates. As Chandler and Gabriel ultimately do, and as Stephen will again and again, they hear or sense "voices" that will haunt them until they force less restricted modes of expression to come into being.

The final scene of "A Little Cloud," an anxious denouement in which Chandler tries to quiet his crying infant, is an powerful metaphor for this hearing of disruptive voices. After Chandler has returned home from his night on the town with Gallaher, his wife Annie puts the couple's sleeping baby in Chandler's arms with the admonishment "Here. Don't waken him" (*D*, 82). Chandler then begins to read a poem by Byron that is reminiscent of the kind of sentimentalized, "Celtic twilight" verse he wants to write, but the infant's screaming voice will not let him focus on his trite poetic thoughts. Joyce uses an ellipsis to mark a clear break in narrative tone and purpose as we shift from Chandler's melancholy thoughts to the loud, insistent, language-defying cries of the waking infant:

> How melancholy it was! Could he, too, write like that, express the melancholy of his soul in verse? There were so many things he wanted to describe: his sensation of a few hours before on Grattan Bridge, for example. If he could get back into that mood . ...
> The child awoke and began to cry. He turned from the page and tried to hush it: but it would not be hushed. He began to rock it to and fro in his arms but its wailing cry grew keener. (*D*, 84)

In a sense, the elliptical silence is being pried open to reveal a voice. Chandler's "mood," an acute case of Irish artistic silence and paralysis, is interrupted by ellipses and, immediately thereafter, by the voice of the sobbing infant. As in "The Sisters," the silence in the house is broken, though this time much more audibly, by an indecipherable voice. Even at face value, we can argue that the screaming child is a metonym for a waking voice that is trying to interrupt the silencing mechanisms of both Chandler's melancholy mood and the narrative itself. But here Joyce adds an important cultural allusion, in the form of the word "keener," which attaches a specific Irish significance to the voice of the crying child. In Irish tradition, to "keen" is to wail prolongedly for the dead.[27] The suggestion, reinforced throughout the scene, is that the insistent voice prohibiting Chandler from maintaining his "Celtic mood" is simultaneously a waking voice and a voice crying, in indecipherable words, for the dead:

> He rocked [the child] faster while his eyes began to read the second stanza:
> *Within this narrow cell reclines her clay,*
> *That clay where once ...*
> It was useless. He couldn't read. He couldn't do anything. The wailing of the child pierced the drum of his ear. It was useless, useless!... The child stopped for an instant, had a spasm of fright, and began to scream. ... He tried to soothe it but it sobbed more convulsively. (*D*, 84)

---

[27] Looking ahead to my arguments about the Irish subaltern woman in "The Dead," it is also worth noting here that keening is traditionally performed by mourning women.

When Annie returns home to find the crying child, she takes the baby from Chandler and "murmurs" comforting words to calm it down. "There now, love!" she says to child, "There now! ... Lambabaun! Mamma's little lamb of the world" (*D,* 85). The word "Lambabaun" is an Irish dialect term of affection derived from the Gaelic *leanbhan*. Translated it means "lamb child," a clear symbol of birth, death and resurrection. The symbol of resurrection is fitting, for as Annie (whose name Joyce would later give to ALP, the harbinger of narrative eruptions in *Finnegans Wake*) whispers Hiberno affections to the child, the infant finally quiets its sobbing and a curious thing happens: Chandler himself begins to cry, and the story ends:

> Little Chandler felt his cheeks suffused with shame and he stood back out of the lamplight. He listened while the paroxysm of the child's sobbing grew less and less; and tears of remorse started to his eyes. (*D*, 85)

A possible new reading here, one we might say is foreshadowed by the "infant hope" that had earlier (although for the wrong reasons) "took life within" Chandler (*D*, 73) is that the voice of the crying infant that refused to be silenced is now just beginning to wake within Chandler. While Chandler's sobbing, his childish submissiveness in the presence of his wife, and his retreat from the light have often been taken as signs of Chandler's weakness, there are also reasons to consider his crying as a moment with some potential. For one, Chandler is undeniably stronger than the other father figure in *Dubliners* who tries to silence a child, Mr. Farrington of "Counterparts," who does so by beating the child. But the main reason that Chandler's silence is worth "measuring" for its expressive potential is that, like the boy narrator, James Duffy, Gabriel Conroy and Stephen Dedalus, he is a version of Joyce as a young artist, or at least a version of the Irish writer whose struggles with language may help point us toward Joyce's own.[28] In fact, the closing image of Chandler crying (an expressive act that blurs the visual, assails the audible, and can stifle or break apart the vocal) suggests a more muted form of the "generous tears" that Gabriel Conroy sheds during his soul's apparently ineffable migration to "that region where dwell vast hosts of the dead" (*D*, 223). Perhaps, then, the point of Chandler's remorseful crying is that he must now force himself, as the child's crying had earlier forced him, to refuse the typical Irish artist's paralysis of poetic clichés. But

---

[28] As Stanislaus Joyce once commented, Joyce's early attempts at writing short fiction, the series of ten "epicleti" about Dublin life entitled *Silhouettes*, anticipated "the first three stories of *Dubliners* . . . and described a row of mean little houses along which the narrator passes after nightfall," the same scene that Chandler tries to write about in "A Little Cloud" (see *JJII*).

again we can only speculate, as the narrative leaves us merely with the suggestion, and not the sound, of an emerging voice.

That the *Dubliners* stories, in particular those which foreshadow "The Dead," ultimately work toward a formal disruption, or a breaking of silence, to register or account for historical and cultural emergence becomes evident when consider them in relation to the closing passages of the collection's final story. During Gabriel's final, lucid confrontation with the liminal space between the living and the dead, changes in narrative tone and perspective and the theme of Irish colonial memory are almost impenetrably mingled. As Donald Torchiana has convincingly demonstrated, an Irish historical understanding of Gabriel Conroy's interior monologue requires a knowledge of "The Confessions of St. Patrick," a pseudo-historical autobiographical narrative that chronicles St. Patrick's conversion and uniting of Ireland. At the end of "The Dead," Torchiana explains, Gabriel undergoes a modern version of St. Patrick's conversion as Joyce likely interpreted it, meaning that Gabriel does not convert the Irish but becomes "converted by them" and drawn back to Ireland by the "ur-Irish," or atavistic "soul" of Ireland.[29]

Among the more compelling passages from "The Confessions" that Torchiana points to is one in which St. Patrick tells of a dream in which he hears a collective "voice of the Irish" speaking to him, as it seems, through the layers of a written text:

> ... in a night vision, I saw a man called Victoricus who seemed to come from Ireland with innumerable letters, and he gave me one of them and I read the beginning of it, containing The Voice of the Irish. And when I read the beginning of the letter aloud I seemed in that moment to hear the voice of those who were beside the Wood of Foclut ... and they shouted out as if with one voice: We beg you, holy boy, to come and walk among us once again and it completely broke my heart and I could read no more, and woke up.[30]

Torchiana is basically concerned with the thematic comparison between the passage and Gabriel's final epiphany, and he points out that after St. Patrick hears the voice of the Irish calling out to him, he returns as Ireland's savior and makes several "journeys westward" from Dublin, just as Gabriel is about

---

[29] Donald Torchiana, "The Ending of 'The Dead': I Follow St. Patrick," *James Joyce Quarterly* 18 (1981): 123-132.

[30] Arnold Marsh, trans., *Saint Patrick's Writings* (Dundalk: Dundalgan Press, 1961), 11.

to at the story's end: "The time had come for him to set out on his journey westward" (*D*, 223). I would argue that the passage also contains multiple figurations of voice, textual representation, and cultural and historical identity that may be essential to understanding, and politically contextualizing, the confrontation with language that is enacted at the end of "The Dead." While the "Voice of the Irish" that St. Patrick hears is simultaneously the voice of a multitude, of the past, and of the dead, that voice is clearly not represented by the words he sees; rather it is suggested, somehow audible to him, from *behind* the words themselves, and discernible only within a suspended state of liminal consciousness which its very utterance terminates.

Clearly, there are important formal and linguistic issues raised by the suggestion that Gabriel's interior monologue—a foreshadowing of Joyce's later prose styles—involves the hearing, or potential presence, of *voices* of the Irish dead. Can we say that *Dubliners* ends on a suggestion, reinforced thematically and structurally, that previously unheard voices are speaking to Gabriel, and to us, through a layer of scrupulous narrative that has so often left us with silence, elliptical gaps, and the paralysis of marginal voices? I submit that we can. But to explain why I am inclined to think so, as well as to demonstrate what is at stake politically and historically in that answer, requires a closer examination of the story.

Like the stories I have read thus far, "The Dead" is haunted by allusions to dead, but potentially speaking, voices from Ireland's past. Like "The Sisters," "A Painful Case," and to some extent "A Little Cloud," it also revolves around the theme of men, here typified by Gabriel and his trite speech on "those great dead and gone ones" (*D*, 203), trying and failing to drag the voices of the dead, dying or forgotten into explicit representation, and, as in "Eveline," often looking to women as a symbol of that which can not be spoken. When the aging Julia Morkan finishes singing her morbidly symbolic version of "Arrayed for the Bridal," Freddy Malins, who has drowned his own voice in alcohol at a "committee meeting" in a Dublin pub, tells her "I never heard your voice sound so fresh and so ... so clear and fresh, never" (*D*, 193). Malins *almost* manages to describe the unusual clarity of the aging woman's voice, but an ellipsis breaks off his praise, leaving us to wonder what is so significant about her voice. During the dinner party discussion on old tenors (another extended scene which suggests that this story is about absent/present voices), Malins again expresses a curiously insightful sympathy with a culturally silenced voice, this time the "grand voice" of a "Negro chieftain" singer in the Gaiety pantomime that no one else at the table recognizes or remembers:

—Have you heard of him? he asked Mr. Bartell D'Arcy across the table.
—No, answered Mr. Bartell D'Arcy carelessly.

> —Because, Freddy Malins explained, now I'd be curious to hear your opinion of him. I think he has a grand voice.
> —It takes Teddy to find out the really good things, said Mr. Browne familiarly to the table.
> —And why couldn't he have a voice too? asked Freddy Malins sharply. Is it because he's only a black?
> Nobody answered this question and Mary Jane led the table back to the legitimate opera. (*D*, 198-199)

Malins is an important choice for the character sensitive to the sounds and implications of the suppressed colonial voice. As Torchiana tells us, his name suggests the Celtic word for monk or disciple, *malean,* as well as a possible spelling of the name of the family that kept St. Patrick's bell in the North of Ireland,[31] but he is also a drunk, pub-going Dubliner whose own voice is silenced by a self-imposed paralysis. Thus Malins is in a sense both a stage Irishman and an atavistic Irish presence in search of a voice. It is interesting that he recognizes with disturbing clarity the political dynamics of a parallel colonial experience (the denied voice of the black singer) even as he participates in the inebriated denial of his own voice. Thus, like Little Chandler, he represents the paradox of Irish colonial identity as Joyce saw it—a condition of silence brought about by an erasure of history from without and an acquiescence to the condition of oppression from within. Because Malins is the only one at the party who insists on trying to speak for or about the fading voices of the Irish (Julia), or their racialized counterparts (the pantomime singer), and because he is constantly interrupted either by other speakers or by his own drunkenness, the presence of a voice of the silenced or the dead is again suggested (and very strongly suggested by this point), but still unheard.

We do, however, begin to hear a voice somehow related to a faded Irish identity when Gabriel, after delivering his trite, scrupulously rehearsed speech on "those dead and gone great ones," finally begins to surrender his obsessive self-preoccupation as he tunes in to the "distant music" that Gretta, whom he sees in the moment as "a symbol of something," listens to as she stands motionless on the stairwell (*D*, 210). It is an old and broken Irish music, sung in an unsteady voice by Bartell D'Arcy, the man who, much to the Morkan sisters dismay, "wouldn't sing all the night," and who, after singing, tells the sisters about "the *history* of his cold" that has "put [him] out of voice" (*D*, 210-211). Thematically, the suggestion that long silent voices

---

[31] Donald Torchiana, *Backgrounds for Joyce's Dubliners* (Boston: Allen and Unwin, 1986), 126.

of Ireland's troubled past are straining to be heard, or that they are present but indecipherable through the evanescent masking language of exactness, is growing undeniably strong by this point in the story:

> Gabriel said nothing but pointed up the stairs toward where his wife was standing. Now that the hall door was closed the voice and the piano could be heard more clearly. Gabriel held up his hand for [Kate, Julia, and Mary Jane] to be silent. The song seemed to be in the old Irish tonality and the singer seemed uncertain both of his words and his voice. The voice, made plaintive by distance and by the singers hoarseness, faintly illuminated the cadence of the air with words expressing grief. (*D*, 210)

The distant music that briefly breaks the silence of this tableau (in which both men and women stand transfixed) is "The Lass of Aughrim," a song that powerfully exemplifies the connection Joyce is beginning to make between female voice, the voice of the dead, colonial memory, and the need for scrupulous narrative authority (represented by Gabriel's boy-narrator-like limited perspective) to be dissolved, or absorbed, if the silence is to be broken.

"The Lass of Aughrim," as Vincent Cheng argues, "is a stunningly appropriate choice on Joyce's part," for, like the long history of male objectification of the female subject that is alluded to in the staircase scene, the song is

> a song about mastery, domination, and mistreatment (even rape) of a peasant woman by a patriarchal nobleman. 'The Lass of Aughrim' is a version (among many, with many titles) of 'Lord Gregory'; ... [a song which] tells of Lord Gregory having forced himself on the Lass ('Sorely against my will'), who then gets with child as a result; the song finds her standing in the rain outside the castle with her cold and dying child as she begs to be let in, only to be refused entrance and recognition by Lord Gregory.[32]

Aughrim is also a town in the West of Ireland about thirty miles from Galway that was the site of a decisive battle, fought the year after the Battle of the Boyne (1691), that figured significantly in the English subjugation of the Irish.[33] Thus the song suggests simultaneously the mythic symbolism of the romanticized West of Ireland, the equally problematic cultural nationalist trope of the abused peasant woman (with whom Gretta is clearly associated)

---

[32] Vincent Cheng, *Joyce, Race and Empire* (Cambridge: Cambridge University Press, 1995), 142.
[33] Ibid., 143.

as a symbol of a wronged race, and the bitter fact of Irish blood spilled in the name of English cultural superiority. In other words, it suggests very clearly the simultaneous difficulty and necessity of speaking accurately about Ireland's past—neither the inspired but ignorant nation-tropes (attempts to render vocal the members of a culture) nor the reality of English violence laid bare (a rendering visible of the silencing mechanisms of imperialism) are adequate forms of representation for what might be called an Irish identity. Neither can truly "speak for" Ireland, though both clearly point to a sentient but cautious awareness, on Joyce's part, of the need for just such an articulation.

"The Lass of Aughrim," and the broken, tired voice in which it is sung, thus occupy the space between colonial memory and the exhaustion of language—a space that Gabriel himself will soon occupy. At the end of the story, Gabriel's ability to understand the significance of the song (to Gretta) marks the turning point between his ravenous desire to drag into explicit speech the "mystery" his "symbolic" wife is guarding and his potential epiphany about his neglected Irish identity. But during the stairwell tableau, the possibility of an articulate voice of the dead is still muted by the (although now dissolving) limited male voice and perspective, as D'Arcy's breaking voice is too tired to continue. The lyrics that manage to drift down the hall soon fade out, which Joyce indicates with another ellipsis:

> *O, the rain falls on my heavy locks*
> *And the dew wets my skin,*
> *My babe lies cold ...* (*D*, 210)

Here it is important to note that the song, which a male voice is struggling to sing and which Gabriel can make out only as "a distant music," is written from the perspective of, and in the voice of, a peasant Irishwoman. Again, Joyce suggests an important connection between the dead (in this case the lines about the dying child are what the ellipses transform into an absence), the past, a subaltern female voice and a silencing of all three within the confines of a limited narrative perspective.

To say that much has been made of the ideological, political, and cultural importance of female voice in Joyce is, of course, an understatement. Suzette Henke, Bonnie Kime Scott, Karen Lawrence and Sheldon Brivic, among others, have advanced arguments about how Joyce's grammatically unrestrained female narrative voices emerge from silence and usurp or subvert certain temporal, linguistic or teleological aspects of conventional storytelling that can be considered complicitous with patriarchal regimes of thought (or, as Margot Norris has argued in *Joyce's Web*, with imperialist and nationalist modes of patriarchal thought in particular). Most of these critics, arguing from a poststructuralist position or with its polysemous ends in mind, are also quick to remind us that what is "feminine," and what is most important, about these voices is not their reification of an essentialized "woman's consciousness," but their resistance to an essentialism, logocentrism, binary epistemology, and narrative ontology that can be historically coded as "male."[34] The unrestrainable voice or compendium of voices that, partly from Joyce and partly from Joyce criticism, we know by the label of "female" may, as Susan Stanford Friedman has argued, best be coded as ungendered, or as a "doubly inscribed" discourse that speaks simultaneously for male (Oedipal) desire and female subversion.[35] But even in its deconstructive resistance to labels, or more specifically *because* of this resistance—because the ever-approaching and finally present lyrical voice(s) in Joyce ultimately engulf and absorb (rather than speak from within) the language of others—the connection between Joyce's modernism and women's voices provides the crucial site for examining the *postcolonial* significance of Joyce's texts.

[34] As Suzette Henke (*James Joyce and the Politics of Desire* [New York: Routledge, 1990]) argues, "the polymorphous resonances of Joyce's experimental canon everywhere ... exhibit a pervasive anti-patriarchal bias. His writing introduces a lexical play-field that challenges the assumptions of traditional culture, including phallo-centric authority and logocentric discourse." She claims that "Joyce subverts the name and the law of the Father and delights in the ...fluid and elusive *semiotexte* that wends its way through the final "Lps" of *Finnegans Wake* and brings us back ... to a lyrical riverrun of aesthetic *jouissance* defusing the patriarchal can(n)on" (ibid., 11). We must note the ultimately deconstructive orientation of the feminist argument here, where "feminine" is not essentialized, but analogized or equated with the unraveling of what Toril Moi calls the false "seamlessly unified self" of patriarchal identities (ibid., 8). Bonnie Kime Scott (*James Joyce, Feminist Reading Series*, ed. Sue Roe [Brighton: Harvester Press, 1987]) argues along similar lines, explaining that Joyce's experiments with voice and gender exhibit a "deconstructive play" that aligns with feminism's own objectives. "Joyce," she claims, "offers much more than the male *symbolic* order, the word of the father, and the virtuoso author. Words verge and depend on erotic and generative principles positively associated with the river, the primordial mud and the mother; they are beyond male mastery. Women in late Joyce react to language and write their own, though it is hidden away, written over and tediously deciphered by the male authorities. *Finnegans Wake* analyses its own intentions with language, and [its] emphasis is upon diversity and multiplicity of sign, language and focus" (ibid., 108-109). For an excellent overview, and further anti-essentialist critique, of feminist readings of Joyce's modernism, see Susan Standford Friedman, "Reading Joyce: Icon of Modernity," *Joycean Cultures/Culturing Joyces*, ed. Vincent Cheng et al. (Newark: University of Delaware Press, 1998). Also see Sheldon Brivic, *Joyce's Waking Women: An Introduction to Finnegans Wake* (Madison: University of Wisconsin Press, 1995).

[35] Friedman, "Reading Joyce," 125.

Few critics beyond Margot Norris have considered the Irish historical and political significance of Joyce's female voices in depth, and no one, including Norris, has based a full reading of the political significance of those voices on the powerful criticism, and accumulating threat, that they pose (as Joyce already suggests in above passage of "The Dead") to the long-established position of the martyred or betrayed woman within the overt symbolic economy of Irish cultural nationalism. From an Irish historical and cultural perspective, the importance of Joyce's women (as compared to, say, Yeats's, Synge's or O'Casey's) lies precisely in the fact that their final speeches and appearances are not only emotionally powerful and lyrical but also formally disruptive and resistant, if not unthinkably defiant, to a singular symbolic purpose. Reading the crisis of silence in *Dubliners*, we are increasingly reminded that this is the occluded voice that must speak, and Joyce's suggestion is that if such a voice is to be heard, it cannot remain subject to the binary thinking and essentialist discourse that underpins the desire, seen throughout *Dubliners*, to drag the voices of the dead and the oppressed into representation without altering the terms and conditions of representation itself.

In the penultimate paragraph of the story, just after Gabriel thinks to himself that "one by one [the Morkan guests] were all becoming shades" (*D*, 223), and just as the prose becomes increasingly fluid, Gabriel seems to achieve a highly uncharacteristic shift of perspective from male to female. This completes the deterioration of his stubborn and obsessive male perspective from the limited view of his "symbolically" silent wife to an even more limited perspective through which he can, with increasing frustration, only see his wife as a sexual being— "he longed to be master of her strange mood" (*D*, 217)—to a moment of relinquished identity and subsequent adoption of her perspective, her consciousness. At this moment the narrative focus begins to pan outward from Gabriel's perspective to an all-encompassing view of Ireland past and present, and the distinction between the dead and the living begins to blur:

> Generous tears filled Gabriel's eyes. He had never felt like that himself towards any woman but he knew that such a feeling must be love. The tears gathered more thickly in his eyes and in the partial darkness he imagined he saw the form of a young man standing under a dripping tree. Other forms were near. His soul had approached that region where dwell the vast hosts of the dead. He was conscious of, but could not comprehend, their wayward and flickering existence. His own identity was fading out into a grey impalpable world: the solid world itself which these dead had one time reared and lived in was dissolving and dwindling. (*D*, 223)

As Gabriel experiences an increasingly unmediated communion with the dead, he begins, not unlike the women Joyce casts in this difficult role, to lose his own identity—to "swoon slowly" into some new world where conventional narrative or linguistic forms are no longer sufficient to mark the trail of experience.

Here we should also recall arguments about gender and narrative voice in "The Dead" that have been raised by critics seeking to locate the origin of Joyce's "feminine prose." R. B. Kershner, who argues that "*Dubliners* records the breaking of silence,"[36] points out that "The Dead," following the patterns of the operas discussed at the table (*Mignon, Dinorah* and *Lucrecia Borgia*), revolves around mysterious, silent women, and contains "a sexual reversal" in which a central male character (in this case, Gabriel) "learns to speak as Woman."[37] What is most important about this "sexual reversal" in Gabriel's perspective is that it is characterized by his sudden ineffable awareness of the identity of the dead (he hears them but can not comprehend them) and the simultaneous dissolution, or "fading out," of his own identity. Thus if Gabriel is now, like Gretta or Eliza in "The Sisters," silently communing with the dead and experiencing a dissolution of his own identity, then to whose consciousness, or to what voice or perspective, may we attribute the final words of the story—the lyrical sentences we get instead of the ellipsis that truncates the boy narrator's otherwise similar attempt to hear the voice of the dead?

Especially when placed next to the exhausted, obsessively paraphrastic and clichéd style of Gabriel's speech—an unfeeling lamentation of Irishness and "those absent faces we miss here tonight" that represents the silencing style of narrating cultural memory at its most acute—it strikes me that these last poetic lines are at least uncharacteristically lyrical and all-encompassing for Gabriel, or for any of the "scrupulous," obsessive male narrative voices that have dominated *Dubliners*:

> His soul swooned slowly as he heard the snow falling faintly through the universe and faintly falling, like the descent of their last end, upon all the living and the dead. (*D*, 224)

There are several reasons I am tempted to say that these words represent both a breaking of the silence I have traced throughout *Dubliners* and the subtle beginnings of the politically significant movement toward decentered narrative authority that will culminate in *Finnegans Wake*. The first is that

---

[36] R. B. Kershner, *Joyce, Bakhtin, and Popular Literature: Chronicles of Disorder* (Chapel Hill: University of North Carolina Press, 1989), 22.
[37] Ibid., 150.

the narrative voice here seems, in several curious ways, to anticipate the all-encompassing female narrative voices that end *Ulysses* and *Finnegans Wake*. As with the possible symbolism of the cloud in "A Little Cloud," we have, in the image of falling snow, a sort of muted or suspended form of water, Joyce's symbol for the language-engulfing female voice. It is oddly suggestive, I think, that Gabriel hears rather than sees the faintly falling snow. Further evidence for this argument comes from examining how similar the words are to some lines from Joyce's early poem "She weeps over Rahoon." The poem, which Joyce wrote after a visit in 1912 to the grave of Nora Joyce's childhood sweetheart, begins "Rain on Rahoon falls softly, softly falling/ where my dark lover lies," and the speaker of the poem, either Nora herself, or an imagined female voice, is clearly a woman, and again a woman contemplating or communing with the dead. As Terrence Brown comments, "it is possibly worth noting that in 'The Dead' Joyce invests Gabriel's consciousness with the poeticism which later seemed apt for [an] imagined female voice."[38] If we can say that this is a Joycean female voice, and I think that is a distinct possibility, then a female voice (which for my purposes, and I think much in line with the full complexities of gender in Joyce, is better described as an unrestrainable voice that deconstructs the binary oppositions and teleology of conventional linear or realist narrative) breaks through the narrative to provide the last words of the story, and of all the stories, just as it does in *Ulysses* and *Finnegans Wake*. Perhaps, then, at the end of *Dubliners*, we also have the subtle beginnings of the "engulfing and absorbing [of] English language"[39] that, as Emer Nolan has explained, characterizes the Irish historical significance of Joyce's most disruptive prose.

    Secondly, the final sentence also follows in the wake of the death, or revealed silencing, of the story's most important identifiable voice from the past, that of Michael Furey. Furey, a young tenor cut down in his prime, is another subaltern Irish voice that has been consumed by a deathly silence, and thus he functions in fitting closure to *Dubliners*. But he also represents a certain resurrectional potentiality, the will toward speech from the other side of silence, hat I have attempted to trace throughout the book. His name (Furey), combined with the fact that, as with so many fading figures in "The Dead," we know him primarily through his voice, makes him the final metaphor for a voice of the Irish dead that is unwilling to accept mortal

[38] Terrence Brown, Introduction and notes to *Dubliners* (New York: Penguin, 1992), 317.
[39] Emer Nolan, *James Joyce and Nationalism* (London: Routledge, 1995), 147.

paralysis—one that is corporally at rest but spiritually defiant and bent on resurrection.

Thirdly, and most importantly, the final words, and the sudden narrative panning-out from the tight confines of the dinner party, seem to suggest, to borrow a phrase from one of Stephen's epiphanies, that "a voice beyond the world [is] calling" (*P*, 167). The description of snow falling first all over Ireland and then "through the universe" are not the immediate impressions of the "exactness" of what Gabriel sees, but are, at the very least, the farthest reachings of his imagination and his ability to contemplate both past and present, dead and living, Ireland and the world at large. Not surprisingly, Joyce uses the same alliteration and words from the final sentence of "The Dead" when Stephen, in *A Portrait*, experiences his famous epiphany after watching a girl wading in the ocean: "his eyelids trembled as if they felt the vast cyclic movement of the earth and her watchers, trembled as if they felt the light of some new world. *His soul was swooning* into some new world."[40] As with Stephen, Gabriel's "swooning soul" and "bold" passage into "some other world" suggest the coming of new forms of expression to account for both the dead and the living—but this need or desire for new forms of expression, for some radically different mode of representation to capture the polyphony of insistent voices, initially springs not from an *ex-nihilo* modernist or cosmopolitan worldview, but from an intense awareness of the simultaneous presence and indecipherable nature of one's own cultural past. Indeed, Joyce's description of the ephemeral but present past in Stephen's defining epiphany could easily be applied to Gabriel's: "He heard a confused music within him as of memories and names which he was almost conscious of but could not capture for an instant; then the music seemed to recede, to recede, to recede: and from each receding trail of nebulous music there fell always one longdrawn calling note, piercing like a star the dusk of silence" (*P*, 167).

For the author trapped between a past and a present that are equally unacceptable, between a desire for a mythic past and the knowledge, gained at the threshold of modernity and postcoloniality, that there is no specific past that is not already confused by the present and inseparable from the desire for its articulation—and that one is therefore unable to provide unstigmatized images or languages in which to know oneself or to catch the conscience of a race—one shining alternative becomes the deconstruction of the scrupulously erected structure of language in which one is trapped. Along with whatever else we may claim it to represent, the deconstruction of

---

[40] Ibid., 137; my italics.

comfortable forms of knowing, the decentering and recentering that Gabriel, and later Stephen, experience, is a deeply Irish experience, and, perhaps most importantly, a fitting depiction of an Ireland on the threshold of emergence (though to what we cannot say).

Perhaps, then, the key to what is "Irish" about the later Joyce lies in understanding how Gabriel, as his stubborn selfhood dissolves into the Irish past and then the universe at large, can simultaneously feel that he needs to "pass boldly into that other world" (*D*, 223) (perhaps of extinction, perhaps of a cosmopolitan life) and also "set out on his journey westward," following the voice of St. Patrick, or the atavistic voice of the Irish identity. What is happening in the final sentence is both a breaking of silence (an emergence) and a merging of the living and the dead, a combining of the silenced voices of the old world and the polyglot "bold new world" of a common humanity. The utterance that ends the story speaks both of and *because of* the blurring of the boundary between the dead and the living, the conscience of a race and one's own obsessive consciousness, and thus, Like St. Patrick's "Voice of the Irish," it is the voice of a multitude. And, also like the voice in St. Patrick's vision, the voice is both beyond and not beyond Ireland itself, in that it speaks of, or for, an Ireland that exists in the imagination, an Ireland as an unaccountable possible, or an uncreated Ireland. Of course whatever it is that is "general all over Ireland," whatever unidentifiable, unspeakable but imaginable thing it is that binds together a people (as the silences bind together *Dubliners*), is an entity, or a voice of humanity, that is probably "general" throughout the universe as well. But one only learns this, Joyce seems to suggest, when one finally hears, as does Gabriel, the voices of one's own dead speaking.

Tennessee State University

SOMETHING FOR NOTHING: BECKETT'S *DREAM OF FAIR TO MIDDLING WOMEN*

JOHN PILLING

This essay examines the negational strategies operative in Beckett's jettisoned first novel, *Dream of Fair to Middling Women,* posthumously published in 1992. From a consideration of the first few pages of the novel it emerges that all the familiar and conventional paraphernalia of narrative—plot, character, causality, continuity, salience of detail, stability of locale and indeed everything that could conceivably contribute to authorial responsibility—are here either artfully eroded as they threaten to come into being or are conspicuous by their absence. As the novel develops the very genre to which it gestures to belong seems to be so continually called into question that all generic determinants and distinctions are effectively suspended, leaving *Dream of Fair to Middling Women* in the oddly appropriate "middling" state of being neither one thing nor another.

"Nothing is closer to the supreme commonplace of our commonplace age" —wrote Robert Martin Adams more than thirty years ago—"than its preoccupation with Nothing."[1] In the work of Samuel Beckett this preoccupation is certainly sufficiently commonplace for commentators to have explored the ways in which negation operates, both within and between works, as a kind of compositional principle, and an unusually productive one, given its potentially destructive effects. But only since Beckett's death has it become clear that this principle was never more vigorously and variously exploited than at the very beginning of his writing career, in 1931-1932, in his first full-length novel, *Dream of Fair to Middling Women,* which failed to find a publisher, was jettisoned, and only appeared posthumously in 1992.[2] Such an extreme experiment as *Dream* could scarcely have been expected to

---

[1] Robert Martin Adams, *Nil: Episodes in the Literary Conquest of Void during the Nineteenth Century* (New York: Oxford University Press, 1966), 3.

[2] All quotations are from the Dublin Black Cat Press edition of 1992, edited by Eoin O'Brien and Edith Fournier, and are incorporated by page number in the text of my essay.

find favor in the early 1930s, as even Beckett himself seems gradually, if reluctantly, to have realized;[3] and it speaks volumes for his (in the event misplaced) ambition that something similar from an unknown writer would almost certainly fare little better in the creative climate of a new millennium.

Beckett's *Dream* makes use of so many negational strategies that they virtually defy classification. Their full effect can only be felt over the novel as a whole, but it is clear from the outset - the two brief paragraphs which constitute section "ONE"— that Beckett is intending to make headway without any of the conventional supports on which fiction customarily relies, or at least as few of them as may be needed to maintain the enterprise as viable. The cavalier manner of *Dream*'s opening puts the reader at a disadvantage from the start, such that even with the benefit of hindsight it is impossible to say whether the narrative has been primed to fizzle out, at any time or for any reason, or cunningly and deliberately designed to seem as if it might do so, or is simply the victim of narrative ineptitude or creative fatigue. The issue is joined, but also left in jeopardy, by the connective around which the two paragraphs of "ONE" pivot, the "And" which will later (in the sections of the novel "UND" and "AND") be used as a kind of structural marker. This first "And" is the type and measure of all subsequent ones, since far from being a genuine connective, it becomes simply the means whereby additional material can be conveyed. By failing to supply the real ground for continuity which it "ought" to do, this "And"-clause proves in practice to be the ideal agent of temporal discontinuity. The first casualty of *Dream* is causality, and with it, inevitably, time, or rather the time-sequence to which narrative is typically tied. We are only a paragraph into *Dream* when we suddenly discover that it is already "some years later" (1), the author having mysteriously neglected to fill in the interim between two disparate narrative events, which are nevertheless contiguous and in some ways comparable. From this point on Beckett can play fast and loose with time, focusing in upon any given "Now" as if each "Now" were a law unto itself, rather than part of any continuum or *durée*. It is in this same spirit that Beckett also calls spatial issues into question, by making section "ONE" too brief for it to be the separate entity it is, and section "TWO" so long that we cannot help wondering why it could not have been more conveniently subdivided.

Dream claims two more victims only a few pages into section "TWO": plot, conventionally a by-product of causality (as it is even in

---

[3] *Dream* was rejected by Chatto and Windus in July 1932. Beckett was still sending his two typescripts to publishers as late as May 1933.

Tristram Shandy), and character, typically (and, once again, even in *Tristram Shandy*) a matter of consistency, coherence and conservation. The omniscient, but far from omnipotent, narrator, who is happy to pose as a plural entity (as if he might at a pinch be on "our" side), finds himself compelled to admit:

> The fact of the matter is we do not quite know where we are in this story. (9)

and this, when we as readers are only a few pages into such little "story" as we have thus far been given. The implications are ominous: from here on we will never quite know "where we are," either in the restricted local sense, or in the more general narrative sense of the phrase. Dun Laoghaire's Carlyle Pier, the setting for the opening few pages (3-8) of *Dream*, section "TWO," is perhaps the most stable location in the entire novel, yet even so it serves Beckett's more destructive purposes wonderfully well. The pier, jutting out from the land toward the unruly sea in which it stands, does not lead anywhere, being nothing more than what Stephen Dedalus would call "a disappointed bridge;"[4] and in any case it proves to be only the backdrop to a scene first of farewell, and then of expulsion.

The pier, and the farewell and expulsion enacted upon it, prove just stable enough for just long enough to generate the illusion of momentum in the narrative. But with the emergence of a now visible author—"consensus, here and hereafter, of me" (5)—Beckett is effectively admitting that the novel is a doomed enterprise which has been deliberately undermined from the outset. This is suggested by his sudden mention of "a rat gnawing its way into a globe" as found on "[a] low capital in the crypt of the Basilica Saint-Sernin in the most beautiful city of Toulouse" (9). Why this particular memory (if it is one[5]) should surface here is at best a mystery, and at worst—considered from the standpoint of convention—a wholly gratuitous reversion to a "short stay abroad" of which "great play" is being made.[6] Yet even on a first reading of *Dream* one may feel that the "point" of this excursion is to bind significance and insignificance together, to make one the mirror image of the other. Beckett achieves this bizarre outcome by alluding to a poem of La Fontaine's ("The Rat Who Was Through with the World"[7]) written

---

[4] James Joyce, *Ulysses* (London : The Bodley Head,1960), 29.

[5] Beckett and his brother Frank visited the Côte d'Azur in July 1931.

[6] Winnie, in "Fingal," *More Pricks Than Kicks* (London: John Calder, 1970), 29.

[7] A source identified by Phil Baker. The poem ("Le rat qui s'est rétiré du monde") is in Book VII of La Fontaine's *Fables*.

several hundred years after the construction of the crypt in Toulouse. From the Basilica to La Fontaine and his *Fables* is so obviously a long haul as to call Beckett's "book-keeping" and his eye for the "analogymongers" into question,[8] but, as soon appears, this is precisely what the narrator wishes to do. The narrator's "We think not" (9)—i.e., we think, as any reasonable person might, that there is actually no connection between the one and the other—admits the inadmissibility of the analogy. The effect of this remarkable paragraph is to make nothing happen,[9] and to show that negation is at once generative but degenerative, organic but disabling, and dynamic but dysfunctional. Not until *Watt* some ten years later would Beckett foreground the fact that "the only way one can speak of nothing is to speak of it as though it were something";[10] yet *Dream* depends on this principle being operative without the principle ever being voiced, as if negation were itself too negative for any abstract proposition or dictum to stand. In thinking of Toulouse, perhaps, Beckett is thinking of all the fictional paraphernalia he will have to lose to achieve his aims, baggage which—once the novel has been brought to book (as in the event it was not to be)—he can happily consider well lost.

With the principle of negation written out of *Dream*, but with "not" written into it, Beckett's task from this point onwards is to create in retrograde fashion, amassing substantial material while all the time "gnawing" away at it. It is in this spirit that Beckett makes what he can of "a little story about China" (10) found in a book about Chinese music[11] which he had been reading. This will later in *Dream*, more than a hundred and fifty pages later, be identified as a "Tale of a Tub" (178), that is, a diversion or lure, although Beckett ensures that this later judgment is actually little more than a gloss on the story as first told. The lure is the possibility that there may be some equivalences between the figures of an ancient Chinese tale—itself a tale of origin, offering an explanation of how music began—and the *dramatis personae* of this book; the truth is that there are none, so that the episode ends in much the same way as the Toulouse excursus: "We take leave to doubt it" (11). A reader not quite so "gentle" (13) as *Dream*'s author would

---

[8] Beckett's own terms, from the opening paragraph of his Joyce essay of 1929, *Disjecta: Miscellaneous Writings and a Dramatic Fragment*, ed. Ruby Cohn (London : John Calder, 1983), 19.

[9] Compare *Watt*, after the incident of the Galls father and son : "nothing had happened [...] a thing that was nothing had happened, with the utmost formal distinctness" (Samuel, Beckett, *Watt* [London : John Calder, 1963], 73).

[10] Beckett, *Watt*, 74.

[11] A source identified by Sean Lawlor: Louis Laloy, *La musique chinoise* (Paris: Henri Laurens, n.d. [1910?]).

like him to be might quite legitimately object at this point that the narrator has taken "leave" from narrative imperatives with which he has no intention of complying. Even in so taking "leave," however, Beckett characteristically favors the possibility of negation latent in a sequence which begins ("Supposing") and ends ("doubt") in a subjunctive mood and mode (10-11). Also latent in Beckett's Chinese tale is a non-equivalence between source and transcription which is presumably the product of carelessness, or too casual an acquaintance with rather recondite raw material.[12] Yet even if this is simply an error, it typifies another of the negational "rules" by which *Dream* abides, if indeed it can ever be said to abide by any rules. *Dream* depends absolutely upon pre-existent texts of very diverse origin, texts which, in transfer from one context to another, suffer not only displacement but a kind of creative disfigurement. This is very much the case, as I have demonstrated elsewhere,[13] with the plays of John Ford as re-configured for the paragraph of *Dream* which was first published as "Text" in *The New Review* in 1932. But there is in fact scarcely a page of the novel on which some transvaluation does not occur, either by way of re-contextualization, or by creating a peculiarly Beckettian alloy from two (or more) unrelated textual origins. Beckett's aim here seems a by-product of his awareness that literature, or anything written, is in endlessly parasitic reflection upon itself, and is consequently the perfect agent to supervise its own demise

The difficulty here (for the negationist) is that some, at least, of these borrowings must be recognized as borrowed for the dismantling of them to have its full effect; the payoff is the suggestion that much else is borrowed and, in the process, transmogrified. If none of the borrowings were visible, there would be little point in performing such an elaborate exercise. But Beckett solves this problem—or refuses to recognize that it might be a problem—by recurrently (but randomly) supplying referents, by hinting that there are others we can find if we care to ("We stole that one. Guess where" [191]), and by burying a whole host of others so deeply into the fabric that, without access to the *"Dream" Notebook,* we might never have suspected they were there.[14] This "flagrant concealment" (148) accords well with the analysis, such as it is, of what Belacqua is, in essence:

---

[12] The "Great Steepleiron" should more properly have been the "Great Arrow of Steel," as Sean Lawlor pointed out to me in a private communication.

[13] See my "A Mermaid Made Over: Beckett's *Text* and John Ford," in *Beckett and Beyond*, ed. Bruce Stewart (Gerrards Cross: Colin Smythe, 1999), 211-216.

[14] See my edited and annotated *Beckett's "Dream" Notebook* (Reading: Beckett International Foundation, 1999).

> At his simplest he was trine. [...] Centripetal, centrifugal and... not. Phoebus chasing Daphne, Narcissus flying from Echo and...neither. Is that neat or is it not? (120)

Beckett's question begs another question: is it neither?[15] The upshot, in any event, is that Belacqua can never be more than a 'precarious ipsissimosity' (113). By the same token, the section which appears to be telling us how we should read *Dream*—"UND," by definition something of a foreign body in what we expect to be fiction—can only ever be something of "a paraphrased abrégé" (117), and even then cannot actually constitute itself as such. Of Belacqua Beckett subsequently observes that "various though he was, he epitomized nothing" (125), and the same holds true of the "abrégé" which purports to be an epitome of *Dream* as a whole. Beckett's editor at Chatto and Windus wrote in a letter to him that "'UND' helped me a lot,"[16] and it was perhaps as well that Beckett came to realize that help was needed, even if ultimately the enterprise was to prove fruitless. However, "UND" is no more typical of *Dream* as a whole than, say, "AND," both of which look as if they ought to be able to make common cause with one another, although neither can resolve itself into, or by way of, the other, as is dramatically rendered by "THREE" interposing itself between them.

In his maturity Beckett spoke of *Waiting for Godot* as a play striving to avoid definition. But nowhere does Beckett strive harder to avoid definition than in *Dream of Fair to Middling Women*, and nowhere else does he employ such a barrage of weapons to reduce or obscure shape, contour and perspective. It was important to the young Beckett's sense of himself— especially so, once he had abandoned the safe haven of academia[17]—that he should write something possibly one day worthy of admission in the book of "ars longa" (168). If *Dream* was not to be an epic poem (which it was not) this ambition obliged Beckett to work in the genre toward which he would ever after gravitate: the novel. But while *Dream* could not, and cannot, be other than a novel, Beckett did everything he could to question its right to belong to any one genre. He announces this early, when Belacqua is "called on to sustain" (19) a letter, written in French, from his French friend Lucien. This letter breaks the unwritten "rule" that, in any novel written in English, such direct communication would almost always also be written in English. It breaks another unwritten "rule" by completely failing to advance or

---

[15] Cf. the text "neither," written by Beckett in 1976.

[16] Letter from Charles Prentice to Samuel Beckett, July 5, 1932 (Chatto and Windus Archive, University of Reading).

[17] Beckett resigned his post of Lecturer in French at Trinity College Dublin over the Christmas vacation of 1931.

promote the plot. And it further breaks ranks by containing within it an enigmatic twelve-line poem which, as late as 1934, Beckett was considering for inclusion in a volume to be called *"POEMS, by Samuel Beckett."*[18] Just as this novel is determined not to be a novel, so this letter is determined to be not, or not just, a letter. This has been hinted at earlier in the letter when Lucien includes extracts from a letter he has supposedly had from Belacqua, containing obiter dicta on "P." [Proust] which have provoked a mutual friend, Liebert, to comment upon them. Lucien, in writing to Belacqua, quotes Liebert's actual words, granting the latter a kind of temporary life within the novel which his later fitful appearances do little to maintain. Lucien's letter seems here to have transgressed the usual boundaries of correspondence; it is almost as if a full-blown play is struggling to emerge. But in any event, Beckett reins in this impulse, rests content with the many defeated expectations which the letter leaves in its wake, and saves the specter of a possible playscript for the burst of conversation between the Alba and the Polar Bear in section "THREE" (162-164).

Almost from the outset *Dream* is inimical to "what one gets from one's favourite novelist" (10), which for Beckett amounts to a "chain-chant solo of cause and effect, a one-fingered teleophony" (10), a work at the furthest possible remove from the "simultaneity" (10) which he so obviously prefers. Without nominating a "favourite," Beckett very clearly identifies one novelist, Balzac, whom he cannot favor. The many and various deficiencies which Beckett perceives in Balzac are summed up in the accusation that he creates a "chloroformed world" (119), a description from which we may further deduce that it is not part of the business of the novelist to create a "world," in spite of the traditional wisdom which suggests otherwise. *Dream*'s rejection of the novel as heterocosm is of a piece with the judgement which sees "[the] real presence" as nothing but a "pest" (11). Far from seeking to create a fictional world as sound and as substantial on its own terms as the real world, Beckett is intent on creating "the object that becomes invisible before your eyes" (12). A sense of place—of "things seen" which differentiate one city from another—is another of the traditional fictional elements which *Dream* fails to supply. As the European venues of section "TWO" float briefly into focus—Paris, Vienna, Kassel—they flicker fitfully, and then recede into the background. Similarly, when in section "THREE" Beckett returns (by way of "the dull coast road home" [143]) to his native Dublin, there is little sense of any social cohesion of the kind

---

[18] This poem appears as "Text 2" in the A. J. Leventhal materials at the Harry Ransom Humanities Resource Center, University of Texas, Austin.

which makes "real" the city of Joyce's *Dubliners* and *Ulysses*. Beckett's Dublin, like his novel, has become "unstitched" (113), which enables him to suggest that all encounters are the product of chance, and that even a Christmas party, toward which everyone but Nemo seems to be making their way in section "THREE," has little to do with community, and is much more a matter of outsize egos intent on being heard above the hubbub.

As a book *Dream* is a "concert of effects" (12) implacably opposed to any "solution of continuity" (6). The concert begins where it will, and ends where it pleases, and in the interim refuses to resolve its disharmonies, indeed insists upon them drowning out anything resembling "chain-chant." All that survives are labels which refuse to stick to the luggage, an "exordium" (39) or a "codetta" (113) here, a "[t]erminal scena" (115, 149) there; but with no end in view except the "END" which ends "AND" (241). Even what offers itself as an "episode" (109, 147, 198) only occupies the limelight for a brief space of time; in *Dream* "the units of continuity have abdicated their unity, they have gone multiple" (138), and everything has been whittled down to "now, this very moment" (178) or an indeterminate "Next" (19, 118, and so forth.). With "audibilities" which are "no more than punctuation in a statement of silences" (102), *Dream* is an open invitation to us to "school ourselves [...] from the desire to bind for ever in imperishable relation the object to its representation" (160). The specter of a "far far better" story (49, 197) materializes from time to time, and it would be an unusual reader who did not wish some parts of the book—for example, the "unsanitary" (109) episode originally called *They Go Out for the Evening* (74-109)[19]—better than they are. The celebratory shenanigans in Kassel were part of the earliest inspiration for *Dream*, and may have prompted Beckett to end *Dream* as a whole with another party scene, although Joyce's *Dubliners* and Proust's *Recherche* supplied him with the literary authority to do so. But the Kassel party depends too much upon the characters establishing themselves as such—by a trick of speech or a turn of phrase, in what is very much the most "voiced" portion of *Dream*—when all the creative or de-creative energies of the novel are engaged in resisting rigidity.

Beckett's refusal to allow *Dream* to be published once he had achieved fame and fortune was in large part a judgment of maturity over what had come to seem juvenilia, although his poor opinion of the novel may have set in soon after *More Pricks Than Kicks* became an alternative way forward. Certainly, once *Murphy* had become the first in what could

---

[19] Letter from Samuel Beckett to Charles Prentice, August 15, 1931 (Chatto and Windus Archive, University of Reading).

gradually be seen as a "series,"[20] Beckett had no desire to admit *Dream* into the canon of his work. It is symptomatic in this connection that, replying in 1967 to an enquiry from the critic Sighle Kennedy, Beckett should choose *Murphy* as an implicit point of origin:

> If I were in the unenviable position of having to study my work my points of departure would be the "Naught is more real...." and the "Ubi nihil vales ..." both already in *Murphy*, and neither very rational.[21]

Both these "points of departure"—the first from Democritus of Abdera, the second from Arnold Geulincx[22]—post-date the débâcle of *Dream*, as it came to seem in the longer perspective. But neither the "Naught" of the one, nor the "nihil" of the other, can disguise the fact that there was a point of departure earlier than either, and that even when (unusually, but by no means uniquely) the highbrow focus of *Dream* relaxes to admit Marlene Dietrich and *Die Blaue Engel* ("Sonst, in the words of the song, gar nix" [11,17]), the not very rational, but very deep-seated, commitment to negation was already in place.

University of Reading

---

[20] Letter from Samuel Beckett to George Reavey, May 14, 1947 (Harry Ransom Humanities Resource Center, University of Texas, Austin); letter from Samuel Beckett to Thomas MacGreevy, January 4, 1948 (Trinity College, Dublin).

[21] Beckett, *Disjecta*, 113.

[22] For a very full account, see Dougald McMillan and Martha Fehsenfeld, eds., *Beckett in the Theatre: The Author as Practical Playwright and Director* (London : John Calder, 1988), 50-58.

JOYCE'S NEGATIVE ESTHETICS[1]
JEAN-MICHEL RABATÉ

Wishing to explore what Joyce means by his esthetic theory, I discover four "paradoxes" or internal contradictions in this concept. The first paradox hinges around a division between "esthetic" understood as individual perception of the world and "esthetic" as a discourse about the beautiful; this accounts for the crucial reduction of "imitation" to a progressive learning process. A second paradox, relayed by Bosanquet's lectures on esthetics, associates the "theoretic" with pure contemplation by opposition to the elaboration of hypotheses (defined as the "theoretical"); this forces us to bring a "theoretic" moment closer to some form of mysticism. The third paradox arises from a divorce between the individual promoter of new theories of art and a context determined by collective political ideals without which no self-authorization can be effective. The fourth paradox comes from the division between esthetics of beauty and esthetics of the sublime. Finally, it seems that only a theory of negative esthetics founded on a redoubling of the heroic by the heretic, both contemplating without flinching the Nothing or the unspeakable Real, can allow us to understand how Joyce solves the previous paradoxes. But, of course, the last paradox resulting from this is that in the process, Joyce entirely lost faith in the project of constituting an esthetic. Starting from earlier formulations of these issues in the first "Portrait of the Artist," *Stephen Hero* and the critical writings, I try to understand how Aristotelian definitions lead to theoretical complexities underpinning the writing of texts like *Finnegans Wake*.

The relation between Joyce's esthetics and his works of fiction has always been a vexed one. We all remember the proud assertion Joyce made in March 1903 when he announced to his mother from his first Parisian "exile" that among his projects, an aesthetic theory would figure prominently in the work-schedule he saw filling up two decades: "My book of songs will be published in the Spring of 1907. My first comedy about five years later. My 'Esthetic' about five years later again."[2] Surprisingly, Joyce managed to be almost right about the first two dates: *Chamber Music* was published in 1907

---

[1] This is a revised version of a chapter in *Joyce and the Politics of Egoism* (Cambridge: Cambridge University Press, 2001).
[2] *SL*, 19.

while *Exiles* (if it can be called a "comedy") was begun in 1913. However, no "Esthetic" was ever published or written, unless we count the reviews and essays collected under the title of *Critical Writings*. One could add a few theoretical passages from *Ulysses,* mostly culled, one supposes, from Stephen Dedalus's ruminations on art, paternity, creation and rhythm. This might produce a Joycean equivalent of what Meschonnic has done with Mallarmé when he edited his "Writings about the Book" and produced a selection of theoretical fragments from letters, reviews and essays that put together provide a strikingly coherent aesthetic.[3] It might be harder to find a workable title in Joyce's case, although one could easily settle for a conservative subtitle such as "post-Aristotelian poetics." Moreover, his decision to incorporate fragments of an esthetic system considered as an independent discourse or a totatilizing system into the very stuff of his fiction entailed a certain disappearance of "theory" as such.[4] It is less a disaffection of the author with his own theories than a refusal to let theories stand on their own, without a strong link with their source of enunciation.

One might be tempted to account for this in terms of a double principle of esthetic apprehension that could bridge the gap between fiction and the general esthetic treatise Joyce never wrote. On the one hand, there would be the concept that Joyce proffers so obtrusively yet obliquely at the beginning of *Dubliners*, when he tantalizingly suggests that our reading will be patterned by a "gnomon"—an incomplete figure in which meaning is made manifest through lack and darkness. On the other hand, one meets early enough the crucial and much debated term of "epiphany" understood as a principle of revelation by which the hidden sense is perceived as groping toward a presentation in full light. I wish less to force well-known concepts into strict dichotomies than to show how both principles bypass, exceed and finally undermine any explicit theory of their meaning, production and functioning. This complex movement also helps redefine the very notion of Esthetics understood as just an "Esthetic theory." However, one of the preliminary questions we can pose is whether there is for Joyce a specific meaning in the term of "theory." As I hope to show, "theory" appears as the site or knot connecting a number of cruxes or paradoxes. I would like to suggest that we need to posit four distinctions in order to understand more fully Joyce's strategic revisions of "theory."

---

[3] Stéphane Mallarmé, *Ecrits sur le Livre*, ed. Henri Meschonnic (Paris: Editions de l'Eclat, 1985).

[4] I have touched upon this issue in the conclusion to *Joyce Upon the Void* (London: Macmillan, 1991), 217-222.

1. The four paradoxes of Joycean esthetics[5]

A first distinction derives from the age-old bifurcation of "esthetics," a term caught up between the meaning of "sense perception" as found, for instance, in Kant's first *Critique* when a "transcendental esthetic" is defined by the coordinates of space and time, and the meaning of "discourse bearing upon beautiful objects" which is the object of Kant's third Critique, the *Critique of Judgment*. The point has been made by many critics that Joyce's Aristotelian point of departure led him to stress the concept of "natural process" as a way of unifying these two levels. For instance, the commentary on Aristotle's *e tekhne mimeitai ten physin* found in the 1903 Paris notebook ("Aristotle does not here define art; he says only, 'Art imitates Nature' and means that the artistic process is like the natural process"[6]) will then lead to the genetic theory of artistic development that will constitute the backbone of *A Portrait of the Artist as a Young Man*.[7] The making of a work of art implies a more complex and detailed process of "artistic conception, artistic gestation, and artistic reproduction" (*APA*, 209), all of which is based upon the idea that personal experience puts the production of artifacts on par with that of living beings. A further paradox is that the male artist will have to imitate or steal even the feminine role in gestation and reproduction. The theory will vanish of its own as soon as it has taught the artist how to "give birth" to art. Much as the theory cannot be abstracted from an experience of revelation, the three stages of its progression become identical with an ideal genesis that transcends sexual division. If Aristotle's *Poetics* define tragic drama as the "imitation of an action" producing pity and terror, the playwright's aim is nevertheless not the creation of a resembling picture of this or that man, but the creation of emotions similar to those inspired by suffering characters like Oedipus. As Butcher's commentary on Aristotle's *Poetics* insists, mimesis is the imitation of an action, of real "men in action."[8] This is why music and dancing can be said to "imitate" passions. Butcher concludes that "imitation"

---

[5] I am borrowing the idea of successive "paradoxes" in order to describe conceptual tensions from Antoine Compagnon's insightful *Les Cinq Paradoxes de la Modernité* (Paris: Seuil, 1990).

[6] *CW*, 145.

[7] James Joyce, *A Portrait of the Artist as a Young Man*, ed. Chester Anderson (New York: Viking, 1968); abbreviated as *APA*. When I quote the 1904 "Portrait of the Artist," I refer to this edition.

[8] S. H. Butcher, *Aristotle's Theory of Poetry and the Fine Arts* (London: Macmillan, 1895), 123.

is synonymous with "producing" or "creating according to a true idea"[9] which suggests a dynamic theory of an imitation linked with a living process and completely divorced from any pre-conception of the beautiful. Joyce's itinerary from Aristotle to Vico thus appears relatively direct, since both philosophers share the belief that imitation is a fundamentally human process and is not based upon any notion of the beautiful or limited to categories of traditional esthetics.

The concept of "imitation" crucial to Aristotelian poetics paves the way to a new psychological realism that has important consequences. As Stephen explains to a bemused Lynch, "Aristotle's entire system of philosophy rests upon his book of psychology" (*APA*, 208) which justifies his effort aiming at paralleling formal structures of the work of art with the stages of the mind's apprehension of it. Psychology and esthetics are both underwritten by what could be called a genetic reason. Esthetics cannot become a "science of the concrete" or a "science of the particular" (and if it fails to do so, it remains a dead letter, pure abstraction devoid of real content) without accounting for its genesis. This generates one of the cruxes of *A Portrait of the Artist as a Young Man,* in which the evocation of esthetic experience explains how any subject is bound to follow in Stephen's steps and apprehend the three stages of the individuating beauty in an object while being also entirely part of a quasi biographical narrative. Such a narrative will chart the course of the subject of enunciation or "I" while remaining fixed at each stage on the desired vision of an essence of beauty, in other words gaining a deeper understanding of theory as such.

The second paradox follows from the first in that it addresses a difficulty arising from the usual definition of esthetics understood conventionally as theory elaborating the modalities by which we apprehend or contemplate the beautiful. Theory is indeed a loaded term, hesitating between the vague idea of abstract discourse while retaining something of its etymological connection with contemplation.[10] It might then be useful to distinguish between the Marxist sense (in its Althusserian version, especially) of "theory" as dialectically joined with "praxis" and the more etymological sense of "contemplative," in the mystical or just artistic use of the term. Any danger of confusion can be avoided if one distinguishes between a "theoretical" and a "theoretic" approach. Such a distinction is not a mere linguistic quibble; it was felt to be quite necessary by a philosopher of

---

[9] Ibid., 153.

[10] See Martin Heidegger's systematic discussion of the Greek roots of "theory" in "Science and Reflection," trans. William Lovitt, in *The Question Concerning Technology and Other Essays* (New York: Harper & Row, 1977), 163-166.

Esthetics whom Joyce read and used with great profit during his Dublin years, Bernard Bosanquet. Bosanquet's explication of these terms is to be found in a collection of lectures published in 1923, the year of his death, *Three Lectures on Aesthetic* (henceforth, *TLA*).[11] Here is what Bosanquet has to say about the idea of "contemplation", in a passage qualifying an earlier definition of the "aesthetic attitude" as that "in which we imaginatively contemplate an object, being able in that way to live in it as an embodiment of our feeling" (*TLA*, 29-30):

> "Now, I am uneasy about this word "contemplate". No doubt it makes a very good distinction against the practical and the theoretical frames of mind; which in contrast with it are very much like each other. For, I think, we must distinguish the theoretical, at least in modern usage, from the "theoretic". "Theoretic" is pretty much "contemplative", while "theoretical" indicates a very busy activity aimed at putting together hypotheses and testing them by facts. It is in this sense that it is so sharply opposed to "theoretic" or contemplative." (*TLA*, 30)

Bosanquet's dichotomy starts off a series of binary oppositions: theoretic is opposed to theoretical as passive is opposed to active and as the fragment is opposed to totality. The theoretical intellect associates facts and ideas, it starts from experience considered as "praxis" and moves toward the conceptual. It aims at a general dialectization of sense experience and general deductive ideas. The theoretic intellect, closer to pure "vision," remains passive and contemplative. It seizes forcibly, in a direct glance, what the mystics attempt to express by the negative way of apophatic revelation. For Bosanquet, Aristotle would represent the theoretical mind while Plotinus would be on the side of the theoretic.

I would like to suggest here another verbal echo, the latent overtones of "heresy" in "theoretic" rendered more plausible by Stephen's reiteration of artistic defiance. Very early, the youthful Stephen Dedalus is presented as a "hero" above all because he manages to link the production of an esthetic theory with an attitude of refusal or subversion of dominant values. Stephen should properly be called a "hero" only insofar as he appears as a theory-hero who is therefore also a "the(o)hretic." It is therefore quite logical that the earliest manifestations of Stephen's theories should be accompanied by acts of negation. His theory of art is thus properly an anti-theory, never very far from Adorno's negative dialectics or from his esthetics of negativity.

---

[11] Bernard Bosanquet, *Three Lectures on Aesthetics* (London: Macmillan, 1923), 30.

In *Stephen Hero* (henceforth, *SH*), however, one can discern quite soon a fetishization of the word "theory"—the term being a shortcut for "aesthetic theory" but brandished in a repeated gesture of distanciation and negation. If, as we have seen, "theory" is never too far from its sense of "contemplation," the subsequent question is the movement that brings the subject from perception determined by the categories of space and time to a heightened sense of revelation—as when Stephen is described exultant, under the shock of the vision of a young girl wading in the sea at the end of chapter IV in *A Portrait of the Artist as a Young Man*. All in all, Stephen could almost appear as a disciple of Ruskin, when the latter opposes "aesthesis" and "theory" in *Modern Painters*: "The mere animal consciousness of the pleasantness I call Aesthesis, but the exulting, reverent and grateful perception of it I call Theoria."[12] *Theoria* provides another name for the artistic task consisting in the apprehension and the subsequent recording of epiphanies seen as these "most delicate and evanescent moments," to quote Stephen's definition in *Stephen Hero*.

Hence a third paradox of esthetic theory will be generated by the forceful link theory establishes between the individual subject and the discourse of the collective body of citizens. As Wlad Godzich stresses in a very useful commentary, "*theoria*" cannot be abstracted from its political function, especially if we remember that "*theoria*" can be construed as a plural, a plural referring to the succession of official witnesses who could testify that such or such an event had actually taken place in Athens. The individual "aesthesis" had to be relayed by the official *theoria*, a *theoria* grounded in a *deixis* of the "here and now" but underwritten, countersigned by the *polis* and the body politic. *Theoria* warrants that any particular event is capable of being narrated, which simply redoubles the task epiphanies leave to the individual.

This points to another gap in Stephen's youthful formulations, since the rewriting of *Stephen Hero* as *A Portrait of the Artist as a Young Man* tends to leave out most social reference from his system. Yet Stephen seems to be in constant search of recognition, at least by his peers, if not from his masters. Hence the dialectical turn of his meditations: Stephen needs a number of "witnesses" before he can authorize himself. The main issue, however, is less the accusation of bourgeois individualism that is leveled against him by his fellow students at the University than the consideration of the mechanisms by which any statement, be it literary, artistic or political, will be authorized. Stephen, like Joyce, often appears in the uncomfortable

---

[12] As quoted by Wlad Godzich in his "Preface" to Paul de Man's *The Resistance to Theory* (Minneapolis: University of Minnesota Press, 1986), xiv.

position of pretending to subvert all types of "authority"[13] while being still caught up in a tremendous effort of "self-authorization."

Finally, a fourth paradox would have to point to the quandary in which post-Kantian esthetic finds itself: is esthetic merely the conventional discourse about judgments of taste and beauty understood as that which "pleases" a social majority, or can it be capable of a more radical approach to negativity? Kant's analysis of the Sublime paves the way for Hegel's critique and reappropriation of an infinity that is perceived when the subject faces certain natural spectacles (a wild tempest tossing ships, distant armies charging across lands, the ineffable symphonies of clouds at sunset) and then understands how these sights exceed the powers of conception of the human imagination. If, as Zizek has shown, we have here in a nutshell the entire revolution produced by Hegelian dialectics,[14] we do not have to follow Kant's return toward the infinite interiority of the moral law. In Kant's well-known analysis of the sublime, the subject, comprehending that he cannot comprehend, ends up transforming his utter abasement facing an excess of magnitude as perceived into a truly ethical infinity. In Joyce's case, we can wonder whether his own esthetic categories can even lead to the previous bifurcation into beauty and the sublime. As Ginette Verstraete's book on the "feminine sublime" has shown, Joyce's deviant theory entails changing the field of reference and abandoning the confrontation between Kant and Hegel in order to use the different model provided by Schlegel's esthetics.[15] A new "feminine sublime" would then be generated, a sublime that might also encompass ugliness and ridicule. Even if Joyce may have remained unaware of Schlegel's theses, he shares Schlegel's basic insight into the duplicity, irony and reversibility of any version of the Sublime. I will now turn to some key passages in the early works so as to suggest that Joyce slowly worked toward a resolution of the esthetic antinomies just sketched. Egoism can be shown to function not merely as a moral or political term but as the keystone of a system of "disappearing" esthetics.

---

[13] For a good analysis of this tension, see the new edition of Vicki Mahaffey's brilliant *Reauthorizing Joyce* (Gainesville: University Press of Florida, 1995).

[14] See Slavoj Zizek, *The Sublime Object of Ideology* (London: Verso, 1989), 201-231. See also Immanuel Kant, *The Critique of Judgement*, trans. J. C. Meredith (Oxford: Oxford University Press, 1952), 90-203.

[15] See Ginette Verstraete, *Fragments of the Feminine Sublime in Friedrich Schlegel and James Joyce* (Albany: State University of New York Press, 1998).

2. Heroism as esthetic negation: "Ego Nego"

In the first "Portrait of the Artist" (1904), the radicalization of esthetic egoism leads to a position of absolute negation: Stephen's consistent "Ego Nego" defines him, in the words of *Finnegans Wake,* as a "Negoist" (*FW,* 488.21). One sentence from the 1904 text finds its way literally in *Stephen Hero:* "It was part of that ineradicable egoism which he was afterwards to call redeemer that he imagined converging to him the deeds and thoughts of the microcosm" (*APA,* 259 and *SH,* 34). His hyperbolic egoism has little to do with acquisitive individualism or hoarding, it is a Stirnerian posturing that also borders on delusion and a rather shrill assertion of one's utter centrality. What accounts for the "redeeming" nature of this egoism is the idea that Stephen does not keep what is given to him since he sees himself as a "spendthrift saint" (*APA,* 258). Sanctity might be the one redeeming feature of the egoist. As an egoist, Stephen is at the same time a "saint" since he desires "an arduous good" (*APA,* 260) and a "spendthrift" since, like his father, he cannot resist giving again what has been offered to him, at least under the form of words. The saint, as Lacan has shown in his television interview[16] manages to own, condense and redeem the essential value of the world by excluding himself from it. The Saint and the Egoist negate everything from their banal surroundings that annoys them in the name of the power of Beauty. Stephen has chosen as his muse "the image of beauty" (*APA,* 260) and it is thanks to this unwavering resolution that he can keep ideological authority and religious conformity at a distance.

A model for this youthful confession documenting a struggle with an ambitious esthetic program could be found in Rimbaud's similar recapitulation of esthetic failure in *A Season in Hell.* Rimbaud's original claims ("I shall now unveil all the mysteries: mysterious religious or natural, death, birth, future, past, cosmogony, void. I am a master of

---

[16] Jacques Lacan, *Television*, trans. D. Hollier, R. Krauss, and A. Michelson (New York: Norton, 1990), 15-16: "A saint's business, to put it clearly, is not *caritas.* Rather, he acts as trash; his business being *trashitas.* So as to embody what the structure entails, namely allowing the subject, the subject of the unconscious, to take him as the cause of the subject's desire. In fact it is through the abjection of this cause that the subject in question has a chance to be aware of his position, at least within the structure. (...)That produces an effect of *jouissance*—who doesn't "get" the meaning along with the pleasure? The saint alone stays mum; fat chance of getting anything out of him. That is really the most amazing thing in the whole business. Amazing for those who approach it without illusions: that saint is the refuse of *jouissance.*"

phantasmagoria"[17]) are soon shattered after he realizes that he cannot "fix" vertigoes or stabilize hallucinations: "My health was threatened. Terror came upon me. (...) I was forced to travel, to distract the enchantments crowding in my brain."[18] Rimbaud's obvious ambivalence facing religion and art is similar to the tone of Stephen's self-critique: "A thousand eternities were to be reaffirmed, divine knowledge was to be re-established. Alas for Fatuity! as easily might he have summoned a regiment of the winds" (*APA*, 261). With *Stephen Hero* and *A Season in Hell,* we would have two identical confessions of "negative esthetics," or of a moment of sheer impossibility met as the necessary limit to theory in the constitution of full-fledged esthetics. What pushes Stephen out of the despair that marks Rimbaud's esthetics is an innate belief in his worth coupled with a Fichtean assertion by negation: "His Nego, therefore, written amid a chorus of peddling Jews' gibberish and Gentile clamour, was drawn up valiantly while true believers prophesied fried atheism and was hurled against the obscene hells of our Holy Mother: but that outburst over, it was urbanity in warfare" (*APA*, 265). This juvenile portrait ends on a socialist plea for revolution that might seem at odds with the previous profession of esthetic isolationism. Nevertheless, a revolutionary position, as we have seen, is the only way of bridging the gap between an individualist rebellion and the collective dimension it needs to acquire, in other words between an early "egoistic mysticism" and Stephen's admission that he is after all also Irish, even if chooses exile.

The bold statement opening the 1907 essay entitled "Ireland, Island of Saints and Sages" ("Nations have their ego, just like individuals..." [*CW*, 154]) suggests that if the Irish Nation's "ego" is aptly summed up by the phrase "Island of Saints and Sages" (a phrase that is unpacked and entirely explicated in the lecture itself), Joyce is also aware that his historical survey of Ireland leads to a critical (or suspensive) analysis of nationalism. When summing up the British conquest of the island or the Act of Union of 1800, he stresses two combined factors that account for Irish corruption and Irish betrayal, adding: "From my point of view, these two facts must be thoroughly explained before the country in which they occurred has the most rudimentary right to persuade one of her sons to change his position from that of an unprejudiced observer to that of a convinced nationalist" (*CW*, 162-163) This illuminating text appears not only as a synthesis of the individual and the collective that was still tentative in *Stephen Hero* but also as a blueprint for the whole of *Finnegans Wake.* For it is only in the *Wake*

---

[17] Arthur Rimbaud, "A Season in Hell," in *Collected Poems*, trans. Oliver Bernard (London: Penguin, 1986), 315.
[18] Ibid., 335.

that Joyce overcomes the paradox of the collective versus the singular "theoretician" and he does so partly by getting rid of any conventional "character" and replacing them with "sigla" or mere narratological functions.[19]

By that time, the term of "theory" needs to be dropped since the new writing in a synthetic language successfully negotiates between the beautiful and the sublime on the one hand, and the sublime and the ridiculous on the other hand. We do find some quasi-Freudian infantile "theories" about the excremental nature of writing seen as Shem's bodily production, but they are couched in such a language and caught in such complex narratological determinations that it becomes impossible to extract them from their context and to ascribe them to an author who might be called "Joyce" in the way so many of the earlier theories could be.

What remains difficult to understand is the link between Joyce's early egoistic estheticism and the revolutionary consequences he ascribes to it—all of which revolves around the recurrent and loaded use of the word "theory". One of the major differences between the first "Portrait"—a text that announces the final *Portrait* in its bold cinematographic montage of different scenes and in its non-chronological, synthetic approach—and *Stephen Hero* is the shift in the meaning of the word "theory." In the first "Portrait of the Artist" of 1904, "theory" has still a negative value; we see this when Stephen opts for "the lower orders" in which a "confessor did not seem anxious to reveal himself, in theory at least, a man of the world" (*APA*, 258). In *Stephen Hero*, on the contrary, the term of "theory" is flaunted with a curious and almost mechanical insistence as we have seen.

Stephen's heroism consists in the ardor and candor with which he strives to reach his goal of artistic self-generation through the egoistic production of a theory. His "ordeal," to use a term Meredith often employed, consists in serial negotiations with figures of authority who can validate his "theories" and also recognize their marginal—or subversive—status. However, Stephen's esthetic theory (understood as a theory of the apprehension of the beautiful) has constantly to be detached from the process of sublimation that produces it. This is why it is crucial for Stephen to refuse to follow the President of the University on his field when the latter attempts to push the discussion of Beauty into a discussion of the Sublime. They are discussing Aquinas's *pulchra sunt quae visa placent,* when the President remarks:

---

[19] See Roland McHugh, *The Sigla of Finnegans Wake* (London: Arnold, 1976).

—But he means the sublime—that which leads man upwards.
—His remark would apply to a Dutch painter's representation of a plate of onions.
—No, no; that which pleases the soul in a state of sanctification, the soul seeking its spiritual good.
—Aquinas's definition of the good is an unsafe basis of operations; it is very wide. He seems to me almost ironical in his treatment of the "appetites." (*SH*, 95)

After all, one doesn't see why a Dutch still life representing onions on a plate could not be called "sublime" or why a plate of onions could not help the soul turn upward in the hope of sanctification. However, Stephen's deft rhetorical move forces the President to leave esthetics and enter into ethics, which proves to be his mistake; the president has then to identify the Sublime with saintliness before adding lamely, in an ironical foreshadowing of one of Ezra Pound's later mottoes: "The cult of beauty is difficult" (*SH*, 96), by which he probably hopes to induce Stephen to confess an impenitent estheticism. Indeed, "difficulty," which is not so distant from the "arduous good" the young esthete was searching after, is a weakened form of sublime, but the saintliness the President has in mind is quite at odds with that Stephen or Joyce see as their goal.

At that juncture, Stephen is eager to avoid any subjective reduction of his theory to its position of enunciation: "My conviction has led me nowhere: my theory states itself" (*SH*, 96) This announces the attitude one sees him taking at the end of his Shakespeare discussion in "Scylla and Charybdis" when he admits that he does not believe in his own theory. It is clearly a "sublime" moment when the author of his theory can renounce the paternity of the discourse, cutting as it were the umbilical cord linking the words to their enunciator, turning away like a saint who wishes to have no truce with earthly goods.

Later in the book, when Stephen argues about the beautiful and the good" (*SH*, 170) with a more amenable interlocutor, Father Artifoni, he has bridged the gap between art and nature, on the one hand, and between the good and the beautiful, on the other hand, by a systematic reference to "process." This process could be called a process of "sublimation": "To talk about the perfection of one's art was not for him to talk about something agreed upon as sublime but in reality no more than a sublime convention but rather to talk about a veritably sublime process of one's nature which had a right to examination and open discussion" (*SH*, 171). The next paragraph states the stakes implied by this qualification: "It was exactly this vivid interest which kept him away from such places of uncomely dalliance as the debating society and the warmly cushioned sodality" (*SH*, 171). If we agree to see in Stephen's fascination for the theory of Beauty the consequence of a "sublime process," it is clear that he is constantly going to be precipitated from the sublime to the ridiculous (as *Finnegans Wake* also states in a revealing parenthesis at 445.27).

What prevents a systematic moving back and fro between moments of sublimation and moments of debunking (a strategy that is fully developed in *A Portrait of the Artist as a Young Man)* is that the text of *Stephen Hero* is open in its middle, and holds precisely by the hole of the Real gaping in its center. It is not a coincidence that a long manuscript beginning and ending with unfinished sentences—at least in the current edition, with the additional pages concluded by "but when he was a few paces" (*SH*, 253) while it jumpstarts with "anyone spoke to him mingled a too polite disbelief with its expectancy (*SH*, 23, beginning of chapter 15) —should be punctured roughly in its middle by the recycling of one of the most painful and cruel epiphanies: the question of an helpless mother asking Stephen whether he can give any advice about the suspicious liquid oozing away from Isabel's (Georgie's in real life) stomach. In spite of the minimal reworking of what was epiphany 19 (Joyce adds in *Stephen Hero* "a voice of a terrified human being" and "like the voice of a messenger in a play"), the sheer horror betrayed by the question limns a limit of language and leads the reader to an unnamable zone, the Lacanian Thing as offering us a glimpse of the Real.

But in fact, what can the "hole ... the hole we all have ... here" (*SH*, 163) refer to? This riddle, after all, seems to be harder to crack than even that of "the word known to all men." If most readers see it as pointing to the navel, some also insist upon seeing it as the anus, in which case "the hole in Isabel's... stomach" would be a distortion attributable to a desire to be polite, a little like the ellipsis in the aunt's question: "Did he ... peacefully?" in "The Sisters." Thus the motto of "Do you know anything about the body?" will insist and disturb, which is why it echoes in *Ulysses* from Buck Mulligan's medical knowledge of how a "dogsbody" can die and rot to Leopold Bloom's curiosity for everything that concerns body orifices. Lacan's Real is called for at the crucial point where gnomonic negativity and epiphanic elision meet. This convergence forges a *deixis* that cannot show, that does not "present" but merely point to the unpresentable or the unspeakable.

This crux is not merely the locus of death and putrefaction, it also leads us by another way to the ineffable *jouissance* that letters and literature attempt to circumscribe. Lacanian metapsychology and Joycean "theoretic" drift merge when they meet a limit, a border—this encounter with the limit could be called, as Wittgenstein once said, the realm of ethics, or the pure function of silence in theory—in a movement that is not too far from what classical esthetics used to call the discourse of sublimity. Joyce's concept of the sublime in *Finnegans Wake* would thus appear very close to what Burke calls a "natural sublime" marked by "difficulty." As Burke noted in his *Philosophical Enquiry into the Origin of our Ideas of the Sublime and the Beautiful*, "Another source of greatness is *Difficulty*. When any work seems to have required immense force and labour to erect it, the idea is grand. Stonehenge, neither for disposition nor ornament, has any thing admirable; but those huge rude masses of stone, set on end, and piled each on other, turn the mind on the immense force necessary for such a work. Nay the rudeness of the work increases this cause of grandeur, as it excludes the idea of art, and contrivance...."[20] Can one say that Joyce attempts to "exclude the idea of art and contrivance" in his new idiom? I would like to suggest that the obvious difficulty of his new work was if not produced, at least enhanced, by an attempt to solve the esthetic paradoxes I have sketched.

3. Theoretic sublimation and the subliminal "language of Night"

Colleen Jaurretche has given us a good idea of how Joyce's language is haunted by its own margins and limits.[21] Her title, *"The Sensual Philosophy,"* suggests that Joyce's negative theology or apophatic mysticism should not be understood as an individual variation or aberration on traditional religion, but as a discourse that addresses all the senses via eroticism, love and desire, and this discourse can be apprehended as the logical consequence of a general esthetic system. Out of the tradition of mystical theology Joyce was tapping from in his Dublin years, out of his interest in occultism and theosophy, his fascination for Blake's visionary powers, his study of Dionysius the pseudo-Aeropagite, we gather a unique and original philosophy of "limit stages" climaxing into an esthetic of negativity. Moreover, this diffuse and vague tradition is presented by Joyce as typically "Irish." Thus, Dionysius, who is quoted in "Ireland, Island of Saints and Sages," is just one among the relatively uncanonical influences who define a tradition of Irish mysticism and link Joyce's "sensual philosophy" with the paradoxical discourse of absence and unknowing.

Joyce found in the *Cloud of Unknowing* and above all in John of the Cross's *Dark Night of the Soul* apt images materializing the almost ineffable process of "forgetting" that leads to a mystical fusion with God. Such a union is not devoid of sexual overtones, as any reader of John of the Cross will

---

[20] Edmund Burke, *A Philosophical Enquiry into the Origin of Our Ideas of the Sublime and the Beautiful* (Oxford: Oxford University Press, 1990), 71.

[21] Colleen Jaurretche, *"The Sensual Philosophy": Joyce and the Aesthetics of Mysticism* (Madison: University of Wisconsin Press, 1997).

know. *The Dark Night* is an erotic poem, and like most mystical writers he puts forward the "pleasure of nothing," the sensual dissolution of the self when it meets with an ineffable divine lover. Joyce's critical writings are also bathed in the light of mystical theology, which links him with a specifically Irish tradition as we saw. In the Wake, Joyce's decision to confront and explore the Night as such shows how negative theology turns into sensuality if not lewdness when Shawn-John faces an enamored and enraptured Issy.

I would also like to stress the role of the cultural context provided by Jolas and the *transition* group of writers who, starting in 1927 and with increasing force in the thirties, stressed the affinities between Joyce's *Work in Progress* and what they called "the language of night". Jolas had started reading Saint John of the Cross early and quite independently of Joyce, and this reading nourished his fascination for all sorts of mystical and paradoxical discourses. In *transition* n° 23 (1935), an issue partly devoted to "James Joyce and his new work," Jolas typically sketches what he calls "a Little Mantic Almageste" in which he lists Blake, Boehme, Madame Guyon and St. John of the Cross among others mystics as the forerunners of the new language of myth and the unconscious developed by the group of experimental writers and artists he is promoting—Joyce representing of course the culmination of such a process in his eyes. The language of the Night confronts the inexpressible: it attempts to posit esthetic discourse in the place once occupied by negative theology. While Rimbaud's "impossible" seemed to mark an unpassable frontier that lyricism could not breach, here language justifies its activity when living up to the task of extending and subverting the usual communicational model.

While pursuing the negative way, Joyce's last book attempts to provide a solution to the four paradoxes of esthetics I have sketched earlier. The first level consisted of the distinction between *aesthesis* as sensual perception and esthetics as a discourse regulating the conditions requested for the production or perception of the beautiful and sublime. This gap is bridged as soon as the reader's perceptions of any word, sentence or paragraph in the book is always suspended between contradictory or undecidable levels of sense. Something is indeed perceived, if vaguely only, but the hesitation that adheres to what would normally be restricted by univocal linguistic functions pushes the reading to the level of the meta-discourse of esthetics as well. Thus any word, sentence, or bit of narrative in *Finnegans Wake* will not only carry several meanings but will always refer to the book itself and its various insights into beauty, and also into the sublime and the ridiculous. Such self-reference does not inevitably provide the more important level of meaning but will often create reflexive potentialities of allegorization.

Among the four paradoxes already posited, theory as social authentication was seen to be conflicting with the individual act of mystic contemplation. As we saw, Joyce's esthetic individualism led him to assume more and more radically the role of the Saint, that is someone who dares to confront the unspeakable Other and become a cultural or collective "Sinthome." Joyce wishes in the end to embody the spirit of a collective ego, to be one with or to "atone", as Stephen would say, with the ethical substance that Hegel called *Sittlichkeit*. This ethical substance is not, in Joyce's case, limited to Ireland and to its divided community, it includes the whole of Europe and tries to reach forward into the linguistic domains of Africa, Asia, Australia and America. As he hoped, individual artistic toil might redeem and perhaps heal the diseases of the collective spirit such as xenophobic nationalism, fascism, and religious bigotry. The new language should in the end create a different reading practice strong enough to subvert the reactionary values that still adhere to any *Sittlichkeit*. Such a movement, with its ethical and political drift, cannot just be comprehended by the purely esthetic categories of the Sublime and the Beautiful. As Eagleton and Verstraete have shown in totally opposite ways,[22] the *Wake* debunks these categories by constantly sublimating and desublimating itself.

The last opposition between the Sublime and the Beautiful is overcome by the "subliminal" provided we agree to see it as a locus of infra-discursive linguistic production: the subliminal is reinforced by sublimation as a process of transformation from the individual to the collective. The subliminal defines the domain of the language of the Night proper while sublimation stresses its social disseminations in a Babelic idiom. In a crucial episode of III, 3, sleeping Yawn replies to the Four analysts by moving from "Yes" to "No." Between the two assertions, the voice shifts from one speaker to another so as to attribute the negation to the "other" embodied by the brother: "—Oyessoyess! I never dramped of prebeing a postman but I mean in ostralian someplace, mults deeply belubdead; my allaboy brother, Negoist Cabler, of this city, whom 'tis better ne'er to name, my said brother, the skipgod, expulled for looking at churches from behind, who is sender of the Hullo Eve Cenograph in prose and worse every Allso's night. High Brazil Brandan's Deferred, midden Erse clare language, Noughtnoughtnought nein. Assass" (*FW*, 488.19-26). The dialectization of the contraries is subsumed by the oppositional logic that stylizes Shem and Shaun as the fighting brothers. Both have recognizable features and voices, but whereas Shaun is

---

[22] See Terry Eagleton, *The Ideology of the Aesthetic* (Oxford: Blackwell, 1990) and Verstraete, *Fragments of the Feminine Sublime in Friedrich Schlegel and James Joyce*, 190-193.

characterized by an oscillation between the Sublime and the Ridiculous, Shem's writerly capacities are attributable to the process of sublimation already mentioned: "...this Esuan Menschavik and the first till last alshemist wrote over every square inch of the only foolscap available, his own body, till by its corrosive sublimation one continuous present tense integument slowly unfolded all the marryvoising moodmoulded cyclewheeling history..." (*FW*, 185.34-186.2) This goes beyond a simple admission of the autobiographical nature of the book, since Shem, who allegorizes the process of creation by the means of his specific writing, also quotes here Gertrude Stein's idea of writing as a "continuous present."

The fourth paradox I examined revolved around the issue of the theoretic versus theoretical. In his last years, Joyce, heartbroken by his daughter's private tragedy, seems to testify to a deep familiarity with the spirit of utter nothingness. This is why he expressed this despair when writing to his son Giorgio, at the age of fifty-three: "My eyes are tired. For over half a century, they have gazed into nullity where they have found a lovely nothing."[23] One might be tempted to stress the irony of the adjective "lovely"—with innuendoes of the "beautiful" and of the "meaningless." The tone of this passage is very close to that of Mallarmé's last letters, especially when the French poet stresses the proximity of Beauty and Nothingness. The "Nothing" Joyce admits of having gazed at for too long could also be called "God", or the Hegelian "absolute master," Death. While it points to the hollowing of Presence that can be ascribed to negativity, there is in this Nothing an irreducible and undialectizable element, a tragic factor that underpins the "writing of the disaster", to quote Blanchot.[24] But it pertains to the theoretic vigilance of the "theo-heretic"—a godlike heretic, as it were—to dare contemplate this negativity without flinching: only then can the theoheretic receive praise meet for Saint or Sage: "Nought is nulled. *Fuifiat!* // Lo, the laud of laurens now orielising benedictively when saint and sage have said their say" (*FW*, 613.14-16).

University of Pennsylvania

---

[23] *Letters III*, 361. The Italian original has: "Ho gli occhi stanchi. Da più di mezzo secolo scrutano nel nulla dove hanno trovato un bellissimo niente" (*Letters III*, 359).

[24] See Maurice Blanchot, *The Writing of the Disaster*, trans. Ann Smock (Lincoln: University of Nebraska Press, 1986).

THE JOYCE OF IMPOSSIBILITIES

FRITZ SENN

> impassible abjects (*FW*, 340.5)

The following sketch tries to outline a dilemma we have with Joyce's works, perhaps without always being aware of it. It focuses on our interactions with Joyce and how essentially necessary and at the same time impossible they are. As always, this holds true of every writer, but much more poignantly in Joyce who incites so much enthralling endeavour and ultimately frustrates it. Some of those futile and all too obvious endeavours will be listed below. To put it all more positively, they testify to the indomitable vitality of Joyce's works in progress.

I begin with the truism that final, clinching assertions are always risky, but even more so in Joyce. Apart from biographical facts, assuming there are such, it appears next to impossible to make a valid, unqualified, abstract statement with "Joyce" as its subject that would be both true and meaningful. Sentences of the sort that "Joyce arrived in Trieste in October 1904 and afterwards taught English at various schools" are probably correct, but to claim that on 16th June 1904 Joyce and Nora first went out together, which has the same appearance, is already more doubtful and conjectural (and scantily documented). But try to verify or falsify assertions like:

> Joyce ... tries to find a way to represent something ideal, permanent, and absolute in writing.[1] ... both Joyce and Freud unceremoniously reject the notion of autonomous subjectivity, ... both Joyce and Freud indicate a mental "liberation" that their works properly should provide their readers ... *Ulysses* insists that we imaginatively move as fully as possible into those historical myths.[2]

---

[1] Stephen Sicari, *Joyce's Modernist Allegory* (Columbia: University of South Carolina Press, 2001), 2.
[2] Brian W. Shaffer, "Teaching Freud through 'Nausicaa'," in *Pedagogy, Praxis, Ulysses,* ed. Robert Newman (Ann Arbor: University of Michigan Press,

It is not that such statements lack validity. In fact, we hardly can avoid them ("Joyce is a humorous writer, a realist, a political writer, a non-political writer, a leg-puller," etc.). It is the air of exclusiveness that puts them out of court. If they were rephrased in a form like: "In my thesis I emphasize the following significant (maybe predominant, or pivotal, or underestimated) aspect ...," then they would make a good deal more sense. The same may be true of critical summaries or axiomatic nutshells: "Joyce's Leopold Bloom is looking for a reunion with his past and the son he has lost."[3] As long as we take them with their implied grain of salt they are harmless, but some indeed strive to achieve quintessential truths.

The first thing we read in Richard Ellmann's preface to the Gabler *Ulysses* of 1986 is a flat "Joyce's theme in *Ulysses* was simple." I always feared that a student would challenge me to explain what that simple theme was. I am equally puzzled by "The sacred is at the heart of Joyce's writing experience,"[4] something I never experienced and which, therefore, if it is that central a notion, would disqualify me as a reader.

Paradoxically, the opposite of any valid statement is often just as true. Joyce may be the most Irish of all writers, but he is also the least Irish and can be appreciated with almost no knowledge of Ireland.

"the rarefied air of the academy" (*U*, 9.107)

As we all know, Joyce is a godsend for the academy, the source for countless books, essays, dissertations, not to mention conferences and promotions. Academics tend to assume they are in intellectual possession of Joyce. To his glory, though he keeps professors busy for those proverbial centuries yet to come, at the same time he remains out of academic domestication and does not fit into any curriculum. Paradoxically, Joyce cannot be bypassed within the area of English Literature, nor adequately be accommodated within it.

In practice it is even hard to allow enough time for his works. Even the luxury of one whole academic unit, say one generous full semester, will not suffice to absorb *Ulysses*, but it is done in much less (which often on top of it includes history, biography, religion, classics, psychology, popular

---

1996), 3.

[3] Peter I. Barta, *Bely, Joyce, and Döblin: Peripatetics in the City Novel* (Gainsville: University of Florida Press, 1996), 17.

[4] Beryl Schlossman, *Joyce's Catholic Comedy of Language* (Madison: University of Wisconsin Press, 1985), ix.

culture, etc, plus the theory *en vogue*). And of course all contextual frames (Irish literature, the epic, commodity, colonialism, psychoanalysis) are self-fulfilling: we will find what we are expected to find.

A habitual easy way out— to select one of two representative works, as at a pinch we may do in the case of most other writers— is not applicable. *A Portrait of the Artist as a Young Man* might qualify best, and often it may be Joyce's only prose work which readers may feel confident to tackle on their own, or in class. But for all its novel departures it would not allow anyone to extrapolate what was yet in store. Each one of the major works is discordantly *sui generi*. The coherent but dynamic evolution from *Chamber Music* to *Finnegans Wake* can be discovered in retrospect only. It could never have been predicted, even by the author himself, whose works took on a life of their own in the workshop. They energetically transgressed their original conception. I called this rapid expansive and devious evolution Joyce's "provection." The works did not keep still in Joyce's hands nor do they ever for us as we interact with them.

"categorically unimperatived" (*FW*, 176.25)

Stephen Dedalus's lyrical, epical, and dramatic forms in *A Portrait* notwithstanding, it is hard to imagine that Joyce would have greatly cared about genre and other distinctions. Creativity does not fall into neat patterns, but scholars need them. Joyce appears to have used most literary genres and hardly left any one untouched. His first (non-) publishers and editors bear witness to the shocking novelty of *Dubliners*, whose legal consequences they were not ready to face. The stories focused on specific details, even actual shops, and they seemed to consist of random slices of ordinary life and at times lacked closure. *A Portrait of the Artist as a Young Man* is a novel within the tradition of the *Bildungsroman*, but, as Edward Garnett found out in its reader's report, does not quite conform to anything known before. Its formal metamorphoses or excrescences, like a long sermon on Hell or a lecture on aesthetics or, for that matter, a shift into diary form do not resemble any prior *Bildungsroman* technique. For this reason, it was considered to lack form and coherence; its Daedalian engineering, so striking now, was not yet visible on the surface. Attempts to classify *Ulysses*, which after all began as a potential addition to *Dubliners*, are bound to fail. As a long prose story it resembles a novel, though that hardly circumscribes its scope and peculiarities; it is based on an epic, and has become one. It amounts to a sociological account of a certain place at a given period. It imitates plays, newspapers, the catechism; it breaks into lyricism and is awarded the attention that normally would only be devoted to poetry. A casual glance at the layout of some episodes alone shows an uneven texture. Our eyes alone can tell Circe from Eumaeus, or Ithaca from Penelope. Shapes, mood, and perspective develop with increasing intensity. Sticking a label on such a Protean conglomerate is our problem, not the author's, whose trademark was transgressing boundaries—and, thereby, losing support and readers. *Finnegans Wake* probably remains the most universal misfit in all literature. It refuses to conform at all. "*Finnegans Wake* is ..." would have to be followed by a list in which each single item would also have to be negated.

"grave approach and painful" (*U*,11.1007)

All our approaches are a matter of preferences or foregrounding. Potentially each method is positive, but none is essentially superior. One may dip into the texts without preparation at all, a normal starting point. Conversely, some framework may be provided beforehand, such as a mere course description. As indicated above, there is no first premise; what particular context is to be provided remains a matter of subjective priorities: Modernism, biography, Irish history/politics, Catholicism, Dublin topography, Irish, English, European, Western literature, psychology, music, Jewishness, mythology, narrative angles, styles, and so forth. The naïve assumption is that in even a short overview of, say, European history of the last three centuries, the French Revolution simply cannot be left out, or the law of gravity in physics, but in dealing with Joyce is there anything corresponding that absolutely *must* be touched?

Introductions and prefaces serve as guideposts to the reading ahead. Constructive as they may be, they tend to precondition what readers pay attention to and find. Even under ideal circumstances guides, instructors, tutors impose set-up frameworks. Emphasis often depends on current fashions. In recent years Irish history, postcolonially packaged, has become increasingly significant, and so have politics, authority, popular culture, body, gender, desire—all excellent starting points. At the other end of the scale it also makes sense to maintain that familiarity with Dublin places or customs is required to "understand" *Ulysses*, or that at least maps or documents have to be substituted. In practice there are numerous fairly competent readers who have never been exposed to the city and have only a vague notion of a particular nation's history. If a grounding of, say, the *Odyssey* or patristic theology were imperative, there would be an increasingly small audience of *Ulysses*. A walk along Bloom's route in Lotuseaters can be beneficially instructive, yet our appreciation of the book does not—*must* not—depend on such experiences (especially now that Hely's and Switzers have gone the way of all shops). We all move from the accidentally known into the more and more familiar, in Joyce's case into arts that had not yet been devised: "*ignotas ... in artes*" as Ovid and the *Portrait* have it.

Joyce works are being absorbed and, in part, enjoyed by readers with little idea what, or even where, Ireland is. Not knowing Homer or Bakhtin, they may still appreciate its humanity, its fun, or underlying sadness, its sheer verbal exuberance. Scholars who write, for example, in *European Joyce Studies*, approach Joyce more systematically and from their expertise throw light on particular aspects, though that light is not always illuminative. Frequently a trendy and necessary impetus is trumped up as a shatteringly new insight. The point here merely is that most of our priorities need not be inherent in the works. For a long time I myself thought that only readers with a certain sensitivity to its language could tune into Joyce's works. I was human, erring and wrong: to judge from many publications, one can and does get along fairly well without even noticing Joyce's language.

To take an example: how is the Wandering Rocks chapter actually read, not by scholars but by the average uninformed reader of fiction? A first impression is likely to be a blur, a teeming conglomerate of streets, vehicles, shops, and people. That no doubt is part of the intended impact, a modern labyrinth. For Dublin readers the experience is entirely different; most sites are familiar (though changed). Even so, 7 Eccles Street, Nighttown, Crampton Court, Lafayette's have gone the way of most ruins, and a place-name like "Temple bar" would have meant something entirely different to inhabitants of Dublin in 1900 than to those of the seventies when the area was in dreary dilapidation; meanwhile it has acquired an entirely different tone with all the gaudy refurbishing and fashionable restaurants.

Plain fares and city tours are generally not included in the price of a book. Did Joyce expect us foreigners to use maps? Did he foresee a hunt for maps of 1900 with the old street names and tram routes? Should we use old photographs or orient ourselves by the *Topographical Guide* or the useful books that have been provided by Dublin Joyceans? An interesting alternative procedure has been detailed in Kathleen McCormick's *Ulysses, "Wandering Rocks," and the Reader*, where a class was invited to read the chapter in the light of Roland Barthes's *The Pleasure of the Text*,[5] and, sure enough, the students' papers were bristling with "pleasure" and "*jouissance*."

According to what we start from and what efforts we may take, the reading will be determined. No single context, including the one imbued by local familiarity, is intrinsically superior to any other.

---

[5] Kathleen McCormick, *Ulysses, "Wandering Rocks," and the Reader: Multiple Pleasures in Reading* (Lewiston: Edwin Mellen Press, 1991).

How Best to Read?

What do we do in front of an open book? First of all a (voluntary) reading of one's own, based on free choice, is distinct from an assignment, say in class, under the shadow of a grading system and the impetus to produce something pertinent or even original within too short a time. Joyce generally slows us down. In a case like *Ulysses* very few readers curl up with it and finish in the small hours of next morning. A major difference is the time to be devoted to a reading. Individuals may grant themselves enough of it, institutions with schedules cannot. So how much time is appropriate? Autonomous, leisurely groups are less pressed for time (in Zurich, for example, a close weekly reading takes about three and a half years); but no matter how compressed or extended the period devoted to *Ulysses* is, every type of reading is essentially inept, is *"contretemps"* (*U*, 16.1880). Speed makes us skip over the surface, while innocent readings with close attention to every trifle tend to lose sight of the whole. Inspecting trees, or even leaves, we become unable to see the forest. "Do you hear what I'm seeing?" as the *Wake* puts it (*FW*, 193.10). As our eyes follow the lines of text they naturally miss a lot that an acute ear could pick up, so one of the best-circulated stereotypical half-truths is that we must read Joyce aloud, or hear the works read out aloud to us. And a great thrill it can be, especially if the voices have the appropriate Irish timbre. Yet neither reading, optical or acoustic, is remotely complete. When we listen to someone reading a text, even under optimal histrionic conditions, we can only absorb what the one reciting puts in, emphases and all. Inevitably we get a streamlined version, with ambiguities often ironed out, reduced to one particular understanding or set of priorities. In silent reading we curtail the text ourselves, within the limits of our minds. We cannot know what we don't know.

Each type of reading misses out. The eye can detect what the voice cannot utter: how does one vocalize "HOUSE OF KEY(E)S" (*U*, 7.141). Is *"voglio"* (*U*, 4.328) to be pronounced in correct Italian (yes, if Bloom knows how) or by Anglo-Saxon trial and error (if he does not)? Since he thinks of asking Nannetti in the newspaper office(*U*, 7.152) it appears he does not know himself, but if so, what incorrect English articulation is appropriate? What phonetic quality is one to give to a cannibal chief's wives who are imagined "in a row to watch the effect" (*U*, 8.747)? Are the wives neatly lined up in a row (like "blow"), or are they jostling to get close (like "now")? The same dichotomy applies to "language of flow" (*U*, 11.298); "flow" clearly is a clipped form of "flower", but the "flow of language" (as at *U*, 8.65) is a subsidiary (or dominant?) theme.[6] Vocal enunciation does not allow such options: "thought through my eyes" (*U*, 31) is more capable of processing them. A reading voice may distinguish phrases in italics, but cannot utter capitalisation or alternative type (as in the Aeolian headings). A sequence like three question marks, "???" (*U*, 7.512), can only be reported, not voiced. And how do we vocally convey the empty space in Ithaca or, above all, the particular size of a final dot? Incidentally, where should the stress fall in "Ulysses," on the first or the second syllable? The eye does not care.

On the other hand we may never hear that some inconspicuous passages are also songs with a melody. For what it is worth, a common phrase like "would you be surprised to learn ..." (*U*, 16.1120) happens to be an echo of a comic Victorian music hall song, "Would You Be Surprised to Hear ...",[7] which in turn was based on a phrase frequently used in the famous Tichborne claimant case (see *U*, 16.1343).Surely not even the best trained acting voice could bring all *this* out, but it could at least convey that the wording departs from plain prose.

All of this is not to say (which is why it is said here) there is anything "wrong" in all possible readings, just that none of them can ever be entirely "right". The not very spectacular point is merely that every type of reading procedure falls short. When Joyce referred to his "usylessly unreadable Blue Book of Eccles" (*FW*, 179.26) it was not *all* ironic fencing. Ironically the one episode that takes place in a library, Scylla and Charybdis of *Ulysses*, almost demonstrates its own factual unreadability. As conscientious or scholarly readers who want to "understand" or at least to unravel some implications, we tend to leave no obvious avenue unexplored. Assuming for the moment that we have all Shakespeare at our erudite fingertips, after only a few lines we would be sidetracked to Goethe's *Wilhelm Meister*, a sizeable novel, to be followed by *Paradise Lost*, the *Divina Comedia* (in the original Italian), *The Sorrows of Satan*, Blake, Yeats, Swinburne, most of the Irish Literary Revival, quite apart from Plato, Aristotle, Thomas Aquinas, Swedenborg, Wilde, Mallarmé and Blavatsky, and many more (Homer is taken for granted). It would also help to assimilate these works in the light of contemporary (or, even more chancy, of Joyce's own probable) understanding. Many of us have been conditioned to apply a Tip of the Iceberg Principle. Any intertextual clue can be followed up and generally produces additional resonances. The snatch of a song may lead to themes of paternity, betrayal, or reconciliation. So many

---

[6] Not to forget echoes like "Tenors get women by the score. Increase their flow. Throw flower at his feet" (*U*, 11.686).

[7] Christopher Pulling, *They Were Singing* (London: Harrap & Co., 1952), 185.

authors are embedded in the chapter that we could not remotely do all the requisite homework. Reading, or writing about, this particular episode is of necessity a largely arbitrary compromise. Even if we could absorb all this background, potentially the whole Western tradition, only a deposit of disjointed fragments would emerge and clarification would not emerge automatically; on the contrary the confusion expand almost exponentially. And yet, interpretations of the chapter often use selected titbits as insightful leverage. In general we brilliantly cheat our way through a profusion of hints. The buffet contains more *à la carte* than we could ever manage in a series of banquets.

Narrative Labeling

Homer had the head start on his theorists: He did not have to worry about delimitations or classifications (prosody probably was another matter). Nor, possibly, did Joyce worry greatly about distinctions that we, his discerning readers, believe we are forced to make. Whether something is interior monologue, stream of consciousness, the product of a narrator (even, heaven forbid, an "omniscient" narrator!), arranger or related agency, Uncle Charles principle, free indirect style, or whatever else, remains our problem, a self-imposed one. No narratological system seems to do justice to Joyce's stylistic polytropy; such systems mainly tend to justify themselves, and the texts had better comply and are forced into Procrustean beds. We cannot neatly separate interior monologue from descriptive passages, at times it is not certain if a phrase is spoken or merely thought. Where exactly, in those long passages in Eumaeus, does Bloom actually say aloud what we read on the page? Debates on what is parody or pastiche or satire, travesty or burlesque can go on incessantly. Joyce seems to invite us to play the futile game of defining literature and reality. What exactly, for example, "is" something like this interpolation in Cyclops:

> They believe in rod, the scourger almighty, creator of hell upon earth, and in Jacky Tar, the son of a gun, who was conceived of unholy boast, born of the fighting navy, suffered under rump and dozen, was scarified, flayed and curried, yelled like bloody hell, the third day he arose again from the bed, steered into haven, sitteth on his beamend till further orders whence he shall come to drudge for a living and be paid. (*U*, 12.1354)

It reassembles fragments from the previous conversation about the British Navy, sums up a supposedly British attitude, and puts it all in the framework of the Creed. A parody, no doubt, or whatever term is suitable, but of what? A kind of creed of what British imperialism is in the view of an Irish nationalist? The passage does not throw the usual sidelight on the main action (as most other interpolations seem to do); it looks like a fairly unique creative, playful expansion. Its complexity prefigures *Finnegans Wake*. Its whatness is likely to elude us, and everyone will find something missing in the futile attempt that has just been paraded.

What is the triple "Deshil Holles Eamus" which introduces Oxen of the Sun? An invocation, we can say, based on a Latin *Carmen arvale*, and on general threefold repetitions of holy formulas. A self-reflexive touch may be at work. But who, if anyone, is doing the invoking, and to whom? No one seems to say it or think of it; a different narrative agency seems to be responsible, and labeling it would not clarify anything. How does the ritual phrase fit the temporal sequence? We can play with the numbers: 3 x 3 also echoes the end of Nausicaa (9 "Cuckoo"s), and this in turn suggests the months of pregnancy. The three main ingredients—Irish, Anglo-Saxon, Latin—are those of English as spoken in Ireland. Is this geographical direction toward Holles Street in the south, even though Bloom arrives *from* the south? Such shots in the dark are a fascinating game and all very well, but the basic question is not answered (and possibly need not be raised in the first place). Of course there are always those who do know and freely tell us with the voice of authority: their own authority.

"Quote the textual terms" (*U*, 17.1824)

In view of the extraordinary amount of attention devoted to every iota within the texts, it would be reassuring to have those texts themselves as a firm basis for all our speculations. Few scholars are *unconditionally* satisfied with the 1922 Paris edition, the subsequent Random House or Bodley Head versions, the *Synoptic and Critical Edition* by Hans Walter Gabler of 1984 (from which "The Corrected Text" emerged, which has become the standard), the Reader's Edition by Danis Rose of 1997—or the expected and non-existent solution augured by John Kidd. The discovery of new draft material may throw light on some issues but is likely to muddy some others even more. The squabbles of recent years, elevated to "Joyce Wars," have probably shattered the illusion that a generally accepted text is possible. The editors themselves, each with diverging notions, are not at fault. It still remains a matter of judgment whether Buck Mulligan "called out" or "called up coarsely" (*U*, 1.6) or if the cryptic intrusion of French, "thievery alors (Bandez!) Figne toi trop" (*U*, 16.1453) should have been retrieved from its anchorage in a Rosenbach manuscript. Because of Joyce's erratic procedure, the lack of documents, conflicting premises and editorial methods, inevitably, a bit of quicksand remains in the foundation of our critical edifices.

For all we can imagine, the case of *Finnegans Wake* may be much worse since an optically handicapped writer's inconsistencies were compounded by transitional errors. For years Danis Rose has been working on a text that comes significantly closer to what Joyce may have had in mind. Because of copyright restrictions this chancy and intrinsically controversial endeavour may never become a reality. Even without the genetic descent that Rose would provide, there is a sense that in the *Wake* we often tread on treacherous textual ground. An erroneous letter can have far-reaching consequences: from accidental probes we know that Joyce did not write "basidens" (as in "basidens, ardree, kongsemma, rexregulorum" [*FW*, 133.36]), or "madhowiatrees" (*FW*, 259.6), but actually put down "basileus" (without any Latin tooth) and "madhowlatrees": the letter "l" lost part of its stem and came to look like an "i," so there is no healing there, as in "psychiatry," and the word is much closer to a (probably intended) mad howling and "idolatries."

"The plot thickens" (*U*, 9.862)

Literary reference works often require summaries for lexica or reference works; these summaries are makeshift at best, inadequate in any case, and in Joyce's case outrageously so. This is not to belittle such handy props as Blamire's *Bloomsday Book*, or the old *Skeleton Key to Finnegans Wake*, or its *Plot Summary*. Joyce is not quite characterized by the action he depicts. Some of the *Dubliners* stories consist of little more than a day's wanderings or an evening out. Take "The Sisters": is it about a priest who died, or is it about a boy whose reactions to the priest we read—memories remembered much later? It features conversations at home, a dream, a look at the house of the dead, a visit to the dead man's house, a visit to his sisters; it is about a twisted biography in which vocation, doubts, a mysterious accident, disease, unpriestly cravings, possibly madness all may play their part. It also has no ending, but just fades out.

Ulysses is even less amenable to reduction. What happens in "Sirens"? A few men pass their time in various rooms of a hotel where the following occurs: gossip, flirting, eating, singing, and traveling to an assignation—not much to write home about, considering the outrageous uniqueness of the episode which made a stout adherent like Ezra Pound exclaim in ironic protest: "The last chapter: a woman ruminating and a short trip to the chamber pot – big deal!" Ithaca contains many summaries, and pedantic ones at that, of *Ulysses* itself, like the recapitulation of Bloom's adventures during the past day and present night: "The preparation of breakfast ...,intestinal congestion ..., nocturnal perambulation ..." (*U*, 17.2042–58). In itself it would give little idea of what happens, some important themes (like Boylan's off-scene doings) are left out. It is as though Joyce wanted to parody our attempt to reduce experience to some quintessence. The "gist of the pantomime" (*FW*, 599.36) —and pantomime is here taken in the sense of miming everything, which Joyce strives toward—is chasing chimeras. Coincidentally, it serves my illustrative purpose that the word "gist" drives from a Latin-French verb that originally meant to lie (books on etymology, like Skeat, agree on this). Summaries, synopses, abstracts all lie, as do all reports, another thing Joyce almost teaches.

For *Finnegans Wake* we hardly even ask the question, knowing that no answer is remotely adequate. Without any disrespect to tutorials, hardly a reader would imagine that *Finnegans Wake* could be as lackluster as mere outlines suggest. True, a plot summary of *Othello* would miss a lot too, but at least it might give some idea, enough perhaps to extrapolate it into an opera or a movie.

"annotations" (*U*, 17.1381)

No single reader knows everything worth knowing, say the local meaning of "curate", "exhibition" or, less obvious, of "bothered" (in the sense of "deaf"); Sabellius, Lentulus, or "*Bous Stephanoumenos*" are not common knowledge. So props are called for—glosses, annotation, something indispensable, useful and eminently problematical. Joyce stands firmly in a long line of commentaries; he supplied some of his own, in his conversation or his letters, above all the "schemas" for *Ulysses*.

Annotation is necessary and intrinsically misleading. Inevitably we have either not enough of it or too much. There is no right way. First of all, what needs or deserves a gloss? Historical names, places, allusions, obsolete phrases? What is possibly relevant rather than burdensome? How much information should be given at each point, and where, on a first occurrence or later on? Notes have to be concise; they have a terminal, clinching air about them and so are the very opposite of what every Joycean passage provokes. Notes pretend to be answers when they ought to lead to new inquiries; they put a full stop where there ought to be (but cannot possibly be) ellipses. When do notes become interpretation, by forcing a view on innocent readers? One note in Gifford attached to Mulligan's "yellow dressinggown," only a few lines into *Ulysses*, imposes the symbolic meaning of "yellow" as jealousy. Fair enough—such notes are potentially helpful, but possibly premature, maybe exaggerating in a particular direction by implanting the notion that every color must have instant, almost mechanical, significance. How, and at which point, should "home rule" be glossed, ushering in, as it does, decades of Irish History which no note can provide?

"Deaf beetle he is" thinks Bloom of Pat, waiter in the Ormond hotel (*U*, 11.911). This is glossed as "beetle ... is slang for blockhead" (Gifford). Fair enough perhaps, though not more than what one would surmise from the context anyway. It would be more helpful to point out the phrase "deaf as a beetle" which hovers behind Bloom's thought; here *beetle* is not the insect but a large mallet. Men working with such tools would presumably become deaf. So the beetle reinforces deafness and the overall theme of noise/music.[8] The echo in Circe, "Bald Pat, bothered beetle" (*U*, 15.506), features "beetle" doing double duty, both in the former sense and also as an insect, within the predominant animal imagery of the chapter. All of this is laid out here to give a vague idea how much verbiage would be required even for a remotely serviceable gloss which this sample display pointedly could not be. Q.E.D.

How much should readers be told about Bloom becoming "Herr Professor Luitpold Blumenduft" (*U*, 12.468)? The very Germanic "Herr Professor" may be taken for granted. "Luitpold" is a form common in Austria, possibly reminiscent of Bloom's origin, Austro-Hungarian. "Blumenduft" in a way is "flower scent or fragrance" (Gifford), but that sounds a bit too euphemistic. Of course it takes up "those jewies does have a sort of queer odour coming off them" (*U*, 12.452) and will lead to "*fetor judaicus*" in Circe (*U*, 15.1796)—connections that might be left to the readers' own minds and memories. Vehemently reverberating behind the slur is the vicious custom of giving Jews in Europe nasty names with evil connotations, so that a whole history of specific anti-Semitism is invoked. This would be far beyond the scope of concise annotation and yet also cannot be passed over entirely. In the same context, Gustav Freytag's novel *Soll und Haben* in Bloom's possession (*U*, 17.1383) is in dire need of elucidation that has not yet been attempted. Some convoluted story seems to be at the back of Bloom having such a crassly anti-Semitic classic in German, a relict of his father, presumably.

It is one dilemma that we as Joyce readers depend on reports by experts in multiple areas outside our ken, and we also know that no report can ever be trusted. Annotations are gratuitous though well-meant impositions from outside. Electronic media, now in progress, will at least be able not to thrust premature, pertinent, or officious information on readers since it can be hierarchically removed and only called up on demand.

---

[8] "Blind" and "Dull as a beetle" also exist; see in this connection "blind as a batflea ... not a leetle beetle" (*FW*, 417.3).

"translation of texts" (*U*, 17.725)

Literary translation is an impossible necessity at best. It reduces meaning, irons out peculiarities, changes tone, loses resonances, distorts—and, for all its inherent shortcomings, also creatively expands and potentially exceeds the originals. Verbal culture is based on flawed translations. In Joyce such truisms are magnified and made much more conspicuous. There is generally no equivalent to real things like the "area" of Bloom's house (that sunken court below ground), nor the "timeball" on Dublin's "ballast office." The flavor of spoken idiom does not travel into any other language. It would be a rare miracle if the ingredients of "Poached eyes on ghost" (*U*, 8.508) could be salvaged in any other language, and in Joyce such verbal overlays are not rare exceptions as with most other writers. No other culture has an equivalent to faked Old English to be parodied in the target language. The fact that *Dubliners* alone has spawned at least nine different Italian translations shows a basic discontent and a constant need for alternatives. There would not be (at least) five different translations of *Ulysses* into Japanese if any of the earlier ones had been considered satisfactory. No one even suspects the possibility of *Finnegans Wake* in another language that would have even remotely the same effect on readers. Few of our meticulous Joycean researches could be based on any translation.

Translation into a different medium—painting, illustration, stage, opera, ballet, movies—is even more complex and yet perhaps also less problematic because no exact correspondences can be envisaged. Things are bound to change, but the changes, visual or auditory additions, are part of the intention. What a dramatization of *Ulysses* has to sacrifice may in part be made up by imaginative elements of a performance that are not present on a printed page. In its nature every performance may clarify and invigorate a text, but it always misrepresents it. It is enlightening to hear Penelope on the stage. We follow with much less of an effort; gestures and intonation tend to enliven the experience, yet, by the same token, everything has been prearranged for us, ambiguities are ironed out and semantic choices evaded. Molly's essentially unuttered thoughts are spoken aloud, even histrionically declaimed. As often as not, the actress moves about, gestures, and exclaims. Punctuation, whose lack is Joyce's most evident departure from norms of writing, will have to be reintroduced by the sheer necessity for breath and pauses, and so the amorphous passages are broken up into palatable phrases. Such medial adaptations are not considered drawbacks as in verbal translation, but taken in good grace and are even required as creative expansions. They nevertheless are substantial alterations.

In the jubilee year 1982 a performance of *Ulysses* in Paris ended by showing two men, Bloom and Stephen, who ended up engaging in a nude wrestling dumb show—fascinating in its own right but still a far cry from Joyce's book, and possibly giving a less than perfect idea of it. Oddly enough, what I thought to be the best performance of *Finnegans Wake* on a stage was done by a group from Berlin in Zürich: words spoken were not necessarily from the book, actors moved about speaking, there was music and ever-changing drawings and transparencies were projected on a big backdrop, and an actress was dancing in a strange oriental way. Almost nothing was taken from the *Wake*, but the continuing metamorphoses seemed to capture some of the kaleidoscopic spirit of *Finnegans Wake* (whatever that is). It was stimulatingly imaginative and somehow in tune with the book, but certainly not what Joyce wrote.

A good way to discover specific features of *Dubliners, Ulysses*, or *Finnegans Wake* would be to sketch out how they might be turned into movies. All attempts so far made are revealing about the technical and esthetic issues. Some parts of Joyce could almost serve as film scripts; the majority could not without strain. Presumably, "their splayed feet sinking in the silted sand" could be shown in closeup, but the verbal effect is likely to evaporate.

"so many unprobables in their poor suit of the improssable" (*FW*, 609.5)

Much more could be added, all in trite illustration of what we knew all along. The samples just served as an expansible string of reminders. Joyce gives us a great deal of insights, information, hints, constructions, structures, schemata, incitements to understand, connect, categorize, and impose order. We need firm foundations and Joyce provides more than most authors: specific places, patterns, analogues such as Homer, the Mass, newspapers, human organs, "technics", Viconian orders, biographical relationships, correspondences, quotations, and so on. Hardly ever were foundations more stable. And hardly ever were they shakier. Joyce offers certainties accompanied by doubts, in turn stimuli for reinterpretation. It may be comforting to realize that whatever we do, it is always wrong. Somehow this is also the fallible world that Joyce evokes.

Nor would we perhaps want it otherwise. Imagine if some authoritative body were to decree catechetic guidance, dogmatic assurance which would spoil all that explorative excitement! As it happens, some studies do in fact provide just that, but we all enjoy a good laugh and proceed on our investigations.

To sum up (this can be summed up!): we cannot quite read, understand, categorize, translate, annotate, dramatize Joyce and yet we have to do it. I was told that there is some similarity to what is called Negative Theology. Theologians may have analogous problems: God is not perhaps the wise old man with a beard at the celestial switchboard, not an idea, not a psychological or anthropomorphic projection, not an abstraction, not a local deity and all that. This is not, however, to equate Joyce's works with any God in any cosmic context, just to point to an inherent dilemma that may best be epitomized in the Wake's *"Hearasay in paradox lust"* (*FW*, 263, left margin).

Zurich James Joyce Foundation

"WANTING IN INANITY": NEGATIVITY, LANGUAGE AND "GOD" IN BECKETT

ASJA SZAFRANIEC

This paper investigates the resemblance of Beckett's discourse to negative theology. It investigates, in part, Jacques Derrida's inquiry into the rhetoric of the *via negativa* that changed the perception of what we mean when we refer to the properties of negative theology. Partly as a result of discussion of *différance*, negative theology no longer merely stands for an immensely rich yet remote tradition, but functions as a kind of rhetoric from which we draw new insights into language and representation. It is this latter content of negative theology that I want to address when examining its resemblance to Beckett's discourse. The echoes of the *via negativa* in Beckett go therewith beyond epigonism—they do not merely testify to a certain nostalgia for an esoteric tradition, but they employ a strategy characteristic of this tradition in an experimental way—to let certain effects become apparent in its working. Beckett's project of experimenting with the rhetoric of "unsaying" may be said to have culminated in is last prose work, *Worstward Ho*. In this paper, I argue that it is possible to interpret the quest of this work as directed toward God. "God" does not address here a Supreme Being but rather the condition of possibility (and the impossibility) of meaning and language and the hidden source of authority obliging us to speak.

This paper investigates the resemblance of Beckett's discourse to negative theology. I think that we can speak of such a resemblance and that the understanding of its function might yield new insights into a vital aspect of Beckett's work, which is his interest in "nothingness" and his commitment to thinking in the negative. At least from *Watt* onward, Beckett experimented with the rhetoric of negation, a practice that culminated in his last prose work, *Worstward Ho*. Fascination with "nothingness" and various attempts to capture it by focusing on language and staging its failure always accompanied this endeavor. This trait, so characteristic of Beckett's writing, can be illustrated by an idea he expressed in the well-known letter to Axel Kaun: "[m]ore and more my own language appears to me like a veil that must be torn apart in order to get at the things (or the Nothingness) behind it."[1] Beckett's remark, also by virtue of the fact that the name of God does not appear in it, is a quintessential expression of the idea of negative theology. According to this idea God, who cannot be named, can only be reached by tearing the veil of language. God thus conceived is, strictly speaking, "nothing."

Negativity and God

In the concluding passages of *Beckett's Fiction: In Different Words*,[2] Leslie Hill indicates the importance of negativity in reading Beckett in the following way:

> The questions of Beckett's writing are questions of negativity, and the fate of Beckett's texts hangs, quite uniquely, on the issue of how the power of the negative in his work is understood. Indeed, the history of reception of Beckett's texts could be written in terms of the different interpretations put forward as to the force and significance of the negative. It leads one to believe that the single most important reason for Beckett's success, with critics and audiences alike, is in the questions his work raises as to the shape and character *of the negative, the different, the other, the something without name* that haunts not only the words and rhythms of Beckett's writing, but also the words with which audiences, too, strive to pattern their lives. (163, my italics)

What is the meaning of "the negative, the different, the other, the something without the name" in Beckett? The idea of God seems not to be very distant from the idiom of this phrase. Leslie Hill must have realized this affinity, for later on[3] he qualified his own position by insisting that the "use of negative constructions" is "not the admission of God by the back passage." In other words, here Hill severs the link between negativity and God, the possibility of which had been opened up by his suggestive words in *Beckett's Fiction*.

I argue that there is more to the link between negativity and God than Hill's denial implies, for the reliance of mystical discourse on negativity

---

[1] A letter to Axel Kaun, 1937; Martin Esslin's translation from the German in Samuel Beckett, *Disjecta* (New York: Grove Press, 1984), 171-173.

[2] Leslie Hill, *Beckett's Fiction: In Different Words* (Cambridge: Cambridge University Press, 1990).

[3] In a presentation made at the "Beckett Against the Grain" Conference, York, England, May 1999.

is by no means accidental. They are mutually dependent—which is well captured by Jacques Derrida when he says that the reading of "God" as "*that without which* one would not know how to account for any negativity (...) will always be possible."[4] While sympathizing with Hill's intention to keep negativity and God apart, I think that this intention reflects just one particular way of thinking of "God"—as presence. The tradition of negative theology permits such a reading. However, this is not the only possible way of thinking of "God" in accordance with this tradition.

The other possible approach is to *resist* lapsing into thinking of Him as presence. On this reading, God would be a name of a certain void and of a process that is propelled by this void. In this paper I want to consider the possibility that Beckett's art was an example of such a discourse, namely a discourse focused on articulating God as absence.

The discourse on God and the negative has a long history. The procedure was known to the Stoics, neo-Pythagoreans, and neo-Platonists. It appears in the hermetic texts of the Hellenistic Gnostics and in the texts of the Judeo-Christian authors.[5] Within the Christian tradition the first known adherent of speaking about God in the negative, the *via negativa,* was Dionysius the Aeropagite (5th century), whose work, translated in the 9th century into Latin by Scotus Eriugena, prepared the way for other apophatic discourses in which the Neoplatonic and, after Aquinas, Thomistic influences prevailed alternately: for example, those of Meister Eckhart (1260-1329), Nicholas of Cusa (1401-1464), or, as late as the seventeenth century, Angelus Silesius.

Recently, the discourse of negative theology has drawn renewed attention, especially since the philosophical project of Jacques Derrida (most notably its part accompanying the introduction of the notion of *différance*) has been repeatedly identified with apophatic discourse.[6] This comparison evoked a number of responses from Derrida[7] that in turn provoked substantial critical discussion about the rapprochement between philosophy

---

[4] Jacques Derrida, "How to Avoid Speaking: Denials," in *Derrida and Negative Theology*, ed. H. Coward and T. Foshay (Albany: State University of New York Press, 1992), 76-77. Originally appeared as "Comment ne pas parler: Dénégations," in *Psyché: Inventions de l'autre* (Paris: Galilée, 1987), 535-595.

[5] R. Sneller, *Het Woord is schrift geworden: Derrida en de negatieve theologie* , with a summary in English (Kampen: Kok Agora, 1998), 52.

[6] See Coward and Foshay, *Derrida and Negative Theology*, 73-77.

[7] Among others, "Comment ne pas parler," in Derrida, *Psychè: Inventions de l'autre*, 535-595, and "Sauf le nom," in Jacques Derrida, *On the Name* (Stanford, Calif.: Stanford University Press, 1995).

and theology[8] and the way other discourses hinge on the apophatic. As a result, the quasi-apophatic thought of Derrida that both subscribes to and questions this tradition cannot be ignored when addressing the topic of negative theology. It is partly in the wake of the above discussion that negative theology is no longer merely an immensely rich, yet obsolete, esoteric tradition, but a kind of rhetoric from which we draw new insights on the functioning of language and representation. It is this latter content of negative theology that I want to address when examining the resemblance of Beckett's discourse to it. The echoes of the *via negativa* in Beckett go therewith beyond epigonism—they do not merely testify to a certain nostalgia of a remote tradition, but they employ a strategy characteristic of this tradition in an experimental way—to let certain effects become apparent in its working.

Negative theology begins with an insight that predicative language (that is, the formulations of the type *S* is *P*) is inadequate to speak about God. In the words of Meister Eckhart, "God is neither this nor that, that man can say" [*Got inist noch diz noch daz, daz man gesprechin mac*].[9] This insight of *in*adequacy is the first step of the *via negativa* as it already indicates the alternative to predicative language in the form of negative attribution.

The next step is from negation to subtraction. The negation of the *via negativa* is not dialectical[10] and thus is irredeemable. That which is excluded by negation is excluded for good and cannot be reintroduced— herein lies the characteristic radicality of the *via negativa*. Since that which is negated is therewith elided from discourse, there remains less and less to be said—or rather to be unsaid. As a consequence, the discourse evolves toward being rarefied to the point of silence. As Pseudo-Dionysius says in his "Mystical Theology": "my argument now rises (...) and the more it climbs, the more language falters, and when it has passed up and beyond the ascent, it will turn silent completely, since it will finally be one with him who is indescribable."[11]

---

[8] See, for example, John D. Caputo, *The Prayers and Tears of Jacques Derrida: Religion without Religion* (Bloomington: Indiana University Press, 1997) and Hent De Vries, *Philosophy and the Turn to Religion* (Baltimore: Johns Hopkins University Press, 1999).

[9] Meister Eckhart, *Die deutschen Werke*, vol. III, ed. J. Quint (Zűrich: Diogenes Verlag, 1979), 431.

[10] A dialectic would promise a third moment in which the positive element, i.e., the first moment, after being negated in the second moment, is finally recuperated via a synthesis or *Aufhebung* in the third.

[11] Pseudo-Dionysius, *The Complete Works*, trans. Colm Luibheid in collaboration with Paul Rorem (New York: Paulist Press, 1987), 139.

By rarefying the discourse, negative theology moves toward a void which can only be filled up with a mystical experience—or so the proponents of negative theology surmised. The favorite image illustrating the void is the one of the desert. It is not by accident that the "desert" which is the image of ultimate rarefaction is also the biblical place of encounters with God: the desert was the ultimate image of renunciation, a self-denial, which by its negative aspect paved the way to the direct intimation of God. The deserted space of Beckett's stage settings reflects this climate of renunciation.

It may be concluded that the discourse of negative theology eventually recuperates the presence of God. After naming everything God was not, it would be somehow possible to experience His sheer presence in the so created linguistic void or desert. Yet Derrida's careful reading of the texts of Pseudo-Dionysius and Meister Eckhart clearly demonstrates that the *via negativa* can only endlessly hover at the threshold of the promised revelation but is unable to step over it. The experience of the presence of God is simply not built into its procedure.

Derrida's radical reading of the *via negativa*, in which he refrains from conceiving the final goal of the apophatic discourse in terms of an experience of presence, allows him to assign it to a larger domain. After detracting the final moment of God's presence, the *via negativa* can be approached as a textual practice proper to many discourses, a procedure of address constructed on the principle of negation. As Derrida says, negative theology is a "language" or an "attitude toward [it]", and:

> By a more or less tenable analogy, one would thus recognize some traits, the family resemblance of negative theology, in every discourse that seems to return in a regular and insistent manner to this rhetoric of negative determination, endlessly multiplying the defenses and the apophatic warnings. ("How to Avoid Speaking: Denials," 74)

This is a reading of apophasis in which that to which the address is directed is effaced. The discourse empties itself in order to arrive at an empty place. Even though empty, or maybe precisely by virtue of being so, this place is of great interest to modern philosophy and theology—and, as I argue in this essay, to Beckett's "writings." The space, which can no longer accommodate the presence of God, and which therefore is home to an originary absence is perceived by Derrida as the locus of that which he calls "writing," "difference," or the "trace"—a quasi-transcendental principle governing our experience. The purpose of the thus modified negative way is then to address something that cannot be isolated in its presence but can only be discerned in its working. This emptying *kenosis* of discourse is the place where the interests of Beckett, negative theology, and Derridean reflection come together.

The Negative Way in Beckett

The negative discourse, so often stigmatized as heresy, was in fact the most critical, consistent, and uncompromising way of speaking about God. It is not surprising that it appealed to Beckett. Several critics stress the relevance of the mystical tradition for his writing. It is known that Beckett read mystics in his youth, that he discussed the writings of Meister Eckhart (1260-1329) with Charles Juliet in 1977, and that he quoted the 5th century mystic Pseudo-Dionysius in his 1931/2 "Dream" notebook and consequently in the *Dream of Fair to Middling Women*. The "Dream" notebook also contains references to St. Augustine, John of the Cross Thomas à Kempis, and Julian of Norwich.

The content of what has been widely referred to as Beckett's "revelation" or "mystical experience" reflects the mode of renunciation so characteristic of negative theology. Beckett restates this experience in the following words: "I realised that my own way was in impoverishment, in lack of knowledge and in taking away, in subtracting rather than adding."[12] It would be an oversimplification to treat this revelatory moment (which took place in the summer of 1945—and thus after *Watt* and before *Waiting for Godot*) as a sharp caesura indicating a radical and unexpected change in Beckett's work. On the other hand, it is undeniable that it reflects a direction that this work pursued and that one aspect of this direction was the radicalization of its apophatic nature.

Beckett's miming of the discourse of negative theology is often playful; it has the nature of an experiment designed more to test the tenacity of language than to bring about its rarefaction. This is especially true of the early texts which tend to mimic the *via negativa* in its rhetorical patterns (various modes of "unsaying"[13]) rather than in its inevitable consequence (silence). Beckett's silence is never far away—but only from a certain point on in his work is language deliberately thinned down in order to expose it in its working, rarefaction becoming an instrument of inquiry. I will discuss two cases of such playful early "unsaying," one in Beckett's early novel *Watt* and one from *Waiting for Godot*.

At first, the "unsaying" in Beckett's work consists not in a retraction but simply in speaking backward, in the reversal of spelling and syntactic

---

[12] James Knowlson, *Damned to Fame: The Life of Samuel Beckett* (London: Bloomsbury, 1996), 352.

[13] The meaning of "unsaying" in Beckett evolves: from neat reversing of the order of what is said (*Watt*), through bringing language in turmoil or "undoing" it (Lucky's monologue in *Waiting for Godot*), to retraction of what has been said (*The Unnamable*).

order. This kind of situation takes place in Beckett's novel *Watt*,[14] a humorously mystical account of the perambulations of the titular character including the description of his stay in the house of the unfathomable Mr. Knott. The "nicest" examples of the *via negativa* in Beckett can be found in *Watt*, even though they are surrounded with red herrings and even though their function is not as clear as in later writings. *Watt* could be, after all, just a parody (of negative theology among other things) and be as good a book. Yet the element of the mystical is undeniably there. Watt starts speaking back to front, as Shira Wolosky reminds us,[15] "in pursuit of Mr. Knott's Nothingness" and in this he imitates "the linguistic breakdown of an apophatic prayer" (*Language Mysticism*, 90, 97). The breakdown here described is not incurable—even though this "unsaying" renders the speaker apparently incomprehensible, there is a code to it. Here is an example of the negative way of thinking from *Watt* that illustrates this:

> Lit yad mac, ot og. Ton taw, ton tonk. Ton dob, ton trips. Ton vila, ton deda. Ton kawa, ton pelsa. Ton das, don yag. Os devil, rof mit. (165)

Which, by following the narrator's instructions (in this case, "invert... the order of letters in the word together with that of the sentences in the period"), could be translated into something like "So lived, for time. Not gay, not sad. Not awake, not asleep. Not alive, not dead. Not body, not spirit. Not wat/Watt, not Knott. Till day came, to go." The narrator's comment is, appropriately, "This meant *nothing* to me" (165, my emphasis). For the objective of the *via negativa* is, precisely, to express the "nothing."

The other mode of "unsaying"—by undoing language irreversibly—can be found in *Waiting for Godot*, written a few years after *Watt*. The incomprehensibility of Lucky's monologue is the more tragic as it is no longer reversible—this time the code is missing. If the essence of negative theology can be said to consist in provoking a linguistic breakdown in order to address God, then Lucky's soliloquy is an extreme case of such an experiment. Wolosky points out that this monologue, while playing with the idea of God "outside time without extension" by a pun on scholastic terminology, links the discourse on God to a linguistic breakdown known as aphasia. This might suggest, among other possibilities, that only through aphasia is it possible to speak about God—or that speaking about God leads to aphasia.

---

[14] Samuel Beckett, *Watt* (New York: Calder, 1998).
[15] Shira Wolosky, *Language Mysticism: The Negative Way of Language in Eliot, Beckett and Celan* (Stanford, Calif.: Stanford University Press, 1995).

Such expressions as "unwording," "unsaying," and even "leastward on" testify to the interaction of Beckett's work with the discourse of negative theology. Mary Bryden mentions the "apophatic" characteristic of Beckett's work and the "kenotic" mode in which Christ is depicted in *En attendant Godot*. Precisely apophatic *kenosis*—draining language of all content by means of "unsaying"—is the essence of negative theology. Wolosky even goes so far as to insist that "the premises and practices of negative theology act as a generative condition of Beckett's books" and that, for example, "*The Unnamable* openly parades this impulse," in stating the procedure to be followed. "First I'll say what I'm not," declares the narrator, "that's how they told me to proceed, then what I am."[16] "The way of negation—of passing to true reality by progressive denial and reduction—is here declared the Unnamable's very method" (*Language Mysticism*, 93).

Yet, if this mimicking was applied as a method, its function has not been sufficiently elucidated. We are familiar with Beckett's ambiguous but mainly negative attitude to religion, which many commentators have qualified as agnostic, his denial of having "religious emotions" or "the least faculty or disposition for the supernatural."[17] On the other hand, as Derrida reminds us, there is always a possibility that "the extreme and most consistent forms of declared atheism will have always testified to the most intense desire of God."[18] But then again, if it is true that the propensity of Beckett's discourse to the rhetorical practice of negative theology testifies (just as the negative discourse itself) to the "most intense desire of God," how is this God to be thought? How is it possible to think God—without lapsing into the metaphysical trap of thinking him as a presence or being?

Thinking God as Language

In its most radical gesture, the *via negativa* addresses God without hoping ever to reach him in his presence or being, without conferring on him the status of being. God addressed in the negative way would be, in Jean-Luc Marion's formulation, a "God without being" (*Dieu sans l'être*).[19] According

---

[16] Samuel Beckett, *Trilogy* (London: Calder, 1959), 326.
[17] Quoted by Mary Bryden in her *Samuel Beckett and the Idea of God* (Basingstoke: Macmillan, 1998).
[18] "Sauf le nom," in Derrida, *On the Name*, 36.
[19] "[I]l faille libérer 'Dieu' de la question sur/de l'Être" (quoted in Jean-Luc Marion, *Dieu Sans l'être* [Paris: Fayard, 1982], 91). This is also how Heidegger may be said to have attempted to speak about God: by crossing out or erasing the notion of being.

to this discourse "God" "is" not; the word "being" does not apply in the discourse on God. About God so thought nothing can be said, except maybe what Hamm says in *Endgame*: "The bastard, he doesn't *exist*"[20] (my italics). Or what we learn about Mr Knott in *Watt*: "Not that Watt was ever to have any direct dealings with Mr. Knott, for *he was not*" (64, my italics).

This God of questionable origin, who "doesn't exist," can be addressed in prayer, but to no avail. The only thing that can be evoked in this prayer is "God's place which is not God" ("How to Avoid Speaking: Denials," 96). In that place, that which we call "God" is visible in its effects. According to the tradition of negative theology, God's place, the place where God appears, is the origin of language: as we read in the Angelus Silesius's *Cherubinic Wanderer*,[21] "*der Ort ist dass Wort*," "the place is the Word."

> *Der Ort ist dass Wort.*
> Der ort und's *Wort* ist Eins, und wäre nicht der ort
> (Bey Ewger Ewigkeit!) es wäre nicht das Wort.
>
> *The place is the word*
> The place and the *word* is one, and were the place not
> (of all eternal eternity!) the *word* would not be.
> (I:205)

God without being and his place—language, are interdependent and neither of the two can be thought without the other. It is impossible to think God independently of language. In the end, what negative theology addresses is language and the fact that it cannot point beyond itself. In other words, negative theology is a rhetorical practice that addresses its own rhetoric. I think that Beckett's gesture toward it is prompted by the realization that the only thing we can speak about are the effects of God in language, and that God is, strictly speaking, "nothing," but a "nothing" that "happens," that has the status of an "event." This was "[w]hat distressed Watt": that "nothing had happened, with the utmost formal distinctness, and that it continued to happen, in his mind" (73).

---

[20] Samuel Beckett, *Complete Dramatic Works* (London: Faber & Faber, 1986).

[21] Angelus Silesius (Johannes Scheffler), *The Cherubinic Wanderer*, trans. Maria Shrady (New York: Paulist, 1986).

The Dependence of God on Language

The thought about God, both in its positive and negative modus, originates in and through language. This is the questionable origin of God, the reason for Hamm to call him a "bastard": God is the consequence of the way our language is. And our language is such that "any expression of an abstract idea can only be by analogy"[22]—to an expression denoting something particular and tangible. Only by analogy that obliterates the tangible, 'primitive' referents does a new, universal and abstract concept enter language. In the words of *Watt*:

> the only way one can speak of nothing is to speak of it *as though* it were something, just as the only way one can speak of God is to speak of him *as though* he were a man, which to be sure he was, in a sense, for a time, an as the only way one can speak of man, even our anthropologists have realised that, is to speak of him *as though* he were a termite. (74, my italics)

If this gesture of trying to account for the sublime, abstract, or baffling by drawing parallels to the everyday and tangible, so well captured here by Beckett, is indeed "the only way one can speak," then it indicates something very elementary about language, namely the intersection of the ontological and the ontic, or of the transcendental and the empirical. By virtue of this intersection one element of the pair is unthinkable without the other.

It is not unconceivable that the principle of analogy "engendered" or "yielded" a couple of abstract ideas, including the idea of God. Our language's ability to express abstract ideas would in this case be the origin of the idea of a transcendent being. This being, by analogy, would be capable of explaining the world.

> AMM: We're not beginning to...to... mean something?
> CLOV: Mean something! You and I, mean something! [*Brief laugh.*] Ah that's a good one!
> HAMM: I wonder. [*Pause.*] Imagine if a rational being came back to earth, wouldn't he be able to get ideas into his head if he observed us long enough. [*Voice of rational being.*] Ah, good, now I see what it is, yes, now I understand what they're at! (108)

---

[22] Anatole France, *Le jardin d'Epicure* (Paris : Calmann-Levy, 1895).

The Dependence of Language on God

As much though as God is the product of language, this language (as Jean-Luc Marion has argued[23]) always already has the structure of prayer and is thus dependent on God. Prayer, as the etymology of the word tells us (the word evolved from Middle French *preiere*, from Medieval Latin *precaria*, from Latin, feminine of *precarius*—"obtained by entreaty"), is a precarious address, a leap into uncertainty. If language has its paradigm in prayer (praise would be a paradigm of predication), all predication is a function of an address to God. This testifies to an interdependence of "God" and language. It is no longer possible to conceive either of them as "a purported Archimedian point outside all textual determinations,"[24] in other words as a transcendental signified.

As mentioned before, Beckett's project of experimenting with the rhetoric of "unsaying" may be said to have culminated in his last prose work, *Worstward Ho*. This remarkable text might be read among other things as a reflection on the human condition, a phenomenological study of experience, or as an account of the persistence of artistic inquiry going on "till nohow on." It seems to me that it is possible to interpret the quest of *Worstward Ho* as directed toward God as the possibility (and impossibility) of meaning and language.

From its very first word, *Worstward Ho* addresses Being: "*on*" is in Greek the very word of being[25] and hence addresses God. What is Being? Introducing this problem in *Sein und Zeit,* Heidegger quotes Thomas Aquinas: "An understanding of Being is already included in conceiving anything which one apprehends in entities."[26] Then he goes on to explain:

> Everything we talk about, everything we have in view, everything towards which we comport ourselves in any way, is being; what we are is being, and so is how we are. Being lies in the fact that something is, and in its being as it is; in Reality; in presence-at-hand; in subsistence; in validity; in Dasein; in the 'there is'. (*Being and Time*, 6-7)

---

[23] Marion, *Dieu Sans l'être*, 259-277.

[24] Kevin Hart, *The Trespass of the Sign: Deconstruction, Theology and Philosophy* (Cambridge: Cambridge University Press, 1991), 47.

[25] Charles Krance, "*Worstward Ho* and On-words: Writing to(wards) the Point," in *Rethinking Beckett: A Collection of Critical Essays*, ed. Lance St. John Butler and Robin J. Davis (London: Macmillan, 1990), 130-131.

[26] Martin Heidegger, *Sein und Zeit* (Tubingen: Max Niemeyer Verlag, 1993). English quotations come from *Being and Time* (New York: Harper & Row, 1962), 3.

This allows us to see that the concept of being is connected to the problems of identity, existence and truth.[27] "Being" is not exactly the same as "God." Heidegger insisted on a clear distinction between Being (the Being of beings) and God as a supreme being. He also said that were he "to write a theology, as I am sometimes tempted to do, the word 'being' ought not to appear there."[28] However, Derrida demonstrated that, under a certain reading, "being" and "God" are indistinguishable. For "what difference is there between writing Being, this Being which is not, and writing God, this God of whom Heidegger also says that he is not?" ("How to Avoid Speaking: Denials," 128) Consequently, some interpreters of Derrida propose to read God as an "example of a universal figure of Being."[29] God is the *es gibt*, which means not only 'there is' but also 'it gives'.

If we keep in mind Stanley Cavell's insistence on the hidden literality of everything that is said in *Endgame*,[30] Clov's question, "what in God's name could there be on the horizon?" (107), anticipates the search of *Worstward Ho*, the search of the content of God's name within the horizon of language. There is nothing representable in God's name, unless the representation itself be addressed. This is what happens in negative theology, and this is what happens in Beckett: his negative way is, in Carla Locatelli's words, a "duel of language" with representation, language trying to shed its function of representation.[31]

The principle of analogy described in *Watt* that is used to account indirectly for that which cannot be accounted for as it is, returns in *Worstward Ho*. One of the images (the "plodding twain") is said to be "bad as it is as it is"(99). The doubling of the phrase "as it is" reflects the doubling inherent in any kind of representation that prevents it from capturing its object in its (unique) essence. Moreover, *Worstward Ho*, as a representation of this doubling, becomes a case of *mise-en-abyme*, an abyss that opens when

---

[27] E. Tugendhat, "Die Seinsfrage und ihre sprachliche Grundlage: Charles K. Kahn, The Verb "Be" in Ancient Greek," in *Philosophische Rundschau* 24, nos. 3-4 (Tubingen: Mohr, 1977), 161-176.

[28] "S'il m'arrivait encore d'avoir à mettre par écrit une théologie—ce à quoi je me sens parfois incité—alors le terme d'être ne saurait en aucun cas y intervenir. La foi n'a pas besoin de la pensée d'e l'étre" (quoted in Marion, *Dieu Sans l' tre*, 5).

[29] Rodolphe Gasché, "God, for Example," in *Inventions of Difference: On Jacques Derrida* (Cambridge, Mass.: Harvard University Press, 1994), 168.

[30] Stanley Cavell, "Ending the Waiting Game: A Reading of Beckett's Endgame," in *Must We Mean What We Say?* (Cambridge: Cambridge University Press, 1976).

[31] Carla Locatelli, *Unwording the World: Samuel Beckett's Prose Works After the Nobel Prize* (Philadelphia: University of Pennsylvania Press, 1990).

two mirrors are facing each other: it is a representation of a representation. Since it is impossible to say "Being as it is"—to capture its essence without a detour of an analogy, or of a negation, or of a metaphor (*God* is precisely the name of this impossibility)—Beckett's way to deal with this is to address the detour itself, by investigating the working of analogy or negation.

The Function of Subtraction in Beckett

Negative theology must address God and language at the same time. On the one hand it demonstrates the origin of language in prayer (and to whom the prayer would be if not to God?), on the other hand it deconstructs God's image by leading it back to its origin in language. In both cases, language interrogates itself. Self-interrogation, interrogation of itself was for Beckett the function of art (and thus the function of art is epistemological): "Art has always been this—pure interrogation, rhetorical question less the rhetoric."[32] In her *Unwording the World: Samuel Beckett's Fiction after the Nobel Prize*, Carla Locatelli concludes from the above passage that in Beckett's view, a "'pure interrogation' can only be structured as a subtraction (of rhetoric from the rhetorical question)" (228).

Hence subtraction, earlier shown to be an essential phase in the *via negativa*, functions in *Worstward Ho* as an "epistemological instrument" for addressing the interdependence of language and God. According to Locatelli, the notion of subtraction stands for a process of emptying language to see what is left. Yet it might also refer to the process of emptying for its own sake. Indeed, the primary concern of language of *Worstward Ho* is to empty itself. "The words too whosesoever. What room for worse! How almost true they sometimes almost ring! How wanting in inanity!"[33] The words seem to be "wanting in inanity" because they "ring" "true". They *are* not true—they *seem* somehow to be saturated with an illusion of truth, a metaphysical illusion. The function of negative representation in Beckett comes to light here: it is to undo this illusion of truth.

---

[32] Samuel Beckett, "Intercessions by Denis Devlin," in *Disjecta* (New York: Grove Press, 1984), 91.
[33] Samuel Beckett, *Nohow On* (New York: Grove Press, 1996), 99.

Language and God in Beckett

The relationship between language and God in Beckett may also be determined by the idea that the fall in Paradise was semantic in nature.[34] On this reading, part of Adam's disobedience was the trespass of a linguistic sign. The punishment was appropriate to the misbehavior: Adam, and with him the whole of mankind, experienced a fall from unmediated knowledge and communication with God to the imperfect mediation by means of (mutable) signs (Hart, *The Trespass of the Sign*, 3-4). This meant that the direct intimation of God was no longer possible, was condemned to failure. In the light of the above it is interesting to consider the failure Beckett addresses in *Worstward Ho:*

> Ever tried. Ever failed. No matter. Try again. Fail again. Fail better. (*Nohow On*, 89)

Granted that *Worstward Ho* is an "epistemic novel" (Locatelli, *Unwording the World*, 230), and taking into account Dante's reading of the mediation of language as the result of the fall, the failure addressed above could refer to the project of overcoming the fall, overcoming the mediation of signs. Failing better would be intended to undo the fall. This was negative theology's problem: "how to talk properly of God when language can only improperly signify Him" (Hart, *The Trespass of the Sign*). The purpose of negative theology would be then to unsay the distance created by the fall. This was how Beckett perceived the function of his discourse in the already mentioned letter to Axel Kaun:

> More and more my own language appears to me like a veil that must be torn apart in order to get at the things (or the Nothingness) behind it. (...) Language is most efficiently used where it is being most efficiently misused. As we cannot eliminate language all at once, we should at least leave nothing undone that might contribute to its falling into disrepute. To fore one hole after another in it, until what lurks behind it— be it something or nothing—begins to seep through; I cannot imagine a higher goal for a writer today.[35]

---

[34] This idea can be found in Dante, of whom Beckett was an avid reader. See Kevin Hart's reading of *Canto XXVI*, *Paradiso* in his *The Trespass of the Sign: Deconstruction, Theology and Philosophy*.

[35] For reference, see note 1 above.

The idea of representation expressed in this letter, discarded later by Beckett, was to "perforate" language in order to get beyond it to the "thing behind [it]."

The acceptance of the position that there is no "beyond" language calls for rethinking of the role of negative theology. The act of emptying of language would no longer serve the purpose of revealing that which is "behind" it but rather would focus on language itself. The purpose of "failing better" would no longer be to undo the fall but rather to analyze failing itself. Saying is failing: "How try say? How try fail?" (*Nohow On*, 96). The function of Beckett's negative discourse in *Worstward Ho* would be to address the saying by unsaying it. As a representation of a representation it could focus on the traces of the unsayable principle called God that is at work in his language.

Original Affirmation as the Source of the Obligation to Express

Obligation recurs throughout Beckett's writing. It manifests itself in various forms of compulsive behavior, of which the most characteristic is the dutiful or fearful obedience of Beckett's characters to what is often no more than a name (Godot, Mr. Knott, Youdi). With time, the names gradually disappear, making the obligation even more prominent. Obligation to express is omnipresent in Beckett's work. Next to the renowned fragment from the "Three Dialogues" to which I will return, it is especially strong in the *Trilogy*, in *How It Is*[36] (as an obligation to quote), and in *Worstward Ho*. To my knowledge, Beckett has always refrained from speaking about the source of or the reason for this obligation.

As Derrida reminds us, language is dependent on a kind of original affirmation, the affirmation of the precarious identity and both power and weakness of a sign. Using language requires a minimal element of faith, by virtue of which I can assume that something means/is "what I think it means/is." This affirmation of a sign despite its vulnerable and imperfect identity (for I can never be absolutely certain that it means "what I think it means") coincides with the acceptance of the "obligation to express." Once we have started to "speak" by acknowledging the mediated nature of all experience it is impossible not to express, that is, to be "silent," in other words, to leave the mediation. In his reading of Joyce's *Ulysses*,[37] Derrida

---

[36] Samuel Beckett, *How It Is* (New York: Grove Press, 1964).

[37] Jacques Derrida, "Ulysses Gramophone," in *Acts of Literature*, ed. Derek Attridge (New York: Routledge, 1992).

compares the interpretive gesture that allows us to experience "the world" to a gesture we make when receiving a phone call. The "yes" uttered into the receiver acknowledges that the mediation is there and that it is successful. This "yes, I receive you" indicates also a certain commitment (and thus faith again): it means "yes, I will. I will respond to what you say next. What you are going to say will not remain without response." In other words, in every interpretive gesture (and that includes all experience) we have said "yes," and in saying "yes" we have promised. It is in this promise that the "obligation to express" is rooted.

The imperative "say on" in *Worstward Ho* reflects this obligation, arising from being thrown into language. It means 'you have (always) already said (even if only in silence). Go on saying'. "One starts speaking as if it were possible to stop at will," laments *The Unnamable* (*Trilogy*, 301). Once we have started to speak, everything we say addresses what has already been said. In Beckett's words, language is "preying (but also 'praying') on foresaid remains" (*Nohow On,* 105). This prayer on or to the remains does not take place within a unifying sphere of a "dome," but is scattered from "temple" to "temple" (*Nohow On,* 107). In other words, there is no single principle or doctrine, cult or ideology, according to which the "remains" could be organized, archived, and "explained away" or taken into account as a totality.

Paradoxically, Beckett's observation that there is impossibility to express does not entail that no expression is possible. This paradox is well known to Beckett readers who are repetitively reminded that the condition of possibility of discourse (and of meaning, truth, and reference) is rooted in its impossibility. There are fragments in Beckett that show not only the impossibility to express but also the gesture of expressing, despite this impossibility.

There is of course Beckett's famous dictum from the "Three Dialogues" that indicates the impossibility to express. Beckett had by then already indicated impossibility (empêchement) as the field calling for artistic investigation.

> There is nothing to express, nothing with which to express, nothing from which to express, no power to express, no desire to express, together with the obligation to express. (*Disjecta*, 139)

The statement that there is "nothing with which to express" may reflect a conviction that reference is not possible (and so it is commonly read). Yet it can also mean that that which must be expressed is not a thing, that it is not something that "is," but, depending on how we call it, "Being,", "God," or some quasi-transcendental principle. In this case, the tool (the "nothing with which to express") and the object of expression (the "nothing to express") coincide—the tool becoming the object of expression. The obligation is then to express the impossible. We might say that all experience begins with this impossibility or impasse, this, as Watt called it, "nothing" that "happened" and that "continued to happen":

> But if he could say, when the knock came, the knock become a knock, on the door become a door, in his mind, presumably, in his mind, whatever that might mean, Yes, I remember, that is what happened then, if then he could say that, then he thought that then the scene would end, and trouble him no more. (*Watt*, 74).

What "troubled" Watt was the unbridgeable gap, the difference between the knock as it was, and its becoming "a knock" to him. Watt's mystical experience of the Galls consisted in the impasse produced by impossibility to express. Precisely this impasse was indicated by Beckett as the object of the obligation to express, when he criticized in the "Three Dialogues" the art that "never stirred from the field of the possible" (139). To *D*'s question: "What other plane can there be for the maker?" *B*'s response was "logically none." This illustrates Beckett's urge to investigate the impossible. And there is no better way to express and explore the impasse than the negative way that consists in the impasse itself:

> Go there where you cannot; see where you do not see;
> Hear where nothing rings or sounds, so are you where God speaks.
> (Silesius, *Cherubinic Wanderer*, I:199)

In this sense Beckett's statement above could be interpreted as attempting to reach through negation to the most radical conditions of experience, language and knowledge, conditions which are not transcendental but co-dependent on the very things they bring about. And these conditions would be arising out of an impasse.

For, despite the fact that the artist is "helpless to paint"—since "there is nothing to paint and nothing to paint with" (*Disjecta*, 142), in *Worstward Ho* we read:

> Nothing to show a woman and yet a woman. (108)
> Nothing to show a child and yet a child. A man and yet a man. Old and yet old. Nothing but ooze how nothing and yet. (115)

Already in *Endgame* Beckett signaled the feeble nature of the sign that is also its strength. The language of Hamm and Clov may be made of "hollow bricks" (if we read with Heidegger the house as language, "the house of Being"), in other words it is constructed from pieces of vacuum yet it does not collapse. Also in *Worstward Ho* the signs are "graves of none'"" in the "old graveyard" of language:

> In that old graveyard. Names gone and when to when. (115)

They refer, properly speaking, to nothing. Despite, or maybe by virtue of this hollowness of the sign, representation is omnipresent. This precarious status of language that originates from "nothing", from "impossibility" (or from so defined God) is addressed in *Worstward Ho*.

The Unnameable Source of Authority

The first word of *Worstward Ho* is not only "the very word of Being". It is also an *imperative* to continue with something that apparently started without us. This injunction to go on might address the Heideggerian notion of *Geworfenheit*, (a state of "thrownness", of "being thrown" into Being, or, as Locatelli puts it, the state of being caught in a "hermeneutical cycle" (Locatelli, *Unwording the World*, 233). It echoes a Spanish poem by Manuel Gutierrez Najera which Beckett translated as "To Be":

> "We crave a single instant of respite / and a voice in the darkness urges: 'On!'"[38]

Much of *Worstward Ho* is written in the same imperative mode, indicating that it comes from some higher yet unidentifiable and absent authority. The modus of authority is already there in language, conferring obligation and hiding its origin in one gesture. "The words too whosesoever" (*Nohow On*, 99). "On. Say on" (89). This is an obligation to speak but who or what says these words?

> All of old. Nothing else ever. Ever tried. Ever failed. No matter. Try again. Fail again. Fail better. (*Nohow On*, 89)

In the above fragment, the demanding yet absent other (speaking in the imperative) is indistinguishable from the one who is called upon to obey (speaking in the constative). They speak in a single voice—the demand speaks through the voice of the demanded. It is interesting to note that Heidegger defines in a similar way the voice of conscience: the call of

---

[38] *Anthology of Mexican Poetry*, trans. Samuel Beckett and comp. Octavio Paz (London: Thames and Hudson, 1958), 135-137.

conscience is from Dasein to Dasein. On this reading, "on" would be the voice of conscience summoning Dasein "to its ownmost potentiality for Being its Self," to authentic existence (Heidegger, *Being and Time*, 273). "Ever tried. Ever failed" is no excuse: "No matter. Try again. Fail again. Fail better" (*Nohow On*, 89). The uttering of the injunction "Say on" and the performance of the duty it confers (to speak, to express) are one. This is not only an act of "saying"—the saying itself is shown, or "said," here.

Worstward Ho is a portrait of the "saying," a portrait of language in its working, a self-portrait of language. Language speaks here itself (compare Heidegger's expression "Die Sprache Spricht"), as through a medium in an oracle—for the origin of the words remains unknown. This almost-autonomy of language reflects the position of God. As Derrida says, "Language has started without us, in us and before us. This is what theology calls God, and it is necessary, it will have been necessary, to speak" ("How to Avoid Speaking: Denials," 99). Yet God himself cannot be named:

> Whose words? Ask in vain. Or not in vain if say no knowing. No saying. No words for him whose words. Him? One. No words for one whose words. One? It. No words for it whose words. (*Nohow On*, 98)

The above passage addresses that which engenders words. Can it be called "God"? That which engenders words is anonymous. Similarly Heidegger says about conscience: "if the caller is asked about its name (...) it (...) refuses to answer" (*Being and Time*, 274). Negative theology might be helpful here: "in negative theology ... that which calls forth speech is called "God."[39] "Whose words? Ask in vain." The question about the identity of the voice is of no avail—unless you know the negative way: "Or not in vain if say no knowing." The only way God can be addressed in His singularity is by negation: "no words for it whose words." The pronoun "it" functions here as it does in Heidegger's "es gibt," which is to say that it is something that "gives" (i.e., produces certain effects) rather than "is." In this it displays a similar structure to Derrida's "difference."[40] "It" lies at the origin of language and representation.

> Say a body. Where none. No mind. Where none. That at least. A place. Where none. For the body. To be in. (*Nohow On*, 89)

On the other hand, again, it is impossible to think "it" as an origin independent of what it originates. "It" can only be made visible in its effects,

---

[39] Caputo, *The Prayers and Tears of Jacques Derrida*, 3.
[40] Although, as Caputo insists, God is not "différance."

that is, in the language, in the words. The words are everything we have to express their origin: "Worsening words whose unknown. (...) Dim void shades all they. Nothing save what they say. Somehow say. Nothing save they" (*Nohow On*, 104).

The anonymous source of authority is protected by a sphere of secrecy. The way to express the "it" is, just as in negative theology, by renunciation: images are rarefied, and words are banned ("pox on bad"). A sphere of secrecy surrounds the origin of words and images. The productive "dim" is described as a "grot" or a "gulf" in the void in which "shadows" appear. Both "grot" and "gulf" carry mystical associations: "grot" is also a "crypt" (from Italian "grotto") and "gulf" can be both a "vault" and an "abyss."

> Whence no knowing. (*Nohow On*, 96)
> At all costs unknown. (101)

According to Derrida the negative discourse is inseparable from the notion of the secret: "There is a secret of the denial and the denial of the secret. The secret, as secret, separates and already institutes a negativity; it is a negation that denies itself. It de-negates itself. This denegation does not happen to it by accident; it is essential and originary."

Beckett's acknowledged fascination with homonyms can be heard also in *Nohow On*: "no knowing" in the expression "whence no knowing" sounds the same as "know no'ing". The meaning is then either there is no way in which the "whence" could be known—or an imperative: "Know how to arrive at the 'whence' by means of negation." Compare Heidegger's description of the call of conscience: "The whence of the calling is the whither to which we are called back" (*Being and Time*, 280). The answer to the question "whence?" seems to be, once again, "it", which, like Derrida's difference, signifies the movement in which all experience is rooted. "It" "secretes," that is, both hides and emanates language and representation.

I have been trying, with the help of Derrida, to approach Beckett in the way Derrida approaches Heidegger. In other words, my intention was not to give an apodictically theological reading of Beckett that would present itself as a necessary truth but rather to demonstrate that under certain conditions such a reading is possible, and to see what this would entail for the understanding of Beckett's work. It is possible to read certain aspects of Beckett's work from within the context of negative theology. To mobilize a corpus of semantic resources to make sense of Beckettian desire for the "least" which propels *Worstward Ho* is not the same as to assign to it an all-explanatory power. I do not wish to propound that Beckett is all about negative theology, even less that his work is about religious experience, which for Beckett, "in the only intelligible sense of that epithet," would have to be "at once an assumption and an annunciation."[41] If religious experience so understood were to be addressed by Beckett at all, it would rather be in its impossibility. Rather, in this paper, some aspects that can be and are associated with religion—like faith, obligation, and its impossible and unnameable source—are shown to permeate language and representation. And that means that *Worstward Ho*, since it is about language and representation, therewith also addresses religion.

I have deliberately omitted what might be taken to be the "characters" of Worstward Ho: the "head," the "crippled hands," the "pain," the "bodies" male and female, "walking" and "kneeling" which, their clothes removed and their limbs taken away, are gradually reduced to the minimum, to be in the end no more than "[t]hree pins. One pinhole" (*Nohow On*, passim). For Worstward Ho is mainly about words: "Worsening words whose unknown. Whence unknown. (...) Dim shades all they. Nothing saves what they say. Somehow say. Nothing save they" (*Nohow On*, 104). In the tradition of negative theology, *kenosis* is supposed to lead to silence that enables the faithful to experience the ineffable. Needless to say, this is not the intention of Beckett's gesture. Beckett's insistence on the obligation to express precludes interpretation of his work as a plea for silence. Rather, silence is being investigated here in the sense of the ineffable, the secret as the source of obligation, as that which is being affirmed by language but at the same time resists any mediation by it, cannot be represented by it.

That which is left of God in Beckett cannot be understood as an absolute, whether linguistic or epistemic—if for no other reason, at least for the one that Beckett's work does not allow us to think in terms of an absolute "beyond." In a consistently developed discourse of negative theology God becomes "a name that no longer names *anyone* or *anything*."[42] At most one might call it a productive absence at work in language, an absence that never fails to manifest itself and thus is both inside and outside language. If we assign to this absence the status of the source, it is only provisionally—for this "source" is always already embedded in language. The analysis of the discourse of negative theology demonstrates that when language becomes an object of inquiry it can only empty itself and show its original desert-like quality. This is consistent with how Derrida defines God: "'God' 'is' the name of this bottomless collapse, of this endless desertification of language."[43]

---

[41] Samuel Beckett, *Proust* (New York, Grove Press, 1931), 51.
[42] De Vries, *Philosophy and the Turn to Religion*, 314.
[43] "Sauf le nom," Derrida, *On the Name*, 55-56.

"It was on the key issue of pain, suffering and death that Beckett's religious faith faltered and quickly foundered," James Knowlson writes in Beckett's biography. At the same time it is difficult to disagree with Christopher Ricks when he observes that "Beckett ... felt the twinges of the quondam believer, as in a phantom limb."[44] Was God a limb that Beckett discarded? Paradoxically, from the point of view of negative theology this would mean the most profound experience of God, the desired end of the *via negativa*, according to which only by getting rid of God can we understand His real nature. In the words of Meister Eckhart's confession: "I pray God to rid me of God."

University of Amsterdam

---

[44] Christopher Ricks, *Beckett's Dying Words* (Oxford: Clarendon Press, 1993), 55. Also, Charles Julliet recounts: "We discuss religion, and I ask whether he has been able to free himself from its influence. SB: 'Perhaps in my external behavior, but as for the rest ...'" ("Meeting Beckett," trans. Suzanne Chanier, in *TriQuarterly* 77 [Evanston, Ill.: Northwestern University, 1989-1990], 27).

FROM IDEOLOGY OF LOSS TO AESTHETICS OF ABSENCE: THE ENDGAME IN BECKETT'S *THE LOST ONES*

YUAN YUAN

This paper explores negative ideology and negative aesthetics of modern writing within the context of Beckett's *The Lost Ones* from both modern and postmodern perspectives. Loss as the cultural unconscious of modernism functions as the dominant trope to configure the modern subject in alienation or decenterment. By tracing ideas of Hegel, Freud, and Kristeva, I construe that Beckett's *The Lost Ones* is composed within the context of this loss mythology, which indicates not only a negative affirmation but also signifies a sublime mode of being, associated with identification, pleasure, and desire. From a postmodern perspective, Beckett engages the art of the negative through a game with the end that functions as a structural principle and an enabling conceptual framework to approach negative poetics: aesthetics of absence. In Beckett's text, the lost space signifies but a universe of linguistic play. The end as the central metaphor both defines the narrative and simultaneously eludes it, constituting the limit and horizon of representation. Like Lacan's "the real" and Derrida's "the infinite Other," Beckett's "end" points to a primal space prior to language, the alterity and impasse of discourse. Hence, the aesthetics of absence is defined by aesthetics of play and ethics of unrepresentability. The end in Beckett's fiction signifies both absence and infinity.

Critics, both past and present, almost unanimously agree about the form that *The Lost Ones* takes: a fable or an allegory. But as to what this fable or allegory signifies, they seldom concur. Many scholars share Jean-Jacques Mayoux's position that "*The Lost Ones* is of the fable type, a fable of a sinister micro-Hades, of the futility of life, of social organizations and institutions, of individual yearning,"[1] while others believe, as Leslie Hill states, "it is more an allegory of its own fabrication or textual production

---

[1] Jean-Jacques Mayoux, *Samuel Beckett*, ed. Ian Scott-Kilvert (London: Longman Group, 1974), 41-42.

than of any stable view of human endeavors."² These two opposing views, I notice, demonstrate two different cultural contexts and theoretical frameworks of interpreting the negative art in Beckett's fiction: the modern ideology of loss or the postmodern aesthetics of absence. That is to say, Beckett's *The Lost Ones* can be read either as a fable of hellish existence or an allegory of writing, either repesentational or metafictional. It is highly possible that Beckett's art of the negative is informed by both the ideology of loss and the aesthetics of absence.

Beckett is well known for his apocalyptic as well as comic visions of our times in terms of "the end." *The Lost Ones* begins with the end: "It is perhaps the end of all."³ What we see in the abode, as represented by Beckett, are nothing but a lot of dead bodies. Indeed, our modern age is marked by end and death: death of God, death of man, death of the author, death of history, death of philosophy, death of humanism, and more optimistically, the end of the century. (The list could be awfully long.) So death or end has been identified and employed by many scholars and artists as a powerful and enabling conceptual framework for critical inquiry or literary representation. In effect, the endgame has been adopted in modern times as a vital strategy of discourse to engage the culture. Beckett knows it very well, so he puts the end to play.

Death or end has different meanings for different people. For Nietzsche, death of God means freedom; for Sartre, anxiety; for Foucault, a contradiction, since to kill God indicates precisely the opposite: negation only affirms its presence; for Derrida, death or end signifies a process of writing in terms of both supplementation and displacement.⁴ Hence, the discourse of loss or end can be put into two different theoretical frameworks and two different cultural perspectives: the framework of the metaphysics of presence or that of the metaphorics of absence; the modern perspective of tragic/apocalyptic vision of doom or the postmodern comic/ironic vision of play.

---

[2] Leslie Hill, *Beckett's Fiction: In Different Words* (Cambridge: Cambridge University Press, 1990), 153.

[3] Samuel Beckett, *The Lost Ones*, trans. Samuel Beckett (New York: Grove Press, 1972).

[4] For further reference to different scholars' responses to death or end, see Nietzsche's *Joyful Wisdom, Beyond Good and Evil*, and *Thus Spake Zarathustra*; Satre's *Being and Nothing*; Foucault's *Language, Counter-Memory, Practice;* and Derrida's *Of Grammatology* and *Writing and Difference*.

I

The zeitgeist of modern age is *Loss*, informed by a tragic vision of suffering, exile, anxiety, alienation, void, and the apocalyptic vision of the end. T. S. Eilot's poems, for example, "The Waste Land," "The Hollow Men," and "The Love Song of J. Alfred Prufrock," all testify to this vision. All these hollow men in Eliot's poems expect the modern age to end either with a bang or a whimper. Similarly, *The Lost Ones* echoes Eliot's prophecy of the culture: "Is not the cylinder doomed in a more or less distant future to a state of anarchy given over to fury and violence?" (52). I argue that it is this ideology of loss that functions as the cultural un/conscious of modernism and configures the modern subject in alienation or decenterment. The modern subject emerges in a paradox: it is constituted in catastrophe through loss of presence, such as death or end. Instead of being destructive, loss is transfigured into a constitutive category as an inherent structure that centralizes the subject. Beckett's *The Lost Ones* is composed in the wake of this loss ideology, recuperating a new mythology of the modern subject: *the subject of loss*.

How could loss, the negative, become a constitutive category of being in the modern context? Perhaps we need to go back to Hegel's *Phenomenology of Spirit* wherein he postulates the central role played by negation as a necessary process of and inaugurating moment of the subject. Hegel's concept of negation is fundamentally related to the configuration of being since, according to him, negation operates within a dialectic process of identification of the subject. In *Phenomenology of Spirit*, Hegel writes: "Spirit is this power only by looking the negative in the face, and tarrying with it. This tarrying with the negative is the magical power that converts it into being."[5] The modern subject is the direct result of "tarrying with the negative" that converts loss into being. Hegel identifies "this tarrying with the negative" as the "moving principle" as he states: "That is why some of the ancients conceived the *void* as the principle of motion, for they rightly saw the moving principle as the *negative*, though they did not as yet grasp that the negative is the self."[6] "*Negativity* is the differentiating and positing of *existence*."[7] Hence, in Hegel's *Phenomenology of Spirit*, negativity precipitates a double process in relation to being, both deleting and instituting the subject.

---

[5] G. W. F. Hegel, *Phenomenology of Spirit*, trans. A. V. Miller (Oxford: Oxford University Press, 1977), 19.
[6] Ibid., 21.
[7] Ibid., 32.

If our modern history is marked by end or death, then it constitutes a culture of mourning, over the death of God, death of man, and end of history. It is not news to us now that with Nietzsche's declaration of death of God, human beings lost their identities as well. It is within the newly discovered void that the modern subject is configured as the subject of loss, born out of catastrophe and consequently suffering from melancholy. And this loss, as represented in Beckett's *The Lost Ones*, constitutes the subjectivity of the subject instead of simply dramatizing an emotional response to the alien and disintegrated universe. So loss not only reveals the emotional affect of the subject, but also articulates the philosophical basis of the subject formation. Instead of being negative or destructive, loss figures as an inherent structure that centralizes and integrates the subject in terms of the void. We might call this process "the negative signification." Thus, *the subject of loss* becomes an ironic and paradoxical concept since loss both disintegrates the subject and simultaneously reconstitutes it, marking the subject as both present and absent: the absurd being of modern times.

If the ideology of loss determines the formation of beings, modern subjects thus inaugurated suffer the constitutional effect of mourning, or worse, melancholy. In "Mourning and Melancholia," Freud makes it very clear that the difference between mourning and melancholy resides in this: mourning indicates a temporary emotional response to loss of the object that is external and in the objective category while melancholy points to the subject loss, implying the identity crisis in the subjective category. Freud writes: "In mourning it is the world which has become poor and empty; in melancholia it is the ego itself."[8] Because the lost object is integrated as part of the subject, the loss becomes permanent and actually functions as the signifier that marks the identification. According to Freud, the melancholic "knows *whom* he has lost but not *what* he has lost in him."[9] Therefore, the melancholic does not recognize the difference between the subjective and objective worlds. Generally he introjects the lost object into the subjective category, "an object-loss was transformed into an ego-loss,"[10] thereby transforming loss into identification. It reminds us of Kristeva's *Powers of Horror: An Essay on Abjection* wherein she says: "The abjection of self would be the culminating form of that experience on the subject to which it is

---

[8] Sigmund Freud, "Mourning and Melancholia," in *Standard Edition of the Complete Psychology Works of Sigmund Freud*, vol. 24, trans. James Strachey (London: Hogarth, 1974), 246.
[9] Ibid., 245.
[10] Ibid., 249.

revealed that all of its objects are based merely on the inaugural *loss* that laid the foundation of its own being."[11]

In *Black Sun: Depression and Melancholy*, Julia Kristeva grounds her discourse of melancholy on loss and despair. According to her, melancholy involves the loss of meaning and despair of life: "empty existence," "unlivable life," "impossible meaning of life," and "a total despair." These are the rhetorics that characterize the psychic state of the modern subject. Instead of seeking meanings of loss, there is meaning only in loss. Thus, loss becomes a strategy for the modern subject to make sense of his existence. In a word, loss becomes a religion, perhaps the last mythology of the obsessional neurotic individuals in Lacanian terms. That is why the lost ones in Beckett's fiction are obsessed with loss; it defines both their identity and destination.

But why does the subject enjoy loss which otherwise would have caused pain and suffering? Historically great thinkers are melancholics: Plato, Socrates, Dante, Petrach, Hölderlin, Dostoevsky, Benjamin, and Freud. According to Juliana Schiesari in *The Gendering of Melancholia*, this pathological affect figures importantly for these men as the pivotal instrument to power or greatness. Is this why melancholy, otherwise a depressed state of psychic condition, "is translated into a virtue" or possibly an ethical choice that qualifies the unique subject? Schiesari writes: "By privileging a nostalgic ideal that is also kept absent and deferred, the self not only reconverts the loss into self-display but also legitimates that display as part of a cultural myth."[12] Eventually, melancholia becomes "an elite 'illness' that afflicted *men* precisely as the *sign* of their exceptionality."[13] Loss thus is transformed from a negation of being into the subject of desire. That accounts for the fact that loss in various contexts has to be endlessly evoked or produced to fabricate the myth of the melancholic subject: something has to be lost; if it is not the objective universe, it would be the subjective world. The disease becomes a gift.

The entire mythology of the modern subject is defined by "the loss narrative." So Beckett writes: "they may crawl blindly in the tunnels in search of nothing" (*The Lost Ones*, 31) and "whatever it is they are searching for it is not that" (36). Eventually, instead of indicating the death of the

---

[11] Julia Kristeva, *Powers of Horror: An Essay on Abjection*, trans. Leon S. Roudiez (New York: Columbia University Press, 1982), 5.

[12] Juliana Schiesari, *The Gendering of Melancholia: Feminism, Psychoanalysis, and the Symbolics of Loss in Renaissance Literature* (Ithaca, N.Y.: Cornell University Press, 1992), 5-6.

[13] Ibid., 7.

subject, this ineffable loss figures as the ideal state of being in a philosophical category or the ideal position of the modern subject.

In effect, end/death in the modern context is transfigured into a fetish, eroticized to entertain the grand narrative of the modern subject. This obsession with death/end uncovers the death wish that can only be gratified through the expression of the repressed—loss as desire. Eventually, loss indicates not only a negative affirmation, but also embodies an ideal state or the sublime mode of being associated with identification, pleasure and desire. Beckett embraces this modern ideology of loss and constructs a myth of "a bode where lost bodies foam each searching for its lost one" (1).

Modernist aesthetics of the sublime attempt to justify the desire for loss, thereby transforming pain into pleasure. According to Jean-Francois Lyotard, "The Sublime sentiment, which is also the sentiment of the sublime, is, according to Kant, a strong and equivocal emotion: it carries with it both pleasure and pain. Better still, in it pleasure derives from pain."[14] So the unconscious lurking beneath the pain of loss is the jouissance of the sublime subject.

Put this way, loss not only embodies the essential spirit of existentialist conditions or the ethos of modern society but also becomes perhaps the last mythology that marks the individual as the unique paradoxical subject in modern culture, despite its anxiety or agony. Instead of resolving loss, modernism embraces and capitalizes it as a sublime mode of identification and the cult subject of desire. When loss as tragic experience is transformed into a sublime mode of being, and when loss is reconfigured as desire instead of effect, it generates pleasure and desire instead of suffering and pain for the modern subject, thereby transforming Thanatos into Eros. It is not so much *the loss of the subject* as *the subject of loss* that becomes the central issue in current discourse. Therefore, loss not only embodies the ethos of the modern age and constitutes the modern subject but also represents the desire for identification.

In *The Postmodern Condition*, Lyotard clarifies that the difference between modern and postmodern aesthetics lies in the different configurations of representation: "Modern aesthetics is an aesthetics of the sublime, though a nostalgic one. It allows the unpresentable [subject] to be put forward only as the missing contents."[15] Therefore loss or end, both missing and missed, emerges as a desire. Whereas Lyotard writes, "The

---

[14] Jean-Francois Lyotard, *The Postmodern Condition: A Report on Knowledge*, trans. Geoff Bennington and Brian Massumi (Minneapolis: University of Minnesota Press, 1988), 77.

[15] Ibid., 81.

postmodern would be that which, in the modern, puts forward the unpresentable in presentation itself, that which searches for new presentations, not in order to enjoy them but in order to impart a stronger sense of the unpresentable."[16] Clearly, according to Lyotard, absence and unpresentability become the focus of postmodern critique of representation.

II

Many critics tend to compare Beckett's *The Lost Ones* to Dante's "Inferno" in *Divina Commedia*. Jean-Jacques Mayoux, in *Samuel Beckett*, states that *The Lost Ones* is "a fable of a sinister micro-Hades, a last circle, gloomier than Dante's, in which creatures of apparently human build, yet dry as insects, mechanical in their motivations, ant-like in their scurrying, climb or do not climb up ladders into niches, and in occupying the ground or ladders must conform to an obscure set of rules and prescriptions, of arbitrary and meaningless purport, but not perhaps more so than those which govern our societies."[17] Similarly, in *The Broken Window: Beckett's Dramatic Perspective*, Jane Alison Hale says: "Perhaps nowhere in the Beckettian oeuvre is there a clearer image of he circular, non-directional, meaningless movement of our existence than in *The Lost Ones*, Beckett's description of life in a closed cylinder where there are no names, no voices, no stories, no reasons—nothing but moving and resting."[18] Apparently, both read Beckett's *The Lost Ones* as a fable of hellish modern life in the context of existentialist ideology and in reference to the meaninglessness of human existence. However, one may ask: what is hell if not the very limit of human imagination of suffering and the very limit of linguistic representation?

But why do the modernists construct the subject of loss and mourn over the loss of identity which, according to the postmodern, never existed in the first place? From the postmodern perspective, the subject of loss signifies an impossible being because it only exists as a state of desire—an absent subject. If we believe, as Judith Butler argues in her book *Subjects of Desire*, that the subject has always been sustained in a state of desire, and the subject has always been defined by what it wants or lacks, then the desire marks the subject as a being of absence. According to Butler, desire is "constitutive of

---

[16] Ibid., 81.
[17] Mayoux, *Samuel Beckett*, 41.
[18] Jane A. Hale, *The Broken Window: Beckett's Dramatic Perspective* (West Lafayette, Ind.: Purdue University Press, 1987), 25.

the subject itself."[19] Jacques Lacan holds similar ideas. In *Seminar II: The Ego in Freud's Theory and in the Technique of Psychoanalysis,* Lacan writes: "Being comes into existence as an exact function of this lack. Being attains a sense of self in relation to being as a function of this lack, in the experience of desire."[20] This lack, primordial and inaugural, re-centers the subject in terms of desire, a desire that points to the impossibility of its realization. For Lacan, this lack constitutes being in the symbolic order in the first place. In addition, if desire is sustained by the linguistic structure in the symbolic order and perpetuated in the chain of the signifiers, then the subject of desire becomes the subject of linguistic fabrication. As Lacan observes in his *Ecrits:* "The psychoanalytic experience has rediscovered in man the imperative of Word as the law that has formed him in its image."[21] In other words, this desire eventually becomes the symbolics of desire in the process of symbolic signification in a Lacanian framework. Loss or end correspondingly is transfigured from ideological concepts signifying existential conditions into narrative strategies or linguistic metaphors in a game of absence. The ideology of loss turns into the aesthetics of absence.

Loss as a cathected signifier is subject to play in various linguistic and cultural contexts. To paraphrase Jean Baudelaire, "human beings are lost in the symbolic forest." If we take this to mean that human beings are lost in the labyrinth of words, we are entering a postmodern space of language instead of a modern world of representation. When loss turns from the real into a symbolic construct for the subject, it is in effect configured in a linguistic game of absence rather than presence. After all, Dante's "Inferno" is a text, and comparing Beckett's *The Lost Ones* to Dante's "Inferno" would only indicate an inter-textual relationship, a return to a prior text, instead of referring to any reality beyond the text. As Derrida reminds us in his *Of Grammatology,* "There is nothing outside of the text."[22] If the modern still maintains the illusory reference to social realities, the postmodern seldom indulges in such an illusion.

On the surface, *The Lost Ones* describes a world organized according to entropic process of diminishing energies and mathematical

---

[19] Judith Butler, *Subjects of Desire: Hegelian Reflections in Twentieth-Century France* (New York: Columbia University Press, 1999), 8.

[20] Jacques Lacan, *Seminar II: The Ego in Freud's Theory and in the Technique of Psychoanalysis,* trans. Sylvana Tomaselli (New York: Norton Press, 1988), 223-224.

[21] Jacques Lacan, *Ecrits: A Selection,* trans. Alan Sheridan (New York: Norton Press, 1977), 106.

[22] Jacques Derrida, *Of Grammatology,* trans. Gayatri Chakrovorty Spivak (Baltimore: Johns Hopkins University Press, 1976), 158.

computation. It seems to be a fiction about pure physicality: bodies, places, temperatures, materials, lights, motions, and so forth. If viewed as a physical universe, one simply fails to take account of the text's reference. The world represented in *The Lost Ones* is surreal with an interior system of recurrent images without reference to any extra-textual reality. Within this enclosed space of loss, language is self-referential. To quote Carla Locatelli in *Unwording the World*: "Beckett does not attempt to describe life, nor to illustrate it; rather, he brings the impossibility of pure description before our eyes."[23]

Similarly, in *Innovation in Samuel Beckett's Fiction*, Rubin Rabinovitz observes: "In *The Lost Ones*, for example, the action takes place within an enclosed cylinder; the size of the cylinder the number of inhabitants, confined in it, the temperature of its interior, and its lighting are described in minute detail. Nevertheless, this precision mocks the verisimilitude it purports to affirm; clearly the inhabited cylinder does not correspond to any object we may have encountered in the physical world."[24] Scrupulous objectivity and clinical detachment are but the pose of the gamer. Even though mutually exclusive, pure physical becomes pure figurative in Beckett's fiction.

Hence there seems to be an insurmountable gap between figuration of language and physicality of the universe. The figurative language's presentation of the end seems to be the "ontologically structured aporia."[25] In fact, instead of the insurmountable gap between figuration of language and the objective end, or instead of the aporia of representation, the end is perpetually fabricated in an infinite space of writing and in the chain of signification. In short, the end is constructed in its irreducible figuration of language that forever postpones it to infinity.

The Lost Ones begins with the end: "It is perhaps the end of all." From a postmodern perspective, Beckett's "end" functions as a rhetorical device to engage negative poetics: the aesthetics of absence. In Beckett's text, the lost universe signifies a space of linguistic play; instead of representing any social realities, the narrative puts itself to test the limit of representation. Hence, the end figures as the starting point of discourse rather than as the last word of existence. Paradoxically, the end as the central metaphor both defines the narrative and simultaneously eludes it, marking the limit and horizon of representation.

[23] Carla Locatelli, *Unwording the World: Samuel Beckett's Prose Works After the Novel Prize* (Philadelphia: University of Pennsylvania Press, 1990), 246.
[24] Rubin Rabinovitz, *Innovation in Samuel Beckett's Fiction* (Urbana: University of Illinois Press, 1992), 16.
[25] Locatelli, *Unwording the World*, 251.

For Beckett, it is the "unthinkable as the end (*The Lost Ones*, 34). Beckett's recurrent return to the same phrase of the end throughout the text simply postpones the end narrative and simultaneously displaces and excludes the end. In other words, the end becomes the unpresentable, beyond the text, and constituting the limit of discourse. As Beckett says in *The Lost Ones*: "All has not been told and never shall be" (51). Therefore, the impossibility threatens the text from within and *The Lost Ones* becomes the allegory of its own impossibility and failure of representation.

Maybe this is a story of absence: no plot, no character, no story, no time, no name, no voice. In a word, absent. "So on infinitely until towards the unthinkable end if this notion is maintained a last body of all by feeble fits and starts is searching still" (60). Thus, the end functions as the central absence defines the narrative. In other words, *The Lost Ones* is defined and structured by absence of end. All the narrative is directed toward the end, but end itself is not represented in it. Absence of the end constitutes the starting point of the narrative that arises to explicate, but which by no means is able to explicate it. In addition, the narrative thus entailed contributes to initiating the displacement of the end. That is to say, absence generates the narrative on the one hand, and the narrative thus emerged can in no way finalize or capture it.

So Beckett's fiction emerges as a paradox; the end that resides at the center of the text and structures the narrative lies beyond the realm of representation. The end that functions as the central metaphor and determines the ultimate signification of the text is denied representation. Even though functioning as the basis of the structure, the end transcends the narrative.

The end is neither allegorical nor parodic because it does not signify a return to something prior. In this context, the representation of the end in *The Lost Ones* signifies a return to something "never there" in the first place. Absence is a figurative turn that promises nothing. It is an empty signifier absent of the signified. So the end as absence can only appear in the form of simulation. According to Jean Baudrillard, simulation differs from imitation in that imitation affirms a primary presence whereas simulation testifies to primal absence, but with the pretension of possessing presence. [26]

Absence and the figuration of discourse are thus incommensurate. Absence, or end in this case, according to the postmodern, informs a primal space prior to language, the alterity and impasse of discourse. Language, while constituting the very contents of the absence, makes it a pure

---

[26] Jean Baudrillard, *Simulations*, trans. Paul Foss, Paul Patton, and Philip Beitchman (New York: Columbia University Press, 1983).

exteriority. Thus the absent end becomes an irreducible space of unrepresentability that renders all narratives about it impossible. As Leslie Hill says: "If what the text says can be accepted as a fictional representation, then its own writing becomes an impossibility. The text of *Le Dépeupleur* becomes therefore an allegory of its own impossibility."[27]

In "Structure, Sign and Play in the Discourse of the Human Sciences," Derrida observes that "this movement of play permitted by the lack or absence of a center or origin, is the movement of *supplementary*."[28] However, absence that requires supplementations that add nothing to its finality or ends ensures the free play of language. Play is always a play of presence and absence as Derrida reminds us. Instead of repeating the obsolete formula "one versus many," I would propose a new paradigm: absence versus infinity.

Therefore, the end in *The Lost Ones* signifies both death and infinity, both nothingness and open space. The modernists point to nothingness when they approach the end while the postmodernists find in the end an infinite possibility for textual production. One fixes the end as the last word of existence, the other finds in it the beginning of text. The existentialist theory is but one response to or constituent of the end. It reflects the limitation of the existentialist philosophy rather than the endless end itself. Absence does not limit us; rather we are limited by our own conceptual framework, our imagination. Existentialism reflects both our restricted understanding of absence and the inadequacy of our language to engage it.

The absent end in Beckett's fiction serves as the organizing principle that entertains the aesthetic play without final recovery of presence. The end, though denied final representation, is forever circulated on the linguistic level as an empty signifier. To deny the final scene is to desublimate the end. The lack of the final scene of the end is consistent with the postmodern aesthetics of comic play and the ethics of unrepresentability. This intranscribability signifies both the incapability of representation and the denial of representation. Desublimation adds nothing to our cognition of totality because representation fails to conceptualize the end. Instead, it deconcepturalizes finality. Against Kant's sublime, Beckett's text affirms the failure of cognition in denial of sublimity. Like Lacan's "the real" and Derrida's "the infinite other," Beckett's end is another signifier without the final signified, a pure metaphor without reference. For Beckett, the end

---

[27] Hill, *Beckett's Fiction*, 155.
[28] Jacques Derrida, "Structure, Sign and Play in the Discourse of the Human Sciences," *Writing and Difference*, trans. Alan Bass (Chicago: University of Chicago Press, 1978), 289.

constitutes the unpresentability itself because the end ends endlessly, forever absent.

California State University, San Marcos

Post/Imperial Encounters
Anglo-Hispanic Cultural Relations

Edited by Juan E. Tazón Salces, Isabel Carrera Suárez

Amsterdam/New York, NY 2005. 239 pp.(Textxet 45)

ISBN: 90-420-1992-1   € 50,-/US $70.-

Spanish and English are two of the most widely spoken languages in today's world, and are linked by a colonial presence in the Americas that has often provoked turbulent relations between Britain and Spain. Despite abundant exchanges between Spain and the British Isles, and evident contact in the Americas, cross-cultural analyses are infrequent, and ironically language barriers still prevail in a world the media and globalization would appear to render borderless: English and Hispanic Studies have seldom converged, the islands of the Caribbean continue to be separated by language, while the new empire, the United States, has difficulty in admitting to its Hispanic component, let alone recognizing that the name "America" encompasses a wider continent. *Post/Imperial Encounters: Anglo-Hispanic Cultural Relations* attempts to bridge this gap through articles on literature, history and culture that concentrate primarily on three periods: the colonial interventions of Britain and Spain in the Americas, the Spanish Civil War and the present world, with its global culture and new forms of colonialism.

USA/Canada: 906 Madison Avenue, UNION, NJ 07083, USA
Call toll-free (USA only)1-800-225-3998, Tel. 908 206 1166, Fax 908-206-0820
All other countries: Tijnmuiden 7, 1046 AK Amsterdam, The Netherlands.
Tel. ++ 31 (0)20 611 48 21, Fax ++ 31 (0)20 447 29 79
Orders-queries@rodopi.nl   www.rodopi.nl
Please note that the exchange rate is subject to fluctuations

A Gorgon's Mask.
The Mother in Thomas Mann's Fiction.

Lewis A. Lawson:

Amsterdam/New York, NY 2005. 435 pp.
(Psychoanalysis and Culture 12)

ISBN: 90-420-1745-7 € 86,-/US $ 120.-

The thesis of *A Gorgon's Mask: The Mother in Thomas Mann's Fiction* depends upon three psychoanalytic concepts: Freud's early work on the relationship between the infant and its mother and on the psychology of artistic creation, Annie Reich's analysis of the grotesque-comic sublimation, and Edmund Bergler's analysis of writer's block. Mann's crisis of sexual anxiety in late adolescence is presented as the defining moment for his entire artistic life. In the throes of that crisis he included a sketch of a female as Gorgon in a book that would not escape his mother's notice. But to defend himself from being overcome by the Gorgon-mother's stare he employed the grotesque-comic sublimation, hiding the mother figure behind fictional characters physically attractive but psychologically repellent, all the while couching his fiction in an ironic tone that evoked humor, however lacking in humor the subtext might be. In this manner he could deny to himself that the mother figure always lurked in his work, and by that denial deny that he was a victim of oral regression. For, as Edmund Bergler argues, the creative writer who acknowledges his oral dependency will inevitably succumb to writer's block. Mann's late work reveals that his defense against the Gorgon is crumbling. In *Doctor Faustus* Mann portrays Adrian Leverkühn as, ultimately, the victim of oral regression; but the fact that Mann was able to compete the novel, despite severe physical illness and psychological distress, demonstrates that he himself was still holding writer's block at bay. In *Confessions of Felix Krull: Confidence Man*, a narrative that he had abandoned forty years before, Mann was finally forced to acknowledge that he was depleted of creative vitality, but not of his capacity for irony, brilliantly couching the victorious return of the repressed in ambiguity. This study will be of interest to general readers who enjoy Mann's narrative art, to students of Mann's work, especially its psychological and mythological aspects, and to students of the psychology of artistic creativity.

USA/Canada: 906 Madison Avenue, UNION, NJ 07083, USA
Call toll-free (USA only)1-800-225-3998, Tel. 908 206 1166,
Fax 908-206-0820
All other countries: Tijnmuiden 7, 1046 AK Amsterdam, The Netherlands.
Tel. ++ 31 (0)20 611 48 21, Fax ++ 31 (0)20 447 29 79
Orders-queries@rodopi.nl www.rodopi.nl
Please note that the exchange rate is subject to fluctuations

Producing the Pacific
Maps and Narratives of Spanish Exploration (1567-1606)

Mercedes Maroto Camino

Amsterdam/New York, NY 2005. 144 pp. + 34 ill.
(Portada hispánica 18)

ISBN: 90-420-1994-8   € 40,-/US $ 54.-

Producing the Pacific offers the reader an interdisciplinary reading of the maps, narratives and rituals related to the three Spanish voyages to the South Pacific that took place between 1567 and 1606. These journeys were led by Álvaro de Mendaña, Pedro Fernández de Quirós and Isabel Barreto, the first woman ever to become admiral of and command a fleet.
Mercedes Maroto Camino presents a cultural analysis of these journeys and takes issue with some established notions about the value of the past and the way it is always rewritten from the perspective of the present. She highlights the social, political and cultural environment in which maps and narratives circulate, suggesting that their significance is always subject to negotiation and transformation.
The tapestry created by the interpretation of maps, narratives and rituals affords a view not only of the minds of the first men and women who traversed the Pacific but also of how they saw the ocean, its islands and their peoples. Producing the Pacific should, therefore, be of relevance to those interested in history, voyages, colonialism, cartography, anthropology and cultural studies.
The study of these cultural products contributes to an interpretive history of colonialism at the same time that it challenges the beliefs and assumptions that underscore our understanding of that history.

USA/Canada: 906 Madison Avenue, Union, NJ 07083, USA.
Fax: (908) 206-0820 Call toll-free: 1-800-225-3998 (USA only)
All other countries: Tijnmuiden 7, 1046 AK Amsterdam, The Netherlands.
Tel. ++ 31 (0)20 611 48 21, Fax ++ 31 (0)20 447 29 79
<u>Orders-queries@rodopi.nl</u>   <u>www.rodopi.nl</u>
Please note that the exchange rate is subject to fluctuations

Innovation and Visualization
Trajectories, Strategies, and Myths

Amy Ione

Amsterdam/New York, NY 2005. 271 pp.
(Consciousness, Literature and the Arts 1)

ISBN: 90-420-1675-2   € 55,-/US $ 77.-

Amy Ione's *Innovation and Visualization* is the first in detail account that relates the development of visual images to innovations in art, communication, scientific research, and technological advance. Integrated case studies allow Ione to put aside C.P. Snow's "two culture" framework in favor of cross-disciplinary examples that refute the science/humanities dichotomy. The themes, which range from cognitive science to illuminated manuscripts and media studies, will appeal to specialists (artists, art historians, cognitive scientists, etc.) interested in comparing our image saturated culture with the environments of earlier eras. The scope of the examples will appeal to the generalist.

Amy Ione is currently the Director of The Diatrope Institute, a California-based group that disseminates information and engages in research exploring art, science and visual studies. She has published extensively on art, science and technology relationships. Ione's artwork has been exhibited in the United States and Europe, and is found in many collections.

USA/Canada: 906 Madison Avenue, UNION, NJ 07083, USA.
Call toll-free (USA only)1-800-225-3998, Tel. 908 206 1166, Fax 908-206-0820
All other countries: Tijnmuiden 7, 1046 AK Amsterdam, The Netherlands.
Tel. ++ 31 (0)20 611 48 21, Fax ++ 31 (0)20 447 29 79
Orders-queries@rodopi.nl   www.rodopi.nl
Please note that the exchange rate is subject to fluctuations

The Theater of Transformation
Postmodernism in American Drama

Kerstin Schmidt

Amsterdam/New York, NY 2005. 230 pp.
(Postmodern Studies 37)

ISBN: 90-420-1895-X   € 46,-/US $ 64.-

The Theater of Transformation: Postmodernism in American Drama offers a fresh and innovative reading of the contemporary experimental American theater scene and navigates through the contested and contentious relationship between postmodernism and contemporary drama. This book addresses gender and class as well as racial issues in the context of a theoretical discussion of dramatic texts, textuality, and performance. Transformation is contemporary drama's answer to the questions of postmodernism and a major technique in the development of a postmodern language for the stage. In order to demonstrate the multi-faceted nature of the postmodern theater of transformation, this study draws on a wide range of plays: from early experimental plays of the 1960s by Jean-Claude van Itallie through feminist plays by Megan Terry and Rochelle Owens to more recent drama by the African-American playwright Suzan-Lori Parks.
The Theater of Transformation: Postmodernism in American Drama is written for anyone interested in contemporary American drama and theater as well as in postmodernism and contemporary literary theory. It appeals even more broadly to a readership intrigued by the ubiquitous aspects of popular culture, by feminism and ethnicity, and by issues pertaining to the so-called 'society of spectacle' and the study of contemporary media.
Kerstin Schmidt is currently Assistant Professor of American Studies and Intercultural Anglophone Studies in the Department of English at the University of Bayreuth, Germany.

USA/Canada: 906 Madison Avenue, UNION, NJ 07083, USA.
Call toll-free (USA only)1-800-225-3998, Tel. 908 206 1166, Fax 908-206-0820
All other countries: Tijnmuiden 7, 1046 AK Amsterdam, The Netherlands.
Tel. ++ 31 (0)20 611 48 21, Fax ++ 31 (0)20 447 29 79
Orders-queries@rodopi.nl   www.rodopi.nl
Please note that the exchange rate is subject to fluctuations

EcoMedia.

Sean Cubitt

Amsterdam/New York, NY 2005. X, 168 pp.
(Contemporary Cinema 1)

ISBN: 90-420-1885-2   € 35,-/ US $ 44.-

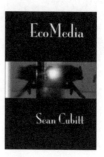

For the last twenty years ecology, the last great political movement of the 20th century, has fired the imaginations not only of political activists but of popular movements throughout the industrialised world. *EcoMedia* is an enquiry into the popular mediations of environmental concerns in popular film and television since the 1980s. Arranged in a series of case studies on bio-security, relationships with animals, bioethics and biological sciences, over-fishing, eco-terrorism, genetic modification and global warming, *EcoMedia* offers close readings of Peter Jackson's *The Lord of the Rings*, Miyazake's *Princess Mononoke*, *The Perfect Storm*, *X-Men* and *X2*, *The Day After Tomorrow* and the BBC's drama *Edge of Darkness* and documentary *The Blue Planet*. Drawing on the thinking of Flusser, Luhmann, Latour, Agamben and Bookchin, *EcoMedia* discusses issues from whether animals can draw and why we like to draw animals, to how narrative films can imagine global processes, and whether wonder is still an ethical pleasure. Building on the thesis that popular film and television can tell us a great deal about the state of contemporary beliefs and anxieties, the book builds towards an argument that the *polis*, the human world, cannot survive without a three way partnership with *physis* and *techne*, the green world *and* the technological.

USA/Canada: 906 Madison Avenue, UNION, NJ 07083, USA.
Call toll-free (USA only)1-800-225-3998, Tel. 908 206 1166, Fax 908-206-0820
All other countries: Tijnmuiden 7, 1046 AK Amsterdam, The Netherlands.
Tel. ++ 31 (0)20 611 48 21, Fax ++ 31 (0)20 447 29 79
Orders-queries@rodopi.nl   www.rodopi.nl
Please note that the exchange rate is subject to fluctuations

Transcultural Graffiti
Diasporic Writing and the Teaching of Literary Studies

Russell West-Pavlov

Amsterdam/New York, NY 2005. 243 pp.
(Internationale Forschungen zur Allgemeinen und Vergleichenden Literaturwissenschaft 87)

ISBN: 90-420-1935-2 € 50,-/ US $ 70.-

Transcultural Graffiti reads a range of texts – prose, poetry, drama – in several European languages as exemplars of diasporic writing. The book scrutinizes contemporary transcultural literary creation for the manner in which it gives hints about the teaching of literary studies in our postcolonial, globalizing era. *Transcultural Graffiti* suggest that cultural work, in particular *trans*cultural work, assembles and collates material from various cultures in their moment of meeting. The teaching of such cultural collage in the classroom should equip students with the means to reflect upon and engage in cultural 'bricolage' themselves in the present day. The texts read – from Césaire's adaptation of Shakespeare's *Tempest*, via the diaspora fictions of Marica Bodrožić or David Dabydeen, to the post-9/11 poetry of New York poets – are understood as 'graffiti'-like inscriptions, the result of fleeting encounters in a swiftly changing public world. Such texts provide impulses for a performative 'risk' pedagogy capable of modelling the ways in which our constitutive individual and social narratives are constructed, deconstructed and reconstructed today.

Russell West-Pavlov is Professor of English Literature at the Free University of Berlin. He is the author of *Conrad and Gide: Translation, Transference and Intertextuality* (1996), *Figures de la maladie chez André Gide* (1997), and *Spatial Representations on the Jacobean Stage: From Shakespeare to Webster* (2002).

USA/Canada: 906 Madison Avenue, UNION, NJ 07083, USA.
Call toll-free (USA only)1-800-225-3998, Tel. 908 206 1166, Fax 908-206-0820
All other countries: Tijnmuiden 7, 1046 AK Amsterdam, The Netherlands.
Tel. ++ 31 (0)20 611 48 21, Fax ++ 31 (0)20 447 29 79
Orders-queries@rodopi.nl   www.rodopi.nl
Please note that the exchange rate is subject to fluctuations

Intercultural Explorations.

Volume 8 of the Proceedings of the XVth Congress of the International Comparative Literature Association *"Literature as Cultural Memory"* Leiden 16-22 August 1997.

Edited by Eugene Eoyang.

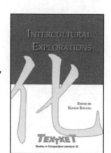

Amsterdam/New York, NY 2005. IV, 292 pp.
(Textxet 32)

ISBN: 90-420-1636-1   € 60,-/ US $ 75.-

Divided into four sections: "Asian-Western Intersections," "Intercultural Memory," "Intercultural Perspectives on Women," "Genre Studies," and "The Intercultural Arts", these essays from diverse hands and multiple perspectives illuminate the intersections, the cross-sections, and the synergies that characterize significant literary texts and artistic productions. Individually, they exemplify the insights available in an intercultural perspective; together they remind us that no culture - even those that claim to be "pure" or those that might be regarded as isolated - has escaped the influence of external influences. As a result, this volume is doubly synergistic: one, because it focuses on intercultural phenomena within a specific culture, and two, because they represent multiple perspectives on these phenomena.

USA/Canada: 906 Madison Avenue, UNION, NJ 07083, USA.
Call toll-free (USA only)1-800-225-3998, Tel. 908 206 1166, Fax 908-206-0820
All other countries: Tijnmuiden 7, 1046 AK Amsterdam, The Netherlands.
Tel. ++ 31 (0)20 611 48 21, Fax ++ 31 (0)20 447 29 79
Orders-queries@rodopi.nl   www.rodopi.nl
Please note that the exchange rate is subject to fluctuations